FEELING GOOD
OR
DOING GOOD
WITH
SANCTIONS

Significant Issues Series
Timely books presenting current CSIS research and analysis of interest to the academic, business, government, and policy communities.
Managing editor: Roberta L. Howard

≈   ≈   ≈

The Center for Strategic and International Studies (CSIS), established in 1962, is a private, tax-exempt institution focusing on international public policy issues. Its research is nonpartisan and nonproprietary.

CSIS is dedicated to policy analysis and impact. It seeks to inform and shape selected policy decisions in government and the private sector to meet the increasingly complex and difficult global challenges that leaders will confront in the next century. It achieves this mission in three ways: by generating strategic analysis that is anticipatory and interdisciplinary; by convening policymakers and other influential parties to assess key issues; and by building structures for policy action.

CSIS does not take specific public policy positions. Accordingly, all views, positions, and conclusions expressed in this publication should be understood to be solely those of the author.

The CSIS Press
Center for Strategic and International Studies
1800 K Street, NW
Washington, DC 20006
Telephone: (202) 887-0200
Fax: (202) 775-3199
E-mail: books@csis.org
Web site: http://www.csis.org/

FEELING GOOD
OR
DOING GOOD
WITH
SANCTIONS

Unilateral Economic Sanctions and the U.S. National Interest

ERNEST H. PREEG

Foreword by Lee H. Hamilton

THE CSIS PRESS

Center for Strategic
and International Studies
Washington, D.C.

The CSIS Press, Washington, D.C. 20006
© 1999 by the Center for Strategic and International Studies
All rights reserved.
Printed on recycled paper in the United States of America
02 01 00 99   4 3 2

ISSN 0736-7136
ISBN 0-89206-349-1

Cover design by Robert L. Wiser, Archetype Press, Washington, D.C.

Library of Congress Cataloging-in-Publication Data

Preeg, Ernest H.
    Feeling good or doing good with sanctions: unilateral economic sanctions and
  the U.S. national interest   /   Ernest H. Preeg : foreword by Lee H. Hamilton
    p.   cm.   —   (Significant issues series ; v. 21, no. 3)
    Includes bibliographical references and index.
    ISBN 0-89206-349-1
    1. Economic sanctions, American.   2. United States—Foreign
  relations—1989–   I. Title.   II. Series.
HF1413.5.P73   1999   99-21602
337.73—dc21   CIP

Contents

Foreword

I N THIS EXCELLENT NEW STUDY of the costs and effectiveness of U.S. unilateral sanctions, Ernest H. Preeg offers a convincing and timely argument that, more often than not, unilateral sanctions let us feel good without doing much good at all.

As of 1997, 75 countries were affected by U.S. unilateral sanctions, representing significant limitations on U.S. commerce with some of the world's largest economies. Increasingly, those sanctions are targeted at changing behavior—such as religious persecution—that we all agree is abhorrent, but whose susceptibility to economic sanctions is unclear. The United States has also begun to rely on extraterritorial sanctions and secondary boycotts, such as those now targeted at foreign firms doing business with Cuba, Iran, and Libya.

Unilateral sanctions are attractive to many because they respond to frustrations and to demands to take action. But as U.S. reliance on unilateral sanctions has grown, so have questions about their effectiveness and their diplomatic and economic costs. In the five case studies that follow, Ernest Preeg carefully examines U.S. unilateral sanctions policy and reaches some disturbing conclusions.

First, the economic impact of unilateral sanctions is usually not what we intend it to be.

Unilateral sanctions have almost no impact on the economy of the target country as long as there are other nations willing to trade. What little economic pain sanctions do create is easily passed on by an authoritarian regime to its people—usually the people we are trying to help. And while the global marketplace can protect the target country from the economic impact of sanctions, it cannot protect U.S. businesses from the loss of commerce or U.S. workers from the resulting loss of jobs.

Second, unilateral sanctions rarely achieve their objectives.

In the five cases analyzed, unilateral U.S. sanctions failed to achieve any significant progress toward their human rights and democratization objectives. As the author points out, these sanctions are intended to change the oppressive behavior of authoritarian regimes that rely on oppression to maintain control and therefore actively resist the objectives we set out. Unilateral sanctions can play only a very small role in accomplishing national security objectives, such as containing weapons programs or preventing proliferation. Multilateral efforts are far more effective in achieving their goals.

Third, at no point in the sanctions decision-making process is there a comprehensive assessment of the impact sanctions will have, either on the target country or on U.S. interests.

One of the most alarming aspects of U.S. sanctions policy is the weak information base on which most sanctions decisions are made. Several dozen laws authorize the president to impose sanctions, but virtually none requires the president to assess the foreign policy, humanitarian, or domestic economic impact of a proposed sanction.

This study offers a detailed analysis of the Sanctions Policy Reform Act, which I introduced in 1997, along with Senator Richard Lugar and Representative Phil Crane. The initiative is intended to provide Congress, the executive branch, and the public with better information about proposed economic sanctions and to establish guidelines for future sanctions proposals and procedures for their implementation. The author includes useful recommendations for additions to this legislation and several policy alternatives to the use of unilateral sanctions.

Ernest Preeg has conducted a comprehensive examination and quantification of the economic impact of unilateral sanctions. His volume should be required reading for those concerned about the use of unilateral sanctions as a tool of U.S. foreign policy.

LEE H. HAMILTON
Director
Woodrow Wilson International Center

Preface

THE UNITED STATES HAS BEEN THE preeminent trading nation during the 1990s to use unilateral economic sanctions as a foreign policy instrument. Occasionally, others have joined with the United States to impose multilateral sanctions, but the United States has been almost alone in going the unilateral route, despite obvious inherent problems and considerable evidence that would militate against it. The momentum toward unilateral sanctions reached a crescendo in 1993-1997, when broadly based sanctions on trade and investment were imposed on Iran, Libya, Myanmar (formerly Burma), and Sudan, extended against Cuba, officially threatened by President Clinton against China, and seriously considered for other countries such as Indonesia and Nigeria. This study examines the recent experience to answer key questions: what explains the U.S. proclivity for unilateral sanctions? Do they achieve their intended objectives, and at what cost to other U.S. interests?

As far as I am aware, this is the first full-length study devoted solely to assessing the experience of unilateral sanctions, and it is certainly the only work on the subject related to the very changed international economic realities of the 1990s. Most broader work on sanctions, which mixes together multilateral and unilateral sanctions and stretches back into earlier periods, comes to the conclusion that unilateral sanctions are less likely to succeed than multilateral sanctions. But previous work has left open the more specific questions addressed here—how much less likely are unilateral sanctions to succeed, and when are they unlikely to succeed at all?

The substantive investigation centers on five in-depth country case studies, which have been a most demanding challenge. They would not have been possible except for wide-ranging assistance from country experts and numerous other public- and private-sector people involved with economic sanctions. This study is, in fact, one part of a broader CSIS project on unilateral economic sanctions, while a second part examines in greater detail alternative policies to unilateral sanctions. The overall project received valuable guidance and commentary from a distinguished steering committee cochaired by four members and two former members of Congress. The committee, whose members are listed in appendix B, has produced its own statement of findings and conclusions.*

The case study work also benefited greatly from an "experts group" of executive branch officials, congressional staffers, policy analysts, and private-sector and nongovernmental organization representatives. The members of this group, who are also listed in appendix B, met six times during the course of the project to review first drafts of the country studies and then the full manuscript. In addition, I conducted between 10 and 30 private interviews for each case study, with some members of the experts group and others, including representatives of the sanction target country governments and current and former senior U.S. government officials.

Invaluable insights on Vietnam and Myanmar were obtained from a memorable trip to those countries in November 1997, which included meetings with government officials, prodemocracy advocates and leaders, private-sector representatives, U.S. and third country resident diplomats, and members of nongovernmental organizations. The evolving struggle of the Vietnamese people to modernize their economic and political systems, in day-to-day dialogue with American officials and private-sector representatives, was striking for a first-time visitor to Hanoi who had followed the tragic Vietnam War from afar. The dangerous ongoing confrontation between the military leaders and Daw Aung San Suu Kyi and

---

* For the report examining alternative policies in greater detail, see Joseph J. Collins and Gabrielle D. Bowdoin, *Beyond Unilateral Economic Sanctions: Better Alternatives for U.S. Foreign Policy* (Washington, D.C.: CSIS, 1999). For the committee's findings and conclusions, see Douglas Johnston Jr. and Sidney Weintraub, *Altering U.S. Sanctions Policy: Final Report of the CSIS Project on Unilateral Economic Sanctions* (Washington, D.C.: CSIS, 1999).

her NLD colleagues in Myanmar left the most indelible impressions, especially from meetings with several of the generals, including the key figure General Khin Nyunt, and Aung San Suu Kyi and other prodemocracy opponents of the military regime. In the Myanmar case study, I do recommend a change in U.S. policy to "proactive flexible engagement," but this honest disagreement with Aung San Suu Kyi in no way diminishes my profound respect and admiration for her courageous struggle to restore democratic government in her country.

Finally, I owe special thanks and gratitude to the massive help from my CSIS colleagues engaged in this project. Codirectors Joe Collins, Bob Ebel, Doug Johnston, and Sid Weintraub all provided sustained guidance and encouragement. My two research assistants during the course of the project, Claudine Chen-Young and Denise Auclair, contributed superb substantive and organizational support throughout the project, including the excellent analysis by Denise of unilateral economic sanctions as they relate to the U.S. Constitution (appendix A in this volume). My dedicated administrative assistant, Dorris Whitford, kept the whole process going, organized the expert group meetings as well as travel and interview schedules, and provided full secretarial support for the numerous drafts of the case studies and other chapters. And last, but assuredly not least, Donna Spitler and Roberta Howard provided their usual high-quality professional editing for this the last of our several collaborations on CSIS book projects.

E.H.P.
April 1999

1

A Deeply Flawed
Foreign Policy Instrument

THIS VOLUME EXAMINES RECENT U.S. experience with unilateral economic sanctions as a foreign policy instrument, a subject of considerable yet ill-informed controversy. The inquiry centers on five in-depth country case studies—of China, Cuba, Iran, Myanmar (formerly Burma), and Vietnam—and from them draws both country-specific and general conclusions about whether such sanctions achieve their intended foreign policy purposes and what their cost is to other U.S. interests.

The focus on unilateral sanctions is important for several reasons. Unilateral sanctions function in very different ways from multilateral sanctions, almost all to adverse effect, and these differences need to be highlighted. In terms of U.S. foreign policy process, the unilateral approach is far more apt to be adopted in ill-considered haste, in response to immediate events and domestic political pressures, because it is not constrained by the need to reach prior international agreement, as is the case for multilateral sanctions. And unilateral sanctions, in part because of the previous point, have become the more frequent U.S. sanctions policy of choice during the 1990s. Nevertheless, other studies on economic sanctions tend to mix together the multilateral and the unilateral, and while generally concluding that the unilateral approach is less likely to achieve the intended foreign policy objective, they may lose or obscure crucial, unique "downsides" of unilateral sanctions.

The choice of the five country case studies has special relevance. The countries range across different regions that have distinct characteristics for U.S. foreign policy objectives in the post–Cold War realities of the 1990s. Cuba is in a Western Hemisphere of otherwise market-oriented democracies, Iran is in the deeply conflicted and explosive Middle East region, and the other three countries are in Asia during a period of fundamental political and economic change. These underlying regional characteristics lead to a corresponding diversity in U.S. foreign policy objectives in the sanctions-targeted countries: human rights/democratization in Cuba, national security interests in Iran, and a combination of political/economic/security interests in Asia. This diversity of regional relationships among the five countries not only enables a broader understanding of the pros and cons of unilateral economic sanctions as a foreign policy instrument, but also facilitates an extrapolation of policy conclusions to other countries in similar circumstances that are or have been the target of actual or threatened sanctions.

Yet another attribute shared by all five case studies is that they involve broadly based or comprehensive sanctions on U.S. commerce with the target country, as distinct from narrowly targeted sanctions that can be limited to individual products or companies. The threat or imposition of comprehensive sanctions have the greatest impact, by far, on U.S. foreign policy and commercial interests, and the countries examined here are among the most important cases in point during the 1990s. Other studies or reports on economic sanctions tally a large number of instances where sanctions were applied—for example, 61 sanctions against 35 countries between 1993 and 1996 alone[1]—but many of them are sanctions of relatively small or noncontroversial consequence. The full range of sanctions activity is pertinent knowledge, but the major impact of recent unilateral sanctions policy on U.S. interests is limited to a relatively small number of countries where broadly based sanctions have been applied or threatened. They include the five selected here (although in China's case targeted sanctions are also exceptionally important and are addressed in addition to the comprehensive most-favored-nation, or MFN, issue). This focus on comprehensive sanctions again facilitates broader conclusions for other country relationships where the United States has imposed or considered sanctions—including Colombia, India, Indonesia, Libya, Nigeria, Pakistan, and Sudan.

Overall, this volume concludes that broadly based unilateral economic sanctions during the 1990s, as assessed in the five case studies and related to experience elsewhere, have been almost entirely ineffective in achieving their intended foreign policy objectives while having a substantial adverse impact on other U.S. foreign policy and commercial interests. The one exception only proves the rule. The lifting of sanctions on U.S. exports to and investment in Vietnam did provide leverage to help achieve the U.S. objective of accountability for U.S. personnel missing-in-action during the Vietnam War. But this unique objective did not require any significant change in the political or economic behavior of the Vietnamese government and was obtained in circumstances where Vietnam, for geopolitical reasons, wanted normalization of relations with the United States more than did the United States with Vietnam. Such narrowly drawn objectives and propitious circumstances do not, however, come close to those prevailing in any of the other actual or potential sanctions-targeted countries encountered in the study.

The remainder of this introductory chapter explains the definition of unilateral sanctions as used here, presents the format for the case studies, and outlines six inherent downsides to the use of unilateral economic sanctions for foreign policy objectives.

The Definition of Sanctions

The subject of unilateral economic sanctions for foreign policy objectives requires reasonably precise definitions of what is meant by unilateral, economic, and foreign policy objectives. The unilateral—as distinct from multilateral—application of sanctions simply means that the United States acts alone or almost alone in applying the sanctions. In most cases, such as Cuba and Iran, the distinction is unambiguous; the United States is acting entirely alone. In some instances, however, the sanctions are not strictly unilateral or fully multilateral, and a judgment is required. For example, a few other countries apply some restraints on investment in and trade with Myanmar, but the U.S. ban on all new investment, because it is not shared by other major trading partners of Myanmar, is treated as a unilateral sanction. In the other direction, the United States and its allies impose sanctions that are generally considered multilateral on the export of armaments and certain dual-use civilian goods and services to China, although Russia continues to export substantial amounts of advanced weapons systems and related technology to China.

An economic sanction is defined as a restriction on normal commercial relations with the targeted country. This basically involves restrictions on trade, investment, and other cross-border economic activities. Denial of MFN status, which arises in the China and Vietnam case studies, is considered a sanction within this definition because the United States grants MFN status or better to countries that account for more than 99 percent of global exports, and thus denial of MFN would clearly be abnormal. Indeed, in 1998, the term "most-favored-nation," or MFN, was officially changed to the more appropriate "normal-trade-relations" or NTR, although MFN is used in the case studies because that was the nomenclature in effect for nearly the entire period under review. Normal commercial relations are also defined to include programs of the Export-Import Bank of the United States (Exim Bank), the Commodity Credit Corporation (CCC), the Overseas Private Investment Company (OPIC), and the Trade and Development Agency (TDA). These programs, which provide official export credit (Exim and CCC), investment insurance/guarantees (OPIC), and preproject technical support (TDA), are included because they are normally available in developing countries in support of U.S. exports and investment, as are similar programs of other industrialized countries.

The reduction or suspension of economic aid can be, and sometimes is, considered an economic sanction, although such official financial support to target country governments is defined here as a positive incentive—or "carrot"—and thus an alternative to the punitive "stick" of sanctions on normal commerce. U.S. bilateral aid, in any event, is not normally provided to all developing countries but is highly concentrated in a relatively few countries, such as in the Middle East, as a positive incentive toward particular U.S. foreign policy objectives. Economic aid, both bilateral and multilateral through the multilateral development banks, is nevertheless addressed in the case studies, for the most part to demonstrate that the providing or withholding of such aid (whether it is called a carrot or a stick) can often yield greater policy leverage than unilateral sanctions on U.S. trade and investment.

The limitation to economic sanctions for foreign policy objectives excludes threatened or actual sanctions within the international trading system related to reciprocal market access and commitments in the World Trade Organization (WTO) and other trade agreements. Unilateral sanctions are, in fact, permitted under certain circumstances within the WTO dispute procedure, and even for non-WTO members, such as China, strictly commercial disputes, as was the case with the United States over protection of intellectual property rights in 1996, can involve the threat or imposition of unilateral sanctions. Such trade disputes can be highly contentious, but they need to be addressed within the more clearly established framework and practices of trade policy rather than in the largely uncharted waters of unilateral sanctions for foreign policy objectives addressed in this study. There are, however, occasional overlapping issues, such as Chinese exports allegedly produced using prison labor and the withholding of MFN treatment for Vietnam linked to a U.S.-Vietnam trade agreement, and these issues are addressed in the case studies.

Case Study Format

The five country case studies have a common format, in part as a convenient structure for addressing the issues, and in part to facilitate reading them. The presentations are in five sections:

1. Narrative account. This is basically a detailed account of the U.S. policy process in formulating, adopting, and implementing the unilateral sanctions. It gives particular attention to the origins and motivations of sanctions proposals in the executive branch and Congress and especially scrutinizes the interaction of U.S. interests in the target country and domestic political considerations. Another focus is the consultative process with friends and allies, especially when unilateral sanctions are being considered for extension to third countries, as in the 1996 Cuba Libertad (Helms-Burton) Act and the Iran-Libya Sanctions Act (ILSA). The record of hard analysis to assess how a proposed sanction would actually affect the target country and U.S. commercial interests is also examined and found to be woefully inadequate to nonexistent. Readers principally interested in policy process and its reform—as proposed, for example, in the 1997–1998 Sanctions Policy Reform Act (Hamilton-Lugar-Crane) proposal—can benefit from reading the five narrative accounts seriatim, although they are warned that it is a disheartening account in terms of a consistent, coherent U.S. foreign policy.

2. Economic impact.   Each case study assesses the economic impact of proposed or actual sanctions for the target country economy and for U.S. commercial interests. Quantitative estimates are provided in almost all cases for the direct impact of the sanctions, while the indirect impact is described mostly in more general terms. The quantitative estimates are subject to a number of qualifications, but they at least provide a rough order of magnitude. They are particularly useful in the sense that in the land of the blind the one-eyed man is king. No comprehensive assessments were undertaken on the impact of proposed sanctions on the target country economy during U.S. government debate over any of the five countries, assessments that are fundamental to a judgment as to whether the sanction will achieve its intended purpose. In fact, there was a consistent pattern by sanctions proponents to overstate in general terms the likely impact on the target country, with a corresponding overly optimistic judgment about the likely success of the sanction. Assessments of the impact of proposed sanctions on U.S. commercial interests tended to be partial or outer-limit maximum estimates and are presented here in a more complete and balanced way.

3. Net assessment.   This section summarizes the impact of the overall sanctions experience, as recounted and analyzed in the previous sections on U.S. interests in the bilateral relationship with the target country and in broader international terms.

4. Alternatives to current sanctions policy.   The alternatives to current sanctions policy are largely formulated on the distinctive circumstances of the U.S. relationship with the targeted country, including specific foreign policy objectives. The two basic alternative courses generally involve a tightening of current unilateral sanctions and a relaxation or termination of the sanctions. In each case, the changes in sanctions policy can be linked to other actions in the diplomatic, economic policy, and national security fields. Specific alternative policy courses currently under discussion are included, as well as bolder and more far-reaching alternatives to give a fuller perspective of the range of policy options.

5. *Conclusions and recommendations.* These author's conclusions and recommendations, drawn from sections 3 and 4 above, are formulated with a view to consistency and mutual reinforcement toward broader U.S. foreign policy and commercial objectives.

The crosscutting issue of economic sanctions and the U.S. Constitution is addressed in appendix A, which is of timely interest in view of the National Foreign Trade Council's legal challenge to a Massachusetts law that sanctions companies doing business in Myanmar. The law was found unconstitutional at the district court level and was under appeal in early 1999.

Six Inherent Downsides

The use of unilateral economic sanctions for foreign policy objectives has a number of inherent, or at least highly likely, downsides that need to be taken into account when considering the use of such sanctions. These downsides do not mean that the imposition of sanctions cannot achieve a given purpose, but rather that they need to be factored into the overall basis for decision, which unfortunately has not generally been done for U.S. sanctions policy during the 1990s. As benchmarks for reading the case studies, therefore, the following annotated listing of six basic downsides is presented at the outset.

1. *The adverse economic impact of sanctions is likely to fall predominantly on the people in the targeted country, especially the poorest, while an authoritarian government tends to become even more repressive.* The purpose of economic sanctions, multilateral or unilateral, is to cause economic pain in the targeted country to the point where the government changes its behavior in some positive way. Experience has consistently shown, however, that the people suffer

most of the economic pain while the government leadership tends to hunker down and, if anything, tighten its oppressive control. This effect reached tragic proportions for recent multilateral embargoes against Iraq and Haiti, and it recurs in each of the case studies here. It received especially high visibility during the Pope's visit to Cuba in January 1998, causing a growing rift in the Cuban-American community.

2. *Unilateral sanctions, in any event, inflict relatively modest economic pain on the target country compared with multilateral sanctions, while adversely affecting U.S. commercial interests.* With the unilateral approach, other nations continue to trade with and invest in the targeted country, to a large extent replacing U.S. firms. As a consequence, the economic pain—induced pressure on the targeted country's government, even assuming, contrary to the general point in the first downside, that such pressure can change governmental behavior, is greatly attenuated. The related consequence is that U.S. commercial interests suffer as third-country competitors displace U.S. exporters and investors in the target country market. When unilateral sanctions are applied to U.S. imports, as distinct from U.S. exports and investment, however, a similar partial impact results as third-country exports to the United States replace those from the target country. Thus unilateral sanctions on U.S. imports tend to have greater adverse impact on the target country economy than do sanctions on U.S. exports and investment.

3. *Domestic political pressures build to extend U.S. unilateral sanctions to third countries, creating problems with friends and allies.* This effect inevitably follows from the third-country displacement of U.S. companies in the second downside and from public frustration over the consequent adverse impact on U.S. companies and jobs. The ensuing response from members of the Congress and a president who support the initial sanctions on U.S. companies can be to seek to extend U.S. sanction laws to third-country competitors, which other governments, in turn, strongly oppose on grounds of sovereignty and, in some cases, breach of trade agreements. The disputes over third-country extension of U.S. unilateral sanctions against Cuba and Iran are described in the country studies.

4. *Sanctions are used as propaganda by target country governments to blame internal economic problems on the sanctions and to appeal to anti-American nationalism.* Although this response applies to multilateral sanctions as well, it is most effective when only the United States applies the sanctions, and especially if the United States is in dispute with third countries over sanction extension. Fidel Castro is preeminent in his skill to maximize such propaganda opportunities, but the issue arises in all five case studies. If the adverse economic impact of U.S. unilateral sanctions is relatively small, as is usually the case, it can be in the net interest of the target country government for the sanctions to continue so as to deflect internal criticism to the external enemy, the United States. Moreover, a mutual interest is created for continuance of the sanction between anti-American nationalist interests within the target country and third-country commercial interests that benefit from the exclusion of American companies, a factor clearly in play in Cuba and Iran.

5. *Adverse impact on other U.S. foreign policy interests and on the U.S. leadership role.* The most explicit broader U.S. policy interest that arises in several of the case studies is in long-standing U.S. support for liberal trade, including a well-functioning World Trade Organization. The U.S.-EU dispute over the Cuba Libertad Act, brought into the WTO, caused some prosanction members of Congress, normally supporters of liberal trade, to denounce the WTO and oppose "fast track" authority for new trade negotiations. In terms of the U.S. international leadership role, unilateral sanctions have been sharply criticized throughout the world as an example of how the United States plays domestic politics to the detriment of shared international interests.

6. *The loss of U.S. private sector engagement in the target country as a positive force for political as well as economic change.* Unilateral sanctions, by definition, reduce or terminate U.S. private sector engagement in the target country, and with it the personal and institutional impact that such engagement has in support of change within the country toward democracy and market-oriented economic policies. Special attention is given to this subject in the case studies, and U.S. private sector engagement is consistently found to have an actual or potential important positive impact for change, in qualitative as well as quantitative terms.

These are the unique and inherent downsides to the use of unilateral economic sanctions as a foreign policy instrument, which arise throughout the case studies contained in chapters 2 through 6. Broader analytic conclusions and policy recommendations are then presented in the final two chapters. Chapter 7 specifically addresses the economic impact of unilateral sanctions, the effectiveness of sanctions to achieve their intended purposes, the policy process, and alternative policy instruments. Chapter 8 takes on the broader issue of doing good versus feeling good, which has much to do with the values and moral principle underlying U.S. foreign policy in the very changed circumstances of the post–Cold War 1990s.

Note

1. National Association of Manufacturers (NAM), *A Catalog of New U.S. Unilateral Economic Sanctions for Foreign Policy Purposes 1993–96* (Washington, D.C.: NAM, March 1997). Senator Jesse Helms, in "What Sanctions Epidemic?" *Foreign Affairs* 78 (January/February 1999), explains why most of the sanctions enumerated in the NAM report were of minor consequence or not really sanctions. The Helms article, however, does not address the issue of whether broadly based sanctions, as in the case studies here, actually achieve their purpose, and at what cost to other U.S. interests.

2

Cuba: A Western Hemisphere Anachronism

1. Narrative Account

U.S. UNILATERAL ECONOMIC SANCTIONS against the Castro government began in July 1960. The United States reduced the Cuban sugar import quota by 95 percent to retaliate for the nationalization of U.S.-owned oil refineries, and by February 1962 an almost total embargo on Cuban trade and travel had been imposed, which still remains in effect. The 39-year experience with economic sanctions against Cuba, however, is sharply divided into two phases—Cold War (1960–1989) and post–Cold War (1990–1998). The discussion that follows presents a brief account of the Cold War years to provide policy context and highlight the contrasting forces at play and then focuses on the circumstances of the 1990s, which form the basis for current U.S. policy.

Although the initial sanctions were triggered by expropriation of U.S. property, the embargo quickly became linked to national security interests as Soviet military facilities were established in Cuba and the Castro government supported communist subversion throughout the hemisphere and elsewhere. In the early years through 1975, diplomatic isolation and trade embargo against Cuba were broadened throughout most of the hemisphere. But Cuba later improved relations with many Latin American countries, and the U.S. policy of detente with the Soviet Union led the Ford and Carter administrations to attempt steps toward normalization of the Cuban relationship. These initiatives failed to produce significant results, however, because Fidel Castro was unresponsive. By the early 1980s, pro-Castro governments in

Nicaragua and Grenada, communist insurgency in El Salvador, and the harder line anticommunist policy of the Reagan administration led to reinforced U.S. sanctions against Cuba through the end of the decade.

This three-decade embargo constituted a Cold War stalemate and a basically stable U.S.-Cuba relationship after the Missile Crisis of 1962. As a result of that crisis, the United States agreed not to attack Cuba militarily, and the Soviet Union committed massive financial support to the Castro regime, which ensured reasonable prosperity within Cuba despite the U.S. embargo and the failures of the centrally planned Cuban economy. There was a mutual interest in restricting the outflow of Cubans to the United States, except for the brief 1980 Mariel boat exodus. The U.S. embargo may have put some financial constraints on Cuban support for communist insurgencies elsewhere in the world, but this is doubtful because the Soviet Union ultimately paid the bills. The only clear, positive result from the Cuban embargo for U.S. foreign policy was the substantial financial burden it placed on the Soviet Union. That burden (along with a similar burden in Vietnam, as described in that case study) significantly contributed to the USSR's financial collapse.

All of these elements of stalemate and stability in the U.S.-Cuba relationship changed with the disintegration of the Soviet Union and the abrupt termination of Russian economic support for Cuba. Such support dropped from $6 billion in 1989 to near zero in 1992, causing a devastating decline in Cuban imports from $8.1 billion to $2.3 billion. Food shortages and blackouts from the lack of imported oil were the politically sensitive immediate effects. The widespread shutdown of industrial and agricultural production and the sharp contraction of the investment sector began the longer-term process of deterioration in the industrial base and economic infrastructure of the Cuban economy that continues today. In terms of U.S. security interests, the Russians left Cuba except for maintaining one intelligence listening post, and the Cuban government lost the financial resources and political standing to support revolutionary movements abroad.

This radically new situation called for a fundamental reappraisal of U.S. policy toward Cuba, as was being done for U.S.

relations elsewhere in the "New World Order," but the Bush administration never did so. Cuba policy received wide-ranging commentary and some public debate outside the government, but the initiative for crafting a post–Cold War strategy gravitated to Congress. U.S. policy finally took the form of the 1992 Cuban Democracy Act, or "Torricelli Act," in recognition of its principal sponsor, Congressman Robert Torricelli, a New Jersey Democrat and chairman of the Subcommittee on Hemispheric Affairs of the House Foreign Affairs Committee.

Discussion leading up to the act revolved around three basic options for U.S. policy toward Cuba in the new post–Cold War circumstances. One option would be simply to declare victory, terminate the embargo, and let the forces of change, including contact with Americans through trade and travel, blow away the failed communist regime and its leader. This was basically U.S. policy toward the Soviet bloc during the late 1980s and was espoused for Cuba in the early 1990s by some conservative experts and press, including the *Wall Street Journal* and the *Journal of Commerce*. The second option was to open a dialogue with the Castro government and offer step-by-step relaxation of the U.S. embargo in parallel with progressive political and economic reforms within Cuba. This option was similar in concept to the Ford and Carter initiatives, with circumstances presumably more favorable in view of Castro's loss of Soviet political and economic support. The third option was to tighten the embargo so as to intensify the economic crisis within Cuba, thereby forcing the communist regime either to yield to democratic elections or face violent upheaval.

The 1992 Cuban Democracy Act was a combination of options two and three—a "carrots and sticks" approach—but with principal emphasis on the embargo-tightening sticks. This outcome derived from an evolution of viewpoint by Chairman Torricelli and the rapid growth in influence of the hard-line anti-Castro majority of Cuban-Americans. During the 1980s, Torricelli had advocated a dialogue with Castro. In 1989 he cosponsored legislation to partially lift the embargo to permit shipments of medicines and medical equipment to Cuba on the grounds that "to have an American policy...based on the idea that we wish the revolution didn't happen, that he'd go away, is foolish going into a fourth decade."[1] The

Cuban American National Foundation (CANF), founded in 1981 under the dynamic leadership of Jorge Mas Canosa, however, steadily built its lobbying capability in support of a tightening of the embargo. Mas Canosa had numerous discussions with Torricelli, and the congressman progressively shifted to the much harder, anti-Castro position of the 1992 act. Its principal provisions were to prohibit subsidiaries of American companies from trading with Cuba, which had been legal since 1975, and to restrict ships that traded with Cuba from docking in U.S. ports. These "stick" provisions were combined with the "carrot" of support for the president to undertake "carefully calibrated" steps toward improved relations with Cuba, although provisions in earlier drafts to ease travel and cultural exchanges were dropped.

President George Bush initially opposed the legislation on the grounds that the prohibition on trade by U.S. subsidiaries was an extraterritorial extension of the embargo and would cause problems with trading partners, particularly in Europe. In April 1992, however, Bush, by executive order, did restrict docking for ships trading with Cuba. Mas Canosa, meanwhile, met with Democratic presidential candidate Bill Clinton to urge support for the Cuban Democracy Act. On April 23 Clinton met with several hundred Cuban-Americans in Miami, announced, "I have read the Torricelli-Graham bill and I like it" (referring to Florida Democratic senator Bob Graham, who was cosponsor of the bill), and left Miami with $275,000 in campaign contributions. Bush, facing the loss of Cuban-American votes in Florida and New Jersey, then reversed himself and signed the Cuban Democracy Act in October 1992.

The Cuban Democracy Act thus became heavily enmeshed in the 1992 domestic election campaign. During its passage little serious attention was given to its potential impact on the Cuban economy and thus its ability to further U.S. objectives of an early democratic transition with a minimum of violence. This lack of economic analysis led to two widespread misperceptions with, in one case, serious consequences.

The first and more serious misperception related to the prohibition of U.S. subsidiary exports to Cuba and its impact on the Cuban economy. Such exports to Cuba had risen sharply from about \$200 million a year in the mid-1980s to more than \$700 million in 1991, and these exports, mostly foodstuffs and pharmaceuticals from Western Europe, which had raised the ire of the CANF, did almost entirely disappear after passage of the 1992 act. What transpired in terms of the Cuban economy, however, was that the earlier buildup of U.S. subsidiary exports resulted from the cutoff of Soviet export finance and a radical shift of dwindling Cuban imports from Eastern to Western Europe. When the U.S. subsidiaries stopped exporting to Cuba, they were simply replaced by French, Swiss, and other European company exports at little extra cost to Cuba. Moreover, although European governments did protest the extraterritorial extension of the U.S. law, as President Bush had anticipated, and ordered U.S. subsidiaries to comply with European law and ignore the Cuban Democracy Act, they did not pursue the issue because of the benefits to European companies at the expense of U.S. subsidiaries. This veiled support for domestic commercial interests by European governments in 1992 went unrecognized in Washington, however, and led to a serious miscalculation by President Clinton and congressional leaders four years later in believing that European trading partners would again roll over for the extraterritorial reach of the 1996 Libertad, or Helms-Burton, Act. The critical difference was that the 1996 act was targeted at European companies, not U.S. subsidiaries, and the European governments this time did not roll over.

The second misperception of the 1992 act concerned the adverse impact on the Cuban economy caused by the restrictions on U.S. docking for ships engaged in trade with Cuba. In fact, the restrictions sharply raised shipping rates by as much as 40 percent for some cargoes and thus cost the Cuban economy \$100 million to \$200 million a year, a substantial amount during the most difficult years 1992–1993. But in this instance President Bush had already imposed docking sanctions to head off the legislation, and thus the act itself, when finally adopted, had no impact.

The provision of the 1992 Cuban Democracy Act that would become an important issue leading up to the 1996 Libertad Act was the U.S. policy objective "to be prepared to reduce sanctions in carefully calibrated ways in response to positive developments in Cuba." The Cuban economy, as explained in the following section, bottomed out in 1993, and interest grew within the first Clinton administration to attempt such "carefully calibrated" moves. An accord on illegal migration was reached in May 1995, with provision to return Cuban boat people directly to Cuba, and initial market-oriented reforms within Cuba were generally considered "positive developments." U.S. business interests became more active in supporting a relaxation of the embargo as European, Canadian, and other competitors took advantage of new opportunities for private investment in Cuba. It was widely anticipated in 1995 that a second Clinton administration would pursue a more comprehensive initiative for improved relations with the Castro government.

In part to head off such an outcome, the more conservative members of the new Republican majority in Congress, together with hard-line Cuban-American groups, developed the Libertad Act proposal. Senator Jesse Helms made this his first major initiative as chairman of the Senate Foreign Relations Committee in February 1995, and Republican congressman Dan Burton, who had succeeded Torricelli as House subcommittee chair, introduced the same legislation in the House, consisting of four titles. Title I, as ultimately adopted, strengthens existing sanctions with respect to international financial institutions, U.S. imports from third countries, and economic assistance programs, as well as providing support for democratic and human rights groups within Cuba, the so-called Track Two. Title II nullifies the "carefully calibrated" objective of the 1992 act and effectively eliminates the president's authority to negotiate any easing of the embargo with the Castro government. The president is prohibited from relaxing the embargo until a post-Castro provisional government is in place that, inter alia, has organized free elections within 18 months under the supervision of international observers, has released all political prisoners, has permitted political parties, and has ceased interference with radio and TV Marti broadcasts from Miami. Title III allows U.S. citizens and companies to file federal lawsuits against foreign companies that have taken control of their former properties in Cuba, a legal recourse that includes current U.S. citizens who were Cuban citizens when their properties were expropriated. Title IV denies entry into the United States of foreign citizens who are corporate officials or otherwise involved in the control of the expropriated properties defined in Title III, as well as of their spouses and minor children.

The formulation of the Libertad Act was done by Helms-Burton staffers in close contact with the three Cuban-American members of Congress—Republicans Ileana Ros-Lehtinen and Lincoln Diaz-Balart of Florida and Democrat Robert Menendez of New Jersey. CANF, of course, strongly supported the initiative. Significant new, active supporters were the National Association of Sugar Mill Owners of Cuba and the Bacardi rum company, major former owners of properties in Cuba expropriated by the Castro government. These sugar and rum interests became strong supporters of the extension of Title III rights to Americans who were Cuban citizens at the time of expropriation, which was their own situation, although this provision was initially developed by Senator Helms's staff.

The Title III extension was especially controversial in policy terms as well as in its potential economic impact among Americans. Extending U.S. expropriation law to claimants who were not U.S. citizens at the time of expropriation conflicts with long-established international practices by all other countries and for existing U.S. law except with respect to Cuba. Polish-Americans and Palestinian-Americans, for example, cannot bring comparable claims in U.S. courts if they were not American citizens at the time of expropriation in Poland or Israel, which probably means that this provision would be found unconstitutional if challenged in court on this basis. The extension of Title III rights to Cuban-Americans was strongly opposed by other Americans whose property in Cuba was expropriated and who have been legal claimants for more than 30 years. These Americans hold more than $6 billion in claims, or 50 percent to 100 percent of today's Cuban gross domestic product (GDP), an unprecedentedly large expropriation situation to begin with, and they will clearly have to settle for a fraction of their claims. To extend Title III rights to Cuban-Americans who owned the sugar lands and the rum and other industrial properties before the revolution would, by likely increasing U.S. claims several times, further delay and diminish the final outcome for other American claimants. And yet the Cuban-American interests, with

strong and effective lobbying by the Sugar Owners Association and
Bacardi, prevailed over the less well-financed and organized
"Certified Claimants" group of former U.S. property holders in
Cuba.[2]

The Libertad Act nevertheless faced an uncertain course. The
Clinton administration position was ambivalent over the 12-
month period until February 1996. Secretary of State Warren
Christopher said that he would recommend a presidential veto on
the grounds that "these inflexible standards for responding to what
may be a rapidly evolving situation [in Cuba] could leave the
United States on the sidelines during a transition," and warned in
general terms that Title III "will be extremely difficult to defend
under international law" and could "create a flood of lawsuits concerning properties located outside the U.S."[3] There was never,
however, an assessment by the administration or the congressional
committees involved of the likely relatively small impact of the proposed legislation on the Cuban economy, nor by the U.S. Trade
Representative or other administration officials of whether and
how the act might conflict with U.S. commitments in the World
Trade Organization.

The real question, of course, was whether President Clinton
would agree to Secretary Christopher's veto recommendation, and
the answer was never clear. The State Department might oppose
the bill, but White House political advisers, looking ahead to the
1996 elections, pressed for some kind of compromise sanctions bill
that would maximize the president's flexibility in implementation
while appearing responsive to Cuban-American voters in Florida
and New Jersey. This tactic appeared to be working because many
Democrats and a few Republicans in the Senate threatened a fili-
buster of anything like the hard-line bill adopted in the House.
Whatever weakened version might come out of the Senate would
then have to be negotiated in conference committee, and the outlook at the beginning of 1996 was for a relatively weak bill that
would probably not greatly constrain the reelected president.
Meanwhile, Cuban-American lobbying efforts intensified in support of the hard-line House version, while U.S. business interests,
with a few exceptions, did not strongly oppose the bill, in part to
avoid protests from Cuban-American groups in the domestic

market and in part because of mixed attitudes and misperceptions about the consequences of its passage.

Then on February 26, 1996, two unarmed aircraft over international waters off the coast of Cuba were shot down by the Cuban Air Force, and four American residents lost their lives. Outrage exploded throughout the United States, and President Clinton came under strong pressure to do something in response. The president rejected one option—a quick punitive strike against the Cuban air force—in the face of strong opposition from the Department of Defense concerned about a retaliatory attack on U.S. facilities at Guantanamo Bay. Instead, he announced almost unqualified support for the Libertad Act, and within days the Republican majority, with ample Democratic support, passed the very hard-line bill, as described above, while administration representatives at the conference markup were transformed from earlier critics to obedient supporters.

A critical factor in this important U.S. foreign policy action is why Fidel Castro shot down the planes. He knew about the flights in advance from an infiltrator in the "Brothers to the Rescue" organization that undertook the flights. He apparently intended to shoot down all three planes (one did escape) and then fabricate a story about flights over Cuba to drop leaflets, which the "Brothers to the Rescue" had done before. Castro was in the process of suppressing the internal dissident grouping, "Concilio Cubano," and reining in earlier market-oriented economic reforms, for which the shootdown would deflect attention, but he also had to know that the shootdown would likely trigger passage of Helms-Burton in extreme form. Many Cuban experts believe Castro, in fact, saw such legislation, with all its extraterritorial ramifications, as in his interest in dividing the United States from its friends and allies, as it subsequently did, a daring if risky foreign policy move characteristic of the Cuban leader over several decades. In contrast, the Clinton administration's policy toward Cuba during 1995–1996 was one of tactical maneuvering with a Republican-led Congress, largely determined by domestic political objectives for the 1996 election.

The follow-on to President Clinton's signing of the Libertad Act on March 12, 1996, was predictable in terms of third-country reactions. The United Nations (UN) condemned the act as affecting the sovereignty and legitimate interests of other states by a vote of 138 to 3, with 38 abstentions—the most severe defeat ever of U.S. anti-Castro policy in that forum. The terms of condemnation were even stronger than the separate rebuke of Castro's shootdown of the unarmed planes. Subsequent UN votes have increased further the opposition to the U.S. embargo, reaching 157 to 2 (the United States and Israel), with 12 abstentions, in 1998. The greater and prolonged problems, however, involved reactions by trading partners, especially within the WTO, where the European Union (EU), with support from virtually all other members, brought a complaint against the United States over violations of commitments within the multilateral trading system. The formal complaint was legally complex, but in essence it was a charge that the United States was applying a secondary boycott against European and other companies for trading with or investing in Cuba. The dispute quickly became bitter, especially with Canada and across the Atlantic. Sir Leon Brittan, the EU commissioner for external relations, summed it up by calling U.S. unilateral embargo policy the biggest obstacle between the United States and the EU: "This dispute should be brought to an end. It is damaging the relationship, and it is damaging to the Western world."[4]

The initial U.S. response to the EU complaint in the WTO was to threaten to boycott the dispute panel procedures or to claim a national security exception to its WTO obligations, either of which, as explained in the following section, would have substantially damaged the newly established dispute procedure and U.S. leadership within the WTO. To avoid this, the EU and the United States negotiated a bilateral agreement, concluded in May 1998. The agreement derives from the fact that foreign direct investment in Cuba in the 1990s breaks new ground in internationally accepted expropriation policy whereby properties expropriated from American companies are resold to other non-American private companies before the expropriation claim has been settled. In the agreement, the EU agrees to establish "disciplines" to inhibit and deter such investment by denying a wide range of government assistance to such transactions, including loans, grants, and political risk insurance. The Clinton administration, in turn, agrees to seek from the Congress waiver authority for Title IV so as not to apply it against EU firms.

The Republican leadership in Congress, however, considers the agreement inadequate, especially for EU investments before May 1998, which are not definitively subject to the disciplines. Thus, as of early 1999, the U.S.-EU dispute was in limbo. President Clinton continued to suspend Title III and had not invoked Title IV against an EU company. Congress appeared unlikely to change the 1996 act as required to activate the bilateral agreement, and the EU had therefore not put the negotiated disciplines into effect and reserved the right to reactivate the WTO dispute panel. Most curious, no significant EU investment in Cuba on an expropriated U.S. property subject to the disciplines has been reported by either side, and there may not be any.

Apart from the U.S.-EU dispute, U.S. Cuba policy evolved significantly during 1998, partly as a result of the papal visit to Cuba in January. The Pope's message of engagement with Cuba to bring about social and economic change and his criticism of the embargo as primarily hurting the Cuban people resonated in the United States. In April, President Clinton, with reference to the papal visit, resumed direct flights to Cuba and eased restrictions on dollar remittances to Cuba by Cuban-Americans. The Cuban-American community also became more openly split, for and against the embargo, to some extent along generational lines. The large majority still supports the embargo verbally, although as explained in the following section, the rapid increase in dollar remittances to Cuba since 1993 tends to undermine the embargo. The number of Cuban-Americans traveling to Cuba has increased rapidly from 40,000 in 1995 to 70,000 in 1997 to an estimated 90,000 in 1998,[5] and the CANF has been weakened by the November 1997 death of its able leader, Jorge Mas Canosa, and by the indictment of one of its members in a plot to assassinate Castro. On the legislative front, Senator Christopher Dodd (D-Conn.) and Representative Esteban Torres (D-Calif.) initiated a proposal to unilaterally lift the embargo on U.S. exports of food and medicines to Cuba that attracted 132 House and 30 Senate cosponsors during 1998. The proposal will likely be reintroduced in 1999.

The U.S. Cuba embargo faces more open debate in 1999–2000 than at any time in its 39-year history. In October 1998, former secretaries of state Henry Kissinger and Lawrence Eagleburger and others called for a bipartisan commission to review Cuba policy, which Senator John Warner (R-Va.) and other senators forwarded to the president. In January 1999, President Clinton rejected the commission proposal, reportedly for domestic political reasons related to Vice President Al Gore's presidential election prospects in 2000. The issues that would be addressed by such a commission, however, remain unresolved. One issue is whether the embargo hurts the Cuban people more than the Castro government, and by how much. Another is whether an easing of the embargo will increase or decrease pressure on Fidel Castro to accede to further political and economic reforms within Cuba. Put another way, does the continuing embargo play to Castro's advantage or disadvantage? These issues are determined largely by the impact of the economic embargo on the Cuban economy, which itself has changed greatly during the 1990s.

2. Economic Impact

On the Cuban Economy

The impact of U.S. unilateral sanctions on the Cuban economy derives principally from the comprehensive embargo dating back to 1961 and to a far lesser extent from the tightening effects of the Cuban Democracy and Libertad acts of 1992 and 1996. From 1961 until 1989, the comprehensive embargo forced Cuba to restructure its trade and investment away from the United States, the preponderant and natural economic partner for smaller Caribbean Basin countries, to the Soviet bloc, a move made possible by huge Soviet financial assistance. The Cuban economy during the 1990s, which is the period addressed here, then experienced, in rapid succession, a devastating free fall, an uneven bottoming out, and an ambiguous, export-led recovery. The major interacting forces at play during this period were the abrupt cutoff of Russian aid, limited market-oriented reforms by the Castro government, the continuing and somewhat tightened U.S. embargo, and the rapid increase in dollar remittances by Cuban-Americans back to Cuba. In overall analytic context, the Cuban experience of the 1990s has been that of a dual economy, whereby the external sector, given priority by the Cuban government so as to generate critically needed hard currency, is distinguished from the much larger domestic sector, for the most part still centrally planned and moribund. This duality has broadened in the late 1990s into a highly distorting interaction between the economy's dollar- and peso-generating sectors that gives prominent advantages to the one-third or more of the population with access to dollars.

The first, free-fall phase was caused by the abrupt termination of Russian aid and lasted from 1989 until 1992. The crisis centered on the precipitous decline in imports from $8.1 billion to $2.3 billion, or by 72 percent. By sector, imports of food and fuels (almost all petroleum) were down less than the average, by 55 percent and 68 percent, respectively, reflecting the immediate political sensitivity of food lines and electric power blackouts, while machinery and transport equipment imports dropped by an even more devastating 81 percent, resulting in a virtual standstill in new investment projects and maintenance of economic infrastructure.[6]

The corresponding decline in Cuban GDP is more difficult to assess. Cuban Central Bank figures show a 35 percent decline between 1989 and 1993, but these figures are in constant 1981 centrally planned peso prices that can have little bearing on real economic value. Quantity-based production figures for key industries indicate a much sharper decline: sugar down by 47 percent, steel by 58 percent, cement by 72 percent, yarns and fabrics by 75 to 84 percent, and fertilizer by 85 percent. Thus, the Cuban GDP probably dropped by considerably more than the 35 percent official figure—probably by 50 percent or more.

Fidel Castro declared the new situation a "special period" of extraordinary austerity and initially pursued a strategy of economic self-sufficiency at a more rudimentary level of development— replacing automobiles with bicycles, delivery trucks with horse-drawn carts, and tractors with oxen. Shortages of food, medicine, and other consumer goods nevertheless spread. The basic economic dilemma was that the Cuban economy over 30 years had been restructured toward ever greater dependence on sugar exports to the Soviet bloc at highly subsidized prices, while the rest of the "New Caribbean Economic Order" was moving away from sugar and other traditional commodity exports toward tourism, labor-intensive industry, and nontraditional farm exports such as fruits, vegetables, and cut flowers.[7] In 1989, sugar still constituted 73 percent of total Cuban exports, while for other Caribbean-island economies, tourism receipts alone had become six times as large as sugar, coffee, and banana exports combined. In this context of a Cuban economy still centrally planned and almost totally out of competitive sync with market opportunities, the continuing U.S. embargo through 1992 had relatively small impact.

The 1993–1994 bottoming out of the Cuban economy was the critical stage for the Castro government's response to the economic crisis caused by the abrupt termination of Soviet financial support, and the U.S. embargo during this time became a more prominent, but not decisive factor in the outcome. The Cuban economy reached its low point in the summer of 1993, with food shortages, blackouts, and, for the first time in more than 30 years, Havana street demonstrations. The Cuban government reacted cautiously, avoiding police violence that would have undermined the fledgling tourism sector and brought international opprobrium. In parallel, several market-oriented reforms adopted beginning in 1992 were starting to pay off in terms of increased dollar earnings and domestic production of foodstuffs and consumer services. New regulations for foreign direct investment attracted foreign investors to the hotel and tourist services sector and to nickel, Cuba's second largest export commodity after sugar. Farm cooperatives were given incentives to produce for newly established farmers' markets, and private family businesses were permitted for various consumer services, from home repairs to small restaurants. The most important economic reforms were the legalization of the U.S. dollar and the establishment of dollar-only stores for tourists and Cubans who received dollar remittances from friends and relatives in the United States and elsewhere abroad. Although little noticed at the time, such remittances grew rapidly, from less than $100 million a year in 1990 to about $300 million in 1993.

The result was some easing of domestic shortages and the severe foreign exchange squeeze by late 1993. Total imports inched up from a low of $2.0 billion in 1993 to $2.1 billion in 1994, and a 1 percent increase in GDP was recorded in 1994. This bottoming out, however, was very uneven. Almost all the gains were in the limited economic reform sectors while the rest of the economy remained stagnant. Sugar production, which dropped from 8.1 million tons in 1989 to 4.0 million tons in 1994, would reach a low of 3.3 million tons in 1995. Most devastating for medium- to long-term recovery was the collapse of the investment sector, with gross capital formation down from 26 percent of GDP in 1989 to an incredibly low 5 percent in 1994. The Cuban economy, in effect, was living off its assets, a reality that would exact a progressively heavier toll over time.

In this shifting orientation of the Cuban economy toward the international market, the U.S. embargo became a more important factor. Sixty to seventy percent of tourism for the northerly Caribbean islands' economies, more than 90 percent of labor-intensive export industry, and a similarly high share of nontraditional agricultural exports derive from the U.S. market. The growing Cuban tourism sector would have grown much faster if Americans could have traveled freely to Cuba, and the free trade zones established by the Castro government remain largely uninhabited without access to the U.S. market. The prohibition on U.S. exports to and investment in Cuba, in contrast, was less inhibiting, because European, Canadian, Mexican, and other firms were readily available to move into what were still limited investment opportunities in Cuba. In any event, the U.S. embargo, however restrictive, was not sufficient to prevent the Cuban government, with some recourse to market incentives, to survive its most severe economic crisis.

The export-led recovery that began in 1995 remains uncertain both in pace and composition. Official Cuban figures for GDP growth were 3 percent in 1995, 7 percent in 1996, 3 percent in 1997, and 1 percent in 1998. The officially recorded growth remains concentrated in the external sector, although unrecorded growth in the gray market private sector has also been substantial. The admittedly bloated public sector has been pared back to bring fiscal deficits and peso inflation under control, but this effort has created a major problem of redundant workers that can only be absorbed by further private sector reforms. The backward-looking obsession with increased sugar production has been costly and basically unsuccessful. Environmental problems are growing, related in large part to the continued neglect of the investment sector.

The course ahead for the Cuban economy will depend on the economic reform program within Cuba and implementation of the continuing U.S. unilateral embargo, both of which are highly uncertain at this point. Fidel Castro and his hard-line communist supporters have restrained and in some respects rolled back the market-oriented reforms during 1996–1998. Private sector businesses, and indeed all Cubans with dollars to spend, depend less on the government and are more difficult to control politically. Fidel Castro thus condemns avaricious capitalists and reiterates that market-based reforms are a temporary expedient, while authorities crack down on unregistered small businesses and impose heavy new taxes on them. Meanwhile, however, a process of economic and political change—largely generational in character—is clearly under way within Cuba. The pervasive shift toward a dollar-based market economy and public disdain for an incompetent communist bureaucracy are hilariously illustrated in *Guantanamera*, a 1995 film that was particularly significant for having been produced and shown within Cuba. Young Cubans, especially the better educated, understand that change will and should come toward a more productive market economy and a more democratic form of government, but they are not prepared to try to expedite the process through violent confrontation.

The role of the continuing U.S. embargo, extended to certain third-country investors in the 1996 Libertad Act, is also undergoing important change. The underlying embargo, as noted above, has a major adverse influence by withholding the U.S. market from Cuban exports of goods and services, and the Libertad Act has had some small additional impact on the Cuban economy. The most important immediate effect of the 1996 act was to increase the cost of export credit by about 2 percent, which affected the sugar sector, in particular, by about $100 million in 1996.

Direct investment in Cuba by third countries, however, which was the act's principal target, has not been greatly inhibited. Hotels and other tourist facilities are not affected because they are not on expropriated U.S. properties, and in fact foreign investment commitments in the tourism sector increased substantially in 1998. The Canadian firm, Sherritt International, has proceeded with its investment program in the nickel sector, which is on expropriated U.S. property, while ignoring the Libertad Act with the full support of the Canadian government. An Israeli firm has invested in citrus production on expropriated U.S. property in defiance of the act. And major foreign investment in the Cuban telephone system, led initially by a Mexican and later by European firms, was extricated from the act's reach when the investors bought out the expropriation claim directly from the American claimant, IT&T. Only a few smaller investments have not gone forward because of the Libertad Act.

The most dramatic change in the U.S. response to the continuing Cuban embargo was the sharp rise in dollar remittances to Cuba, estimated at $600 million to $800 million a year for the period 1995–1997, the same years the Libertad Act was being adopted and implemented.[8] The enormity of the $600 million to $800 million figure is evident in its relationship to other sources of dollars flowing into Cuba. Cuban tourist receipts in 1996 were $1.4 billion, sugar exports $1 billion, and all other exports less than $1 billion combined. The dollar inflow from foreign investment was much lower still, probably $100 million to $200 million, although the exact amount is kept secret. These figures, however, are gross dollar receipts and do not reflect the import component for tourism and merchandise exports, which is especially high in Cuba. Cuban hotels import most of their food and other supporting goods, while the sugar industry has to import fertilizer, oil to run tractors and trains, and machinery and parts to service them. The net dollar inflow for Cuban tourism is as low as 30 percent of the gross, or only $400 million in 1996, while that for sugar exports is about 50 percent, or $500 million of net inflow. For remittances, in contrast, all of the dollars stay in the country, and gross receipts equal net receipts—in other words $600 million to $800 million of net dollar inflow. Thus, in 1996, the estimated remittances were larger than the net dollar inflow from tourism or sugar exports, and the $800 million upper limit was almost equal to tourism and sugar exports combined. If a similar gross/net adjustment is made for other exports, up to one-third of the total net inflow of dollars into Cuba was from remittances.

The motivation for these remittances, of course, is humanitarian, to alleviate the serious economic deprivation of relatives and friends in Cuba, a situation that did not exist during the period of massive Soviet financial support through 1989. But at the same time, the large dollar remittance inflow offsets the financial squeeze on the overall economy from the embargo and makes it easier for the Castro government to manage the country despite the failures of the centrally planned economy. The remittances go directly to the Cuban people, facilitated by the dollar-only stores established by the Cuban government. But the dollars are for the most part fungible, and as Cubans abroad, mostly Cuban-Americans, pay for much of the food and basic needs of the people, they free up considerable financial resources for the government to use on other priorities.

The outlook for the Cuban economy in 1999 and beyond, as influenced by U.S. embargo and Cuban economic policies, is thus for continued slow growth or stagnation and progressive decline in the country's industrial base and infrastructure, more powerfully expressed in Spanish as *desmoronamiento*. U.S. sanctions policy is largely self-defeating in its implementation because the very large remittance payments by Cuban-Americans, still mostly illegal even with the easing of official restrictions in May 1998, tend to offset the adverse impact on Cuba from the embargo on trade and investment. The dilemma for economic policy within Cuba is fundamental and apparently irreconcilable over the longer term without a basic systemic change. The extraordinary 20:1 dollar-peso dual economy—that is, maintaining a 20:1 or more convertible dollar exchange rate to the peso with a 1:1 official exchange rate—creates enormous distortions within the economy, and, in particular, provides little incentive to raise gross investment from the moribund 7 to 8 percent in 1998 (less than the depreciation of the existing capital base) to the targeted 25 to 30 percent needed to achieve a sustained 4 to 5 percent annual GDP growth.[9] The fact is, the dollar-based sector of the economy centers on tourism and "exports within the borders" (that is, dollar remittances spent within Cuba) that are not investment-intensive, while the predominant peso-based, centrally planned sector of the economy, where investment and job-creating productive enterprises and infrastructure should be concentrated, offers no incentives to foreign or domestic investors.

On U.S. Commercial Interests

The adverse effects of the unilateral embargo against Cuba on U.S. exports and foreign direct investment have also changed greatly in market context and have become far larger in the post–Cold War 1990s. Throughout the 1980s, Cuban trade, while much larger than it is today, was predominantly on highly subsidized contract with the Soviet bloc. In 1989, only 11 percent of Cuban imports came from Organization for Economic Cooperation and Development (OECD) countries and another 6 percent from Latin America, and many of these imports were financed by official export credits that would not have been available to U.S. exporters even in the absence of the embargo. The annual loss of U.S. exports from the embargo was therefore not likely to have been more than $200 million to $300 million.[10] Private foreign direct investment opportunities in Cuba were close to nil for everybody.

In sharp contrast, the opportunities for U.S. exports to Cuba in the late 1990s would be substantial in the absence of the embargo. U.S. market share for imports of other Caribbean countries is mostly in the 60 to 70 percent range, and under normal circumstances it would, if anything, be higher in Cuba in view of geographic proximity and ethnic ties with the Florida business community. Total Cuban imports of goods and services in 1996 were $4.2 billion, but in the absence of the U.S. embargo this figure would be considerably higher as greater dollar revenues into Cuba were generated by American tourists, Cuban exports to the United States, and a possibly even higher level of remittances. A conservative estimate for total Cuban imports, absent the embargo, is $5 billion to $6 billion, with a corresponding 60 percent U.S. market share in the order of $3 billion. Such exports would be wide-ranging in capital, consumer, and agricultural goods, as well as all manner of services. This U.S. market share, of course, is based on normal commercial relations, including a positive political relationship, which would not be the case if the embargo were lifted while the communist regime continued.

The adverse impact on American companies from lost investment opportunities in Cuba in the late 1990s is more difficult to assess and has a longer-term time dimension. European and other investments in hotels and related tourism facilities are generally profitable under existing circumstances, but the potential for prime beachfront and Havana locations once relations are normalized with the United States is far greater. The foreign investment in the Cuban telephone system of several hundred million dollars during the initial years could develop into a much larger financial position over time, as could the nickel and related mining investments by Sherritt. In all of these cases, absent the embargo, American companies would have been active and largely successful competitors. There is also, of course, a high risk factor for investing within the legal framework of a communist regime that will likely change sometime soon. Sherritt's situation is particularly vulnerable in view of the outstanding U.S. expropriation claim. The track record for private companies that invested in former Soviet bloc communist countries, however, has generally been good in terms of legal transition, and certainly tourist and other export-oriented Cuban investments offer potentially great mutual interests for the current foreign investors and a future democratic government in Cuba. In sum, losses of investment opportunities for U.S. firms from the continuing embargo are currently likely to be relatively small in dollar equity terms—perhaps $100 million to $200 million a year—but the loss of strategic market position in Cuba over the longer term is much greater.

There are also indirect adverse consequences for U.S. commercial interests from the Cuban embargo, both for specific contracts and in broader policy terms. In the specific example of service contracts related to international airports throughout the world, a U.S. company cannot bid on an exclusive contract because it is illegal for a U.S. company to service a Cuban aircraft landing in the airport. Other specific examples relate to sourcing of component production and R&D out of the United States to Europe and elsewhere so as to avoid U.S. export controls related to the Cuba embargo.

The broader policy consequences are most important for the extraterritorial dimension of the Cuban embargo in the 1996 Libertad Act, which has had significant adverse impact on U.S. interests in the WTO.[11] A priority U.S. trade policy objective for more than 20 years was to strengthen the GATT—and now the WTO—dispute settlement mechanism so as to obtain compliance by other governments to trade-liberalizing commitments. The extraterritorial reach of Titles III and IV of the 1996 act, however, provoked a WTO complaint against the United States by the EU, with wide support from other WTO members. The initial U.S. response, by the Clinton administration as well as congressional leaders, was that the Cuba embargo is foreign policy, not trade policy, and therefore the WTO dispute panel has no jurisdiction. Such a claim has no basis of support within the WTO and indeed would open a Pandora's box for other countries to ignore trade commitments. The EU, for example, in its dispute with the United States over preferential access for banana imports from Caribbean countries, could claim foreign policy considerations related to former colonial relationships. The WTO, under GATT article XXI, does provide for a national security exception under the narrowly defined circumstances of "war or other emergency in international relations," but the United States, as the preeminent global power, would look foolish and be juridically vulnerable to claim such a current relationship with the small, withering communist regime in Cuba.

A significant negative consequence for U.S. trade policy has thus been the considerable denigration of the WTO by members of the U.S. Congress normally supportive of a liberal trade policy and the WTO—and with no other members of Congress or the Clinton administration disagreeing with them.

The extraterritorial dimension of the Libertad Act has also complicated and slowed down negotiation of a multilateral agreement on investment in the OECD, which was the forum within which the United States and the EU carried out the prolonged negotiation of the bilateral agreement on expropriated properties. Bitter European attitudes about the Title IV ban on travel to the United States by European corporate executives and their families played into the hands of European interests opposed to the investment agreement on other grounds and contributed to the ultimate demise of the OECD agreement in December 1998.

In sum, the Cuba embargo is negatively affecting U.S. commercial interests in the 1990s far more than it did in the earlier Cold War decades. Annual U.S. export losses range up to $3 billion, lost investment opportunities of $100 million to $200 million a year now have much greater long-term significance, and adverse effects in third-country markets and for the global trading system, although not quantifiable, are substantial as well.

3. Net Assessment of U.S. Unilateral Sanctions Policy

As in the narrative account, a net assessment of U.S. embargo policy against Cuba over 39 years has to be divided into two very distinct periods—Cold War (1961–1989) and post–Cold War (beginning in 1990). Again, the assessment here concentrates on the new situation of the 1990s after a brief comment on the earlier period for perspective.

An assessment of the U.S. unilateral embargo against Cuba for 1961–1989 is complex and centers on U.S. national security interests vis-à-vis the Soviet Union and related Third World relationships. Attempts by the Ford and Carter administrations to negotiate step-by-step normalization of bilateral relations failed because of the lack of a forthcoming response by Fidel Castro, which supports the view of many Cuba experts that Castro has always seen the U.S. embargo as in his interest. The embargo could mobilize Cuban and international public opinion against the United States and take the blame for the failures of the centrally planned Cuban economy, a view that remains relevant for the Castro foreign policy during the 1990s. An early unilateral lifting of the U.S. embargo on trade with and travel to Cuba would have cut both ways—providing a dollar inflow to support the Cuban government while exposing the Cuban people to American political thinking and economic accomplishments—and the net effect is left for historical conjecture. As noted earlier, the hard-line U.S. embargo policy of the 1980s did contribute to the economic collapse of the Soviet Union, as one element in the comprehensive Reagan strategy of forcing higher levels of Soviet defense, foreign aid, and counterinsurgency expenditures to the point of internal and external financial crisis.

The experience of U.S. embargo policy against Cuba in the 1990s is fundamentally different from the earlier period while less ambiguous in its results. The change can be presented most clearly in terms of three categories of U.S. interests: (1) the central policy objective of an early democratic transition in Cuba with a minimum of violence; (2) the immediate impact on other U.S. interests, mainly commercial interests, WTO objectives, and U.S. world leadership capability more broadly; and (3) post-transition interests in Cuba of illegal migration, drug trafficking, and budget requirements for economic aid.

1. The central policy objective.   The central U.S. embargo objective of fostering respect for human rights and an early democratic transition in Cuba with a minimum of violence has clearly not been achieved and almost certainly will not be. The embargo policy, as tightened through the 1992 and 1996 acts, is designed to squeeze the Cuban economy to the point of suffering or collapse whereby the Castro government is forced to hold democratic elections or is violently overthrown. Fidel Castro, however, has not capitulated and has rather consolidated his authoritarian control at home while capitalizing on disputes between the United States and its allies over the extraterritorial extensions of the 1992 and 1996 acts. There is also no apparent prospect for the violent overthrow of the Castro regime from fledgling opposition groups within Cuba. Of course, Castro, at age 72, will likely pass from the scene during the coming decade or two, but the proponents of the U.S. embargo cannot take credit for his declining physical grip on power, however that may evolve.

The embargo policy of squeezing the Cuban economy to the point of collapse came closest to fruition in 1993, but the expedient economic reforms of the Cuban government and the beginning of the surge of dollar remittances from the Cuban diaspora, especially Cuban-Americans, enabled Castro to weather that crisis. The current outlook for lackluster growth, which parallels a gradual deterioration of the country's industrial structure and economic infrastructure, poses little political threat to the regime even while making eventual economic reconstruction costs higher. Indeed, authoritarian regimes generally are more able to maintain control under stagnant yet stable economic conditions than in the more dynamic circumstances of strong growth and private sector job creation.

As for fostering the transition with a minimum of violence, the current U.S. embargo policy faces a dilemma. If the embargo economic squeeze will not itself force Castro's capitulation to democratic elections, the only implicit rationale for keeping the embargo is that the overall economic suffering will trigger the violent overthrow of the government. In view of the extensive and heavily armed security forces within Cuba, such a transition could be very violent. A successful violent overthrow could entail a split among the various security forces, which would likely increase the level of initial armed conflict, not to mention a continuing aftermath of retribution.

Finally, the major conflict in U.S. embargo policy—condoning private aid, through mostly illegal remittances, while prohibiting trade—undermines any continuing hope that the Cuban government will be financially squeezed into early democratic transition. The remittances relieve the most severe economic suffering of the people, which constitutes the most politically sensitive edge of the squeeze. A related question is whether this "private aid but not trade strategy" is likely to lead to a more or less violent transition when the inevitable change finally occurs. This is a more complex question, but there is good reason to believe the answer is more rather than less. The rapid growth of dollar remittances has led to an unhealthy dichotomy among Cubans—between a large minority who receive dollars from abroad to meet their basic needs without having to rely on daily work in Cuba and the majority of Cubans who must work ever harder under worsening conditions while suffering great economic deprivation.[12] This economic dichotomy, which breeds frustration and enmity among the latter against the former, potentially undermines an eventual democratic reconciliation among all segments of the Cuban population. The alternative of creating at least some productive jobs now through trade and investment, with less reliance on remittances, could produce more favorable circumstances for such reconciliation.

For all these reasons, the overall impact of continued unilateral embargo for fostering democratic transition needs to be compared with the basic alternative of increased U.S. private sector engagement absent the embargo. The conclusion drawn here is that the earliest and fullest engagement of such private sector contacts would be more beneficial for setting the stage for the inevitable economic and political changes that will take place in Cuba. Castro's communist Cuba is an anachronism in the Western Hemisphere of the 1990s. The more the Cuban power structure and the Cuban people in general are exposed to the forces of market-oriented economic reform and democratic government under way in all the other 34 nations of the hemisphere, the faster the transition already occurring in Cuba will gather momentum—and with less likelihood of violence.

2. Immediate impact on other U.S. interests.   The impact of the continued embargo on these interests, as explained in the foregoing section, are unambiguously negative on all counts. The adverse impact on U.S. commercial interests is assessed as ranging up to a $3 billion annual loss of U.S. exports to Cuba plus substantial though less quantifiable losses in U.S. investment opportunities in Cuba and exports to third countries. The negative effects on U.S. interests in the WTO, and for U.S. liberal trade policy in general, is significant as well. The ongoing disputes with European and other trading partners over the extraterritorial reach of the 1996 Libertad Act tend to damage the credibility of the WTO dispute mechanism, while attacks on WTO procedures by congressional proponents of the 1996 act and by the Clinton administration have negatively affected U.S. public support for a liberal trade policy, contributing, among other things, to the president's failure to obtain fast-track negotiating authority from Congress in November 1997 when the U.S-EU dispute was most intense.

The broadest adverse effect on U.S. interests in the post–Cold War setting has been the reduced confidence in and support for U.S. global leadership among friends and allies. The almost total opposition to U.S. embargo policy against Cuba in the United Nations and the WTO is coupled with continued criticism of the inconsistency of U.S. policies with respect to unilateral economic sanctions and the arrogance with which the administration and congressional leaders have defended such policies. The most frequent line of attack on U.S. global leadership is the accusation that U.S. Cuba policy is driven principally by domestic politics, with relatively few Cuban-American votes concentrated in Florida and New Jersey taking precedence over U.S. foreign policy interests. Indeed, although domestic politics are involved in all country studies examined in this work, Cuba policy stands out as the most strongly driven by domestic political considerations. Moreover, the domestic political motivation within the U.S. government has provoked a corresponding domestic political response in other countries. Canadian attacks on the U.S. Cuba embargo are very popular on the Canadian domestic political scene, as are continual criticisms by other Caribbean governments of overbearing economic pressures by the United States against its small and vulnerable Caribbean neighbor. French and other European nationalists have likewise made U.S. Cuba policy an easy target for undermining confidence in U.S. global leadership among domestic constituents. U.S. unilateral economic sanctions against Cuba clearly illustrate a recurring theme of this study as to how good domestic politics can make for bad foreign policy, not only in the United States but in responses generated among allies and trading partners as well.

3. Post-transition U.S. interests.   Preoccupation with the immediate effects of U.S. embargo policy against Cuba during the 1990s—its impact on the Cuban economy and the problems it creates with trading partners—has tended to preclude serious discussion of other important U.S. interests in the Caribbean region that will only come fully into play for Cuba after normalization of the bilateral relationship. The three prominent interests in this category are illegal migration, drug trafficking, and budget requirements for economic aid. The outcome will depend on how the transition to a market economy and democratic government takes place within Cuba, but the tentative assessment here is that the continuing embargo policy will have adverse consequences in each case.

Illegal migration from Cuba is currently controlled by the 1995 bilateral accord, but in the context of almost no direct transportation between the two countries. Once relations are normalized, however, air and sea transportation will expand dramatically, and the consensus expert opinion is that pressures for illegal northward migration of Cubans to the United States will far exceed any return flow of Cuban exiles to permanent residence in Cuba, with potential substantial disruptive impact, economically and socially, on Florida in particular. These northbound migratory pressures will only be strengthened, however, by the continued deterioration of the Cuban economy and the substitution of productive employment in Cuba by remittance payments from abroad. Moreover, if the embargo and related hostile U.S. actions were to provoke a violent confrontation within Cuba, the flow of Cubans into the United States would be stimulated further, with a far stronger legal case by arriving Cubans to claim resident refugee status.

Drug trafficking from South America to the United States through Cuba is also now greatly restricted by the absence of direct transportation and travel between the two countries, but this situation too will change abruptly with normalization, creating a nightmare challenge for U.S. drug enforcement and other border authorities. The official policy of Cuba today is to denounce drug trafficking and to claim vigilant enforcement efforts, but these verbal assertions are deeply suspect in the absence of such collaborative programs as the United States has developed with other countries throughout the hemisphere and elsewhere. The embargo policy, however, greatly inhibits first steps toward such collaboration while the stagnation and isolation of the Cuban economy present a breeding ground for drug traffickers to position themselves for business once the U.S. border opens to Cuba.

The future demands on the U.S. budget for aid to Cuba once relations are normalized grow as the Cuban economy continues to deteriorate. The collapse of the investment sector since 1990 is a clear indicator that the economy is living off assets that will have to be replenished at some later time, and the longer the economy runs down, the greater will be the demands for external assistance. In contrast, an expansion of exports, investment, and productive jobs through U.S. as well as third-country private sector engagement leading up to the political transition will tend to decrease future demands on the U.S. taxpayer.

4. Alternatives to Current Unilateral Sanctions Policy

The three basic policy alternatives for U.S. policy toward Cuba introduced earlier in the context of the immediate post–Cold War circumstances of the early 1990s continue to define the policy direction: (1) terminate the embargo and let the forces of change take their course; (2) open a dialogue with the Castro government for a negotiated step-by-step normalization of relations; and (3) continue or strengthen the current unilateral embargo policy. The third alternative was assessed in the previous section, and the first two are elaborated as follows. The two are not mutually exclusive and could be pursued to some extent in parallel, but the sequence and relative importance of specific actions would make a major difference in distinguishing the one from the other. This point as to basic thrust is emphasized by referring to the first alternative as "terminate the embargo with an enhanced multilateral strategy," and to the second alternative as "step-by-step bilateral negotiations."

Alternative 1: Terminate the Embargo with an Enhanced Multilateral Strategy

This approach would follow the pattern of U.S. economic policy toward the Soviet bloc and China during the 1980s. The ban on trade with, investment in, and travel to Cuba would be lifted unilaterally without commitments by the Cuban government linked to democratization, human rights, and economic reforms, and diplomatic relations would be normalized. Important bilateral commitments in the economic field with respect to normal trade relations, or NTR (formerly MFN), the Export-Import Bank, OPIC, and bilateral aid programs would be withheld subject to follow-on negotiations with the Cuban government, and the overarching issue of U.S. expropriation claims, explained more fully in the second alternative, would greatly limit early progress in these areas.

A central judgment under this option is that U.S. private sector engagement at this time would have a net positive effect on the process of economic and political change under way within Cuba. The contact of American citizens and companies with all segments of the Cuban population, and particularly with the younger generation within the political and professional power structures, would be conducive to a faster pace of change with less likelihood of violence. This judgment is based on the record of private sector engagement throughout the emerging market economies in Latin America, Central Europe, and Asia over the past decade, as elaborated in the Vietnam and China case studies.

Under this policy option, a major change in U.S. Cuba policy would be used to develop stronger, more unified diplomatic and other pressures against the Castro government among the United States, its European allies, other Western Hemisphere democracies, and Japan. Such pressure would push for basic human rights, early democratization, and related market-oriented economic reforms. Strong support could be given to nongovernmental organizations (NGOs) operating within Cuba, including the Catholic Church and other religious groups. A pre-membership advisory relationship with the international financial institutions would be encouraged. Membership in such institutions, as well as in the Organization of American States, however, would be withheld until definitive political and economic reforms took place.

The benefits of this option, in addition to the judgment about U.S. private sector engagement, would be a policy of positive collaboration with friends and allies under U.S. leadership rather than the current divisive disputes, the end of Castro's propaganda capability inside and outside of Cuba to blame the failures of his centrally planned economy on the U.S. embargo, and substantial gains to U.S. commercial interests. The principal disadvantage is that the increased inflow of dollars into Cuba would provide a financial cushion for the Castro government to resist economic reforms, although within the context of other pressures building for such reforms. The Castro government could also declare victory in having the embargo lifted, but it would be less than Pyrrhic for the last communist regime in an otherwise democratic and market-oriented Western Hemisphere.

The Dodd-Torres congressional initiative of 1997–1998 to lift the embargo unilaterally for U.S. exports of food and medicines to Cuba would be a significant step within this option and, if enacted, would create pressures for further actions in this direction. Another even more dramatic selective unilateral step would be to terminate travel restrictions for Americans who wish to travel to Cuba.

Alternative 2: Step-by-Step Bilateral Negotiations

This less radical departure from the long-standing unilateral embargo policy has precedents in the initiatives during the Carter and Ford administrations as well as in the provision of the 1992 Cuban Democracy Act calling for "carefully calibrated" mutual steps toward normalization. Initial steps offered by the United States could involve a selective easing of trade and travel restrictions, perhaps beginning with exports of food and medicines as in alternative 1, although the offers would be linked in this case to corresponding actions by the Cuban government. Such actions on the Cuban side, however, are difficult to formulate and are subject to skepticism. Some further market-oriented reforms by the Castro government—for example, to permit small and medium-sized private businesses by Cubans hiring Cubans (as distinct from the current family-based limitations)—could warrant moves on the U.S. side, but more definitive steps by Cuba, particularly in the political field relating to human rights and democratization, appear less likely in 1999 than they might have in 1993 when the Cuban economy was under its most severe stress. Even modest U.S. proposals to ease the embargo, however, together with an offer to go further based on corresponding actions by the Castro government, should enable greater U.S. solidarity with European and Western Hemisphere governments to pressure for reforms on the Castro regime and would put Castro more on the defensive internationally and domestically to defend his intransigence about reforms and transition.

A major obstacle to progressive steps toward normalization through direct bilateral negotiations are the huge outstanding expropriation claims by the United States and how to relate these to the step-by-step negotiations. Depending upon an estimated Cuban per capita income, the more than $6 billion, including accumulated interest, of claims by American citizens and companies (leaving aside the far greater potential claims of Cuban-Americans as provided in Title III of the Libertad Act) are roughly comparable to between half and the entire Cuban GDP in the economy's current depressed state. There has not been anything remotely comparable since the Weimar Republic's unpaid reparation debt following World War I, and as a practical matter any ultimate settlement is unlikely to bring American claimants more than 10 to 20 cents on the dollar. In this context it is almost inconceivable that progress in resolving the issue could be made with the current Castro government, whose unyielding position has been to link any expropriation settlement to Cuban counterclaims for damage caused by the U.S. embargo over the past 39 years.

On the benefit side, this alternative would offer a start for U.S. private sector engagement in Cuba, broader dialogue between Americans and various segments of the Cuban population, a more positive basis for resolving existing disputes and strengthening collaboration with friends and allies so as to press for reforms within Cuba, and some support for U.S. commercial interests. As for the disadvantages, results are likely to be modest at best, and an early impasse could lock in the current embargo relationship even more deeply.

≈   ≈   ≈

Both of these alternatives would require congressional action because Title II of the 1996 Libertad Act terminated prior presidential authority to relax or end the embargo along these lines. This is, of course, the legislative route followed by the Dodd-Torres proposal for food and medicine exports to Cuba. Broader initiatives under either option would require a corresponding broader authority for the president to further ease or completely lift the embargo, which would represent a fundamental reversal of almost four decades of unilateral embargo policy against Cuba. The practical question is whether such a change is politically feasible in the near term, during 1999–2000 in particular. The answer depends on shifting attitudes within the United States and parallel change under way in Cuba.

Within the United States, a substantial weakening of support for the embargo by Cuban-Americans has already been noted. The recently organized active campaign by U.S. business through

USA*Engage to denounce unilateral sanctions as counterproductive to U.S. interests is having an effect, especially on some Republican members of Congress. The Pope's overarching criticism of economic sanctions on humanitarian grounds puts supporters of sanctions, including the Cuba embargo, on the defensive. These mutually reinforcing trends are reflected in press and other media commentary increasingly critical of the Cuba embargo, including some Floridian and conservative press earlier staunchly supportive of Helms-Burton, and the *New York Times*.

Within Cuba, the trend is less clear, both in terms of a political opening and economic reforms. Time is running against the aging communist regime, however, and the economic storm clouds ahead are particularly threatening. One especially striking circumstance in Cuba is connected to shifting attitudes in the United States. The majority of fledging prodemocracy and human rights groups within Cuba have called for a lifting of the embargo to stimulate greater U.S. engagement at the personal and private sector levels and to deprive Fidel Castro of the propaganda argument that the embargo is the principal cause of Cuban problems. The best-known dissident, Elizardo Sanchez, the head of the Cuban Human Rights Watch who has spent eight years in Cuban prisons, attacked the embargo in an outspoken article in the September 14, 1998, edition of the *Washington Times* (an example, incidentally, of a more questioning approach in the conservative press):

> Paradoxically, some politicians in the United States are rowing in the same direction as the hardline sector within our own government. Both are rowing against the current now prevalent in the world which favors reduction of tensions, dialogue and democratization.

> After four decades of strained relations, it is time to explore new avenues in our relationship. Washington should put an end to this absurd cold-war climate, fed by legislation such as the Helms-Burton Act and now the "Solidarity Act." It could achieve much more if instead its Cuba policy, in concert with its allies in Europe, Latin America and the Caribbean, aimed at

engendering an atmosphere of cooperation and confidence. This, in the final analysis, is the only way to encourage a process of gradual democratic and modernizing reforms. Given that the present totalitarian model has no future in Cuba or anywhere else, the most intelligent and practical thing would be to ease the way for the present Cuban government to initiate and lead such a process without fear of endangering the independence, sovereignty or stability of the Cuban nation. Washington could hardly accomplish less than it has with its present approach.

5. Conclusions and Recommendations

The U.S. embargo against Cuba may have benefited the United States in some ways during the Cold War, but no longer does so, and it is now having a net adverse impact on U.S. foreign policy and economic interests. The primary foreign policy objective is to bring about the earliest transition of Cuba to a market-oriented democracy with a minimum of violence. Some embargo proponents claim that lifting the embargo will prolong the Castro communist dictatorship, but this claim is contradicted by the near unanimous view of Cuba experts that Fidel Castro, under current embargo circumstances, can maintain power as long as he is physically able and willing to do so.

In terms of economic interests, the United States is losing in two ways through the continued unilateral embargo. First, U.S. export and investment interests suffer as third-country companies capture the entire export market to Cuba and buy up the most attractive beachfronts and other properties. Second, the U.S. taxpayer will have to pay more for economic aid to Cuba after the transition to the extent the continued embargo contributes to the further decline of the Cuban economy, or is even perceived to do so. The eventual democratically elected Cuban government, in its anticipated nationalist self-interest, will blame the U.S. embargo, probably to a greatly exaggerated degree, for the economic devastation it will inherit. The $4 billion to $8 billion aid package offered by the Clinton administration to a future democratic government in Cuba, in response to a provision of the Libertad Act, is an excessive preemptive capitulation in this direction.

In a more positive light, change is under way in Cuba, and large, wide-ranging mutual benefits await even first steps toward normalization of U.S.-Cuba economic relations. This is clear not only to third-country investors in Cuba today, but to U.S. business leaders who visit Cuba and to their Cuban interlocutors. Indeed, just as other nations in the Caribbean Basin had reason to fear a communist Cuba in the 1970s and 1980s, they now express comparable concern as to how they will cope with an inevitably capitalist Cuba. The answer entails a yet broader mutual interest throughout the region to be unleashed by a Free Trade Agreement of the Americas (FTAA), but this subject goes beyond the scope of this study.

The recommended U.S. policy response thus involves a change of direction toward lifting the unilateral sanctions and engaging in open trade, investment, and travel as early as possible. Alternative 2 above—step-by-step negotiations with the Castro government—however, is not the way to go. It is unlikely to get anywhere and also plays into the hands of the Cuban propaganda machine. Attempts at step-by-step normalization failed during the Carter and Ford administrations because Fidel Castro was not willing to make commitments for change on his part, and the same attitude prevails today. As noted earlier, current circumstances logically imply that it is in the interest of the Castro government for the embargo to continue. In any event, negotiated steps toward normalization would entail unnecessary positive recognition of a discredited communist government and provide Fidel Castro the basis for hailing diplomatic victory, with all its inherent adverse propaganda value.

The better route is the unilateral lifting of the embargo, by steps or all at once, as in alternative 1. The staged approach, beginning with food and medicine exports and/or a lifting of travel restrictions, may be the most practical way to proceed, but it should move forward in parallel with a more fundamental reappraisal of U.S. Cuba policy within the U.S. government. Such a reappraisal, as recommended by Secretaries Kissinger and Eagleburger, would indeed be an agonizing one for some members of Congress. The unilateral lifting of the Cuba embargo would be a bold policy initiative that would have direct and pervasive positive impact on the process of political and economic change under way in Cuba, and linking this move to a more forceful multilateral approach with European and Western Hemisphere allies to press for democratization and respect for basic human rights in Cuba would be a critical component of the overall strategy. The initiative could justifiably be presented, in Elizardo Sanchez's words, as a victory for "dialogue and democratization" in Cuba and in the United States, including in Florida.

Notes

1. Patrick J. Kiger, *Squeeze Play: The United States, Cuba, and the Helms-Burton Act* (Washington, D.C.: Center for Public Integrity, 1997), 33. This report provides a detailed account of the legislative process leading to the Cuban Democracy and Libertad Acts and is drawn on in several instances in this report.

2. Ibid., 48–49, describes in detail the lobbying efforts in support of the Title III provisions.

3. From a September 13, 1995, letter to House Speaker Newt Gingrich, quoted by Congressman Lee Hamilton in the *Congressional Record*, September 20, 1995.

4. *Washington Times*, September 29, 1997.

5. The figures for Cuban-American travel to Cuba are from a conversation by the author with a high-level Cuban official.

6. This free-fall phase is described in detail in Ernest H. Preeg, *Cuba and the New Caribbean Economic Order* (Washington, D.C.: Center for Strategic and International Studies, 1993), chapter 2.

7. Ibid., chapter 1, contains an assessment of the rapid restructuring of the Caribbean regional economy.

8. The UN Commission on Latin American and the Caribbean, in its 1997 report, *La Economia Cubana: Reformas Estructurales y Desempeno en los Noventa*, estimated remittance payments, mostly but not all from Cuban-Americans, at $600 million in 1995 and $800 million in 1996. The estimates were based on a sharp increase in the residual net capital inflow, or "errors and omissions," in the Cuban balance-of-payments, and the lack of any plausible reason for this increase other than the widely reported surge in remittance activity and related purchases in dollar-only stores in Cuba. The surge in "errors and omissions" has also been explained by some observers as

money-laundering through Cuba by drug traffickers. This is analytically unsustainable, however, because such money-laundering would involve dollars passing through Cuba to some safe haven elsewhere rather than a net dollar inflow to finance imports, and there have been no credible reports of large amounts of drug money entering Cuba. The Cuban government estimated $700 million of remittances in 1997 based, in large part, on sales in dollar-only stores. The gross-net differential for dollar inflow of remittances as compared to Cuban exports is described in greater detail in Ernest H. Preeg, "U.S. Embargo: The Illusion of Compliance," *Washington Post*, November 2, 1997.

9. An interesting analysis of the Cuban economy, with high, medium, and low projections for the period 1997–2005, is contained in Claes Brundenius and Pedro Monreal, "The Future of the Cuban Economic Model: The Longer View," presented at a workshop in Copenhagen, June 11–13, 1998. Monreal is an economist at the Center for Research on the International Economy in Havana. The authors project an increase in the investment share of GDP from 8 percent in 1997 to 20 to 30 percent in 2005, but do not specify how this will be achieved.

10. The 1989 market share figures are from Central Intelligence Agency (CIA), *Cuba: Handbook of Trade Statistics, 1994* (Washington, D.C.: CIA, August 1994). The estimate of $200 million to $300 million is based on the assumption that without the official export financing that OECD and Latin American governments were providing, the United States would have obtained only a relatively small share of the $1.3 billion of Cuban imports from these countries.

11. The substantial adverse impact is described more fully in Ernest H. Preeg, "The Helms-Burton Law and U.S. Interests in the World Trade Organization," a statement before the House Committee on International Relations, Subcommittee on International Economic Policy and Trade, March 19, 1997.

12. The increasing resentment of Cubans who do not have access to dollars is described in a November 29, 1998, *Washington Post* story on the surging crime rate in Cuba. A Cuban is quoted: "There is more crime because we are getting more desperate every day. It is so unfair that many people like me cannot eat good food and drink good coffee because we do not have dollars or barely any pesos."

3

Iran:
National Security Interests at Bay

1. Narrative Account

U.S. UNILATERAL SANCTIONS AGAINST Iran have been directed principally at national security interests—international terrorism, the development of weapons of mass destruction, and a buildup of conventional armaments—all related to the Middle East peace process. Democratization and human rights, which have been primary objectives for sanctions applied elsewhere, have been a very small part of the Iran equation even though human rights abuses have been and remain prevalent. Recent U.S. unilateral sanctions, moreover, are a component of the 1993 "dual containment" strategy whereby Iran and Iraq were treated on comparable terms as "outlaw" or "rogue" states. Almost all other nations disagreed with the dual containment strategy, however, which has led to a dichotomy in policies toward Iran between multilateral sanctions narrowly targeted on Iranian weapons capability and U.S. unilateral sanctions of comprehensive scope on trade and investment. A central judgmental issue underlying these differences—as in several of the other case studies—concerns the potential impact of U.S. private sector engagement on developments within Iran, the circumstances of which changed significantly with the election of President Mohammad Khatami in May 1997.

The January 1981 Algiers Accord to release the American hostages included agreement to restore full commercial relations, but the economic opening was short-lived. In 1984, the United States designated Iran as a supporter of international terrorism, which triggered several economic restrictions, and in October 1987 President Ronald Reagan, by executive order, banned almost all imports from Iran, again with principal reference to Iranian links to terrorism. These steps had only limited impact, however, because U.S. imports from Iran then consisted overwhelmingly of oil that could be purchased from other suppliers while Iran simply shifted its exports elsewhere. U.S. petroleum companies remained fully engaged with Iran, which included the marketing of large amounts of Iranian oil to third countries.

The Bush administration initially tried to improve relations with Iran, based on the president's inaugural statement that "good will begets good will," but the good will initiative bore little fruit. In 1992, in the face of continuing evidence of Iranian weapons development, the Iran-Iraq Nonproliferation Act was adopted to substantially tighten U.S. export controls, especially for broadly defined "dual-use" products. The Clinton administration took an even harder rhetorical line associated with Secretary of State Warren Christopher's bitter feelings toward Iran dating back to the hostage crisis and his deep involvement as deputy secretary of state. The "dual containment" strategy, put forward in May 1993, treated Iraq and Iran as "recalcitrant and outlaw states" (along with only Cuba, North Korea, and Libya) that "not only chose to remain outside the [international] family but also to assault its basic values." Iran was singled out as the foremost state sponsor of terrorism, doing its best to thwart the Middle East peace process, engaged in acquiring offensive weapons, and developing weapons of mass destruction so as to dominate the Persian Gulf militarily.[1]

European and other nations did not agree with the dual containment strategy. Iraq was an outlaw state subject to a multilateral oil embargo and UN weapons inspection teams as a result of the Gulf War, but Iran was engaged through "critical dialogue," with sanctions limited to narrowly targeted restrictions on exports to Iran of weapons-related goods and services. This basic difference in approach toward Iran created problems for implementation of the U.S. containment policy, particularly with respect to nonstrategic trade and investment. The United States, besides imposing targeted multilateral sanctions, wanted to exert an overall squeeze on the Iranian economy so as to limit Iran's financial capability to develop nuclear weapons and delivery missiles and rebuild conventional armaments after the prolonged Iraq-Iran War. A principal specific objective was to impede revenue-producing investment in the petroleum sector. The lack of support for multilateral trade and investment sanctions against the Iranian petroleum sector, however, limited the initial policy response. The United States accepted continued trade and investment on commercial terms—including for U.S. firms—while objecting to economic aid and official export finance. In effect, "dual containment" never involved the same degree of containment for Iran as it did for Iraq.

This limited economic squeeze component of the U.S. containment strategy had some impact through 1994, assisted by the depressed state of the Iranian economy and the lack of economic reforms by the government. The World Bank, under U.S. pressure, ceased new project lending to Iran that had been on the order of $400 million to $500 million a year, and Japan was pressed to suspend aid projects. Unable to service massive outstanding foreign debt, Iranian merchandise imports dropped by half, from $23.1 billion in 1992 to $11.6 billion in 1994. In the process, Iran was forced to cut back planned purchases of conventional weapons while investment in the petroleum sector languished.

The economic squeeze was nevertheless undermined from the outset by European allies, with Germany out front, and Japan, who agreed to provide large new official export credits to repay existing debt arrearages, a clear circumvention of "Paris Club" norms for rescheduling official debts that normally require, inter alia, an IMF-approved financial stabilization program. Many of the new loans, moreover, were made at the Libor rate of interest, which for Iran equated to a considerable element of subsidy. When the United States complained about the subsidized loans to Iran, the Europeans responded that U.S. policy was hypocritical because the United States was Iran's largest trading partner while European exports to Iran plummeted. The rallying point for this charge was the $4 billion per year of Iranian oil exports—30 percent of total oil exports—that American companies marketed to third countries. In February 1995, German chancellor Helmut Kohl visited Washington and at a White House press conference was asked about German exports to Iran and growing concerns among U.S.

officials that Germany might inadvertently be helping Iran to develop weapons of mass destruction. Kohl responded that reports about Germany were wrong and referred to a magazine article about the oil sales that "said a number of things this week about American oil companies, not German oil companies . . . [and] these oil companies export into other countries, not our country."[2]

The Kohl attack was unjustified and disingenuous at best. The $4 billion figure, while large in absolute terms, had limited commercial value because profit margins for marketing Iranian oil were small. In terms of exports to Iran, which was the real commercial interest at stake, the United States exported only $330 million in 1994, far behind Germany ($1.7 billion), Japan ($1.0 billion), France ($910 million), Italy ($790 million), the United Kingdom ($480 million), and the European Union as a whole ($5.2 billion). Germany was still clearly the number one exporter to Iran even if it did not have any oil companies. The U.S. policy of continuing normal, competitive trade and investment relations while withholding aid and official trade finance was reasonable and balanced under the circumstances of clearly established international security threats by Iran and the lack of agreement on more restrictive multilateral sanctions. The Clinton administration, however, was in no position to respond effectively to the Kohl criticism. Iran policy was under attack domestically for being weak and ineffective, and the newsworthy $4 billion figure could not be defended as simply one element of an overall level playing field business relationship. A more legitimate charge of hypocrisy in U.S. Iran policy was the contrast between the strong "recalcitrant and outlaw state" dual containment rhetoric and the reality of a largely normal trade and investment relationship.

In these conflicted and discouraging circumstances, two developments in the early months of 1995 propelled the United States down the path of comprehensive unilateral economic sanctions against Iran. The first development was the shift in control of the Congress to the Republicans in January. The new Senate Banking Committee chairman, Alphonse D'Amato, proposed legislation on January 25 to ban all U.S. trade and investment with Iran. Such proposals had long been under discussion, and the New York senator, with strong support from Jewish-American voters in his state, had been at the forefront. Now the likelihood of passage of such legislation became far greater, and the administration came under increased pressure to tighten trade restrictions against Iran. It is noteworthy, however, that the January proposal by D'Amato was limited to a prohibition on U.S. trade and investment and contained no provisions against third-country investments in Iran, which would become the sole substance of the later Iran and Libya Sanctions Act, or ILSA, referred to as the D'Amato Act.

The second development was the March 6 announcement that the Iranian government had awarded the American company Conoco a $600 million contract to develop oil and gas in the Persian Gulf near Sirri Island, which triggered eight hectic days of policy deliberations within the U.S. government and the decision to ban all such investments in Iran. The Sirri project had been under discussion for three years with Conoco and other non-American companies, including the French company Total. Conoco was favorably positioned in commercial terms because of its technical capability and its ongoing adjacent operations in Qatar-controlled waters. It had kept the State Department informed of these negotiations and was told that the U.S. government preferred the project not go forward, but that it was legal to do so. This amounted to tacit approval for Conoco to proceed, but also reflected a lack of clearly established policy in the event a contract was actually signed.

The decision to award the project to Conoco was made by Iranian president Hashemi Rafsanjani, with the support of his oil minister and over the opposition of the more anti-American members of his government. He thus made the decision on a sound commercial basis but also to convey a political signal to the United States of a willingness to strengthen bilateral contacts, at least through the private sector. This was the first major foreign investment contract offered by the Iranian government since the 1979 revolution, and for it to be awarded to an American company was a significant message indeed.[3] The government of Iran and Conoco had agreed to wait 10 days before publicly announcing the contract, among other things to permit Conoco to brief its board and the U.S. government, but the agreement was immediately revealed in a story on Iranian television, presumably leaked by opponents within the Iranian government.

The U.S. government was taken by surprise and was totally unprepared to respond to the news, which drew sharp criticism, especially from Republican congressional leaders. On March 7, White House press secretary Michael McCurry said the contract "does not appear to be illegal or prohibited under U.S. law at this time," and the president, caught off guard, merely commented that the deal was "not a helpful development."[4] Secretary of State Christopher, in Tel Aviv at the time, was also surprised and angered by the news. On March 9 he condemned the agreement as "inconsistent with the containment policy that we have carried forward," adding that "wherever you look you will find the evil hand of Iran in this region."[5] Interagency discussion in Washington, meanwhile, produced opposition from senior officials at the Commerce, Defense, Energy, and Treasury departments to a change of policy that would prohibit U.S. investment in Iran, on the grounds that such a prohibition would have little impact on Iran while harming U.S. commercial interests and disrupting oil markets. Secretary Christopher, upon his return, recused himself from meetings on the subject because the law firm that represented Conoco's interests was also Christopher's former law firm, but the secretary had already effectively preempted the policy outcome with his Tel Aviv statement. No serious consideration was given to the Rafsanjani political message. On March 14, the White House announced that the president would issue an executive order under the International Emergency Economic Powers Act (IEEPA) barring all investments by U.S. firms in the Iranian petroleum sector. Members of the board of the DuPont company, of which Conoco was a subsidiary, also opposed the agreement.[6] The Conoco project was dead.

This unilateral sanction on U.S. investment added momentum to ban trade with Iran as well. The other agencies continued to resist State Department support for trade sanctions, and President Clinton was personally ill-disposed toward economic sanctions in general, but congressional pressure, together with active lobbying by the American Israel Public Affairs Committee (AIPAC), was decisive. On April 30, the president announced his decision to ban U.S. trade with Iran, including the infamous $4 billion oil marketing relationship. He made the announcement at the annual dinner meeting of the World Jewish Congress (WJC) in New York, where he was introduced by WJC president Edgar Bronfman, the prominent DuPont board member who had opposed the Sirri project. President Clinton denounced Iran as a "rogue" state and explained, "Many people here argued persuasively that the best route to change Iranian behavior is by engaging the country. Unfortunately there is no evidence to support that argument."

A more complex issue that inevitably arose from these unilateral sanctions was whether they could or should be extended in some way to third countries so as to prevent others from simply replacing American companies with little net adverse impact on Iran. Iran, for example, quickly awarded the Sirri contract to Total after Conoco was excluded. A new congressional initiative was put forward by Senator D'Amato on March 27 to impose sanctions against third-country companies who invested in or traded with Iran. AIPAC shifted into high gear in an all-out campaign in support of the D'Amato bill.[7] This proposed secondary boycott unleashed a 16-month debate leading to the enactment of ILSA in August 1996.

The legislation proposed in March was sweeping in its coverage. All non-American persons and companies engaged in trade with Iran in any goods or technology would be sanctioned through a prohibition on U.S. government procurement, the issuance of U.S. export licenses, and the importation of any of their products. Very limited exceptions related mostly to defense procurement. The president could only waive the sanctions by certifying that Iran had ceased efforts to acquire nuclear weapons and to support international terrorism and had improved its human rights record. President Clinton initially opposed the extension of the embargo to third countries. In his April 30 WJC speech, he stated, "I do want you to know I do oppose the suggestion some have made that we impose a secondary boycott and prohibit foreign firms doing business with Iran from doing business with the United States. . . . I think that decision would cause unnecessary strain with our allies at a time when we need our friends' cooperation." Administration officials soon backtracked, however, taking no position for or against the legislation while keeping open the option of a presidential veto. Domestic politics in the run-up to the 1996 elections became a growing concern for White House political advisers wanting to avoid being outflanked by Senator D'Amato with Jewish-American voters in particular. State Department interest in cooperation with friends and allies was downgraded.

Prolonged deliberations through 1995 and early 1996 centered on administration efforts to reduce the scope of the proposed sanctions and to increase the president's flexibility in imposing them. Similar issues were raised by congressional members as the legislation worked its way through the responsible committees. On the House side, the International Relations Committee adopted a relatively strong bill, but the Ways and Means Committee then reduced the scope of possible sanctions so as to avoid possible conflict with WTO commitments and disruption of financial markets. Libya was added late in the process through appeals by relatives of victims of the 1988 terrorist bombing of PanAm Flight 103 over Lockerbie, Scotland, with the strong support of Senator Ted Kennedy. By the summer of 1996, a much more narrowly drawn but still potent bill had broad support in both houses. Public sentiment against Iranian terrorism was running high, especially after a U.S. military apartment building in Saudi Arabia was bombed, reportedly through Iranian connections, and TWA flight 800 went down off Long Island in an explosion initially believed to be possibly linked to terrorism. The legislation passed the Senate and the House by unanimous assent and on August 5 was signed by the president in a White House ceremony with former Iran hostages present. The president referred to Iran and Libya as "two of the most dangerous supporters of terrorism in the world," and in a follow-up speech the same day he declared: "You cannot do business with countries that practice commerce with you by day while funding or protecting terrorists who kill you and your innocent civilians by night. . . . I hope and expect that before long our allies will come around to accepting this fundamental truth."

The final version of ILSA was limited to sanctions against relatively large investments in the Iranian petroleum sector. For such investments of $40 million or more—which were lowered to $20 million after the first year—the president should impose against the foreign company two or more of six specified sanctions, including the withholding of Exim Bank facilities, export licenses, and designation as a primary dealer in U.S. government debt instruments, and prohibition of loans from a U.S. financial institution. The president, however, was given broad authority to waive the sanctions for an entire country that undertakes substantial measures to inhibit Iranian support for terrorism and the development of weapons of mass destruction [section 4(c)] and for a particular company investment when the president determines it is "important to the national interest" [section 9(c)].

Other nations, especially EU members, did not "come around" as the president expected and strongly protested the secondary boycott against their companies that invested in Iran. France called for a discussion of possible retaliation, and an official EU protest denounced the legislation as "completely unacceptable." German foreign minister Klaus Kinkel expressed a widely held European view: "Part of what is going on in America has to be seen as part of the election campaign. . . . This is a measure that the Europeans cannot accept. . . . We agree with America on most issues. . . . On the issue of how to treat Iran—with or without talks—we have a different view."[8] It was initially unclear, however, exactly what the Europeans and others would do if an investment took place and was sanctioned. The ILSA sanctions were drafted so as to avoid conflict with WTO commitments, and there were precedents for secondary boycotts.

The big question was whether the threat of sanctions would, in fact, deter third-country investors, and there was some evidence that it was doing so. Even during the 1995–1996 legislative process, the potential threat of sanctions was causing companies to hesitate. Banks that might finance projects were especially vulnerable to some of the specific sanctions under consideration. When reports surfaced of companies negotiating with Iran, warnings went out, including from Senator D'Amato.[9] After the Sirri project, the Iranian government listed 11 more projects open to foreign investors, but through the summer of 1997 no contracts were concluded. The deeply troubled Iranian economy, the large foreign debt payments that were coming due, and the unwillingness of the

Iranian government to offer attractive terms to potential investors were strong deterrents to new investment in any event, but the threat of U.S. sanctions was an additional negative factor. Uncertainty about how the United States would react if and when an investment took place was itself a deterrent.

The uncertainty about ILSA implementation was challenged decisively in September 1997 when Iran announced a $2 billion contract to develop natural gas in the South Pars field in the Persian Gulf. Total was again the lead contractor, teamed with Russian Gazprom and Malaysian Petronas. Iran has the second largest gas reserves in the world, after Russia, and this project would produce substantial financial benefits for the beleaguered Iranian economy. It was difficult to conceive of a more clear-cut case of what ILSA was designed to sanction.

The South Pars project presented President Clinton with a major lose-lose policy decision. Imposing sanctions would produce conflict with the EU and Russia, in particular,[10] because a waiver on this very large project would effectively make ILSA inoperable against most other projects while producing domestic outcries from Republican leaders about failure to carry out the intent of the law. In any event, the project would go forward even if sanctions were imposed because Total had divested its relatively small U.S. holdings to avoid any adverse effects from sanctions.

Another dimension of the decision concerned political developments within Iran. In April 1997, a German court found the Iranian leadership responsible for the September 1992 assassination of four Iranian exiles in Berlin, causing bitter exchanges between Iran and European governments, the recall of EU ambassadors, and a temporary halt to the "critical dialogue." In May, however, Mohammad Khatami, campaigning on a platform of tolerance and social reform, was elected president with a surprising 70 percent of the vote. Khatami had only limited authority, especially in international affairs, but President Clinton called the election result "at least a reaffirmation of the democratic process . . . and it's interesting and it's hopeful."[11] This was a very different assessment from his "rogue state" speech two years earlier, and his decision on the South Pars project would be a concrete test of a significant change in attitude.

The administration "studied" the South Pars project for eight months before deciding whether to impose sanctions on the three companies. The State Department resisted imposition as other foreign policy issues, including the renewed crisis with Iraq in the spring of 1998, required cooperation from EU members and Russia, while Republican congressional leaders urged the president to impose sanctions. The issue was decided through negotiations with the EU that linked ILSA sanctions to Cuba sanctions under the 1996 Helms-Burton legislation. As explained in the Cuba case study, the EU had brought the Helms-Burton sanctions before a WTO dispute settlement panel. The U.S. case was not promising, which led to prolonged negotiation of an agreement whereby the EU would not support certain investments in Cuba on expropriated U.S. properties if the United States modified the Helms-Burton legislation so as to waive sanctions against European companies. The EU linked this outcome to a parallel agreement on ILSA sanctions. The principal negotiators, U.S. under secretary of state Stuart Eizenstat and EU commissioner Sir Leon Brittan, finally produced a draft on both matters that was agreed at the U.S-EU summit meeting in London on May 18, 1998.

The South Pars decision was explained in a May 18 statement by Secretary of State Madeleine Albright. The project was found sanctionable under ILSA, but the sanctions were waived under the project-specific section 9(c) as being important to the national interest. Account was taken of enhanced ability to work with Europeans, Russians, and Malaysians "on a host of other bilateral and multilateral concerns," with several examples listed. Concern about the Asian financial crisis and the impact of sanctions on Malaysia was included as a reason for the waiver. Although countrywide waivers under section 4(c) were specifically rejected, such a waiver—conditional on continued cooperation on nonproliferation and counterterrorism—was in effect granted to EU companies through the statement, "We would expect that a review of our national interests in future ILSA cases involving Iran similar to South Pars, involving exploration and production of Iranian oil and gas, would result in like decisions with regard to waivers for EU companies." Finally, a more ambiguous statement was included about U.S. strong opposition to oil and gas pipelines that transit Iran—with explicit reference to proposals for Caspian Sea oil[12]—for which the United States "will continue to encourage alternative routes and, in the event of a trans-Iranian proposal, will carefully examine . . . possible implications under ILSA and take whatever action is appropriate."

Thus, as of early 1999, U.S. unilateral sanctions policy against Iran is in flux. Secondary boycott sanctions through ILSA have been largely vitiated through the South Pars decision. Republican leaders are displeased with the decision and could attempt to tighten the legislation to force the president to impose sanctions in the future, but it is unlikely that they could override a virtually certain presidential veto. American companies are more upset than ever with being shut out of the Iranian market, while Total and other European companies, in particular, thanks to the South Pars decision, can now move in and position themselves long term for large oil and gas production and marketing once largely engaged by American companies. The ambiguity about a Caspian Sea oil pipeline will face an early test by the Iranian request for bids on a $400 million project.[13] The short-term outlook for the Iranian economy nevertheless is deeply troubled in light of the substantial adverse impact from lower oil prices and the continued lack of an effective economic reform program. A key factor will be the incentives offered to foreign investors for new projects announced by the Iranian government on July 1, 1998. The economic impact of continued U.S. unilateral sanctions on the Iranian economy and on U.S. commercial interests is examined in the following section of this study.

Even more fundamental is the uncertainty about overall U.S. Iran policy. Initial steps toward bilateral engagement with Iran under President Khatami have involved wrestlers and a few academics. Proposals from American companies for some renewed private sector engagement followed in the wake of the South Pars decision. In a more negative direction, the nuclear weapons tests by India and Pakistan will tend to encourage further Iranian aspirations to join the nuclear club, with apparent support from Russian experts. As for change in stated U.S. policy toward Iran, Secretary Albright, in the May 18 statement, was noncommittal but decidedly less confrontational than the "evil hand . . . rogue state" formulation of her predecessor, in explaining: "While there are indicators that the Iranian government may be trying to improve its relationship with the West, we have not seen substantial change in Iranian policies of greatest concern." Then in her speech before the Asia Society on June 17, she went significantly further by stating that the United States is "ready to explore ways to build mutual confidence . . . [and to] develop with the Islamic Republic, when it is ready, a road map leading to normal relations." On May 19, President Clinton, at a press conference, commented that Iran is "changing in a positive way" and the United States seeks "a genuine reconciliation."[14] The dual containment strategy thus became rhetorically inoperative, but the unilateral economic sanctions inspired by it remain in place. The policy implications of this new situation are the subject of the concluding sections of this case study.

2. Economic Impact

On Iran

The issue here is how much adverse impact U.S. unilateral trade and investment sanctions have had on Iran. The Iranian economy during the 1990s has been severely troubled, mostly for reasons of internal mismanagement and, more recently, sharply lower world prices for oil, but the question remains as to whether the additional economic pain caused by U.S. sanctions has made a significant difference in these vulnerable circumstances.

The Iranian economy was devastated by the 1980–1988 war with Iraq, and Iran pursued a five-year recovery program from 1989 to 1993.[15] This program produced high economic growth of 7 percent a year, but it was based on large and unsustainable short-term borrowing from abroad. The external debt/GDP ratio increased substantially from 1992 to 1994, and although European and Japanese creditors effectively rescheduled $11.5 billion of loans during this period, the Iranian government was forced to adopt a more austere and financially balanced five-year program for 1994–1999, the period when U.S. unilateral sanctions were brought fully into play. As a result, Iranian imports of goods and services dropped from $29.2 billion in 1992 to $15.9 billion in 1995 (or by 46 percent), before recovering to $18.9 billion in 1996. Economic growth was correspondingly reduced to 1.6 percent (1994), 3.2 percent (1995), and a somewhat better 4.5 percent (1996). Surging inflation was also brought down from 35 percent (1994) and 49 percent (1995) to 23 percent (1996).[16]

This improving picture received a severe blow from sharply declining oil prices beginning in 1997. Oil revenues fell from $19 billion in 1996 to $16 billion in 1997 and to $12 billion or less in 1998. GDP growth dropped to +3 percent in 1997 and an estimated -2 percent in 1998. Because oil income accounts for up to 40 percent of government revenues, public sector expenditures for investment projects and consumer subsidies need to be cut sharply to contain resurgent inflation, while already high unemployment is increasing to 20 percent or more of the workforce. The deeply troubled outlook is compounded further by the absence of a coherent economic program by Khatami's economic team and the perceived lack of knowledge about, or interest in, economic issues by the president.

One other development in the Iranian economy of relevance to the impact of U.S. sanctions is the growing importance of non-oil exports, which increased from only 5 percent of total exports in the mid-1980s, when the United States placed an embargo on imports from Iran, to 15–25 percent in the mid-1990s. Non-oil exports recently declined, however, from a high of $4.8 billion in 1994 to $3.2 billion in 1996 as a result of an anti-export exchange rate policy (in which hard currency export receipts have to be "repatriated" to the banking system at an unfavorable rate of exchange). Carpet exports were especially hard hit, declining from $1 billion to $2 billion per year in 1992–1994 to $602 million in 1996, although some recovery probably took place in 1997 and 1998. Other large categories of non-oil exports in 1996 were fruits and nuts (largely pistachios) $608 million, textiles and apparel $231 million, and inorganic or petrochemicals $196 million.

In this overall economic context, the adverse impact on the Iranian economy from U.S. trade and investment sanctions consists of four distinct components: (1) The prohibition of U.S.

ties within the economy, and foreign investment policy, in particular, has been highly restrictive. Between 1993 and October 1997, 50 joint-venture projects were approved, 10 with foreign majority shareholders, but they led to only $40 million of actual investment inflows, including $14 million in 1996–1997.[19] Until 1995, the lack of incentives by the Iranian government was the sole reason for the extremely low level of foreign investment inflows.

The turning point in Iranian foreign investment policy was the March 1995 "buyback," as distinct from equity ownership, contract offer for the Sirri project, followed in 1996 by similar offerings on other projects, which could lead to a much higher level of investment inflows in the late 1990s on the order of $1 billion to $2 billion a year. Iran is still a difficult country for foreign investors, however, and the question addressed here is, to what extent have U.S. sanctions since 1995 slowed down such foreign investment? The answer requires distinguishing between oil and gas production within Iran and the transportation of Caspian Sea oil through Iran, as well as between the period 1995–2000, about which relatively specific conclusions can be drawn, and more speculative projections for the following decade.

For oil and gas production within Iran for the period 1995–2000, the impact of U.S. sanctions has been relatively small, principally to delay two or three large projects by two to three years. The Sirri and South Pars offshore projects have gone forward, and the latter would have gone forward even if ILSA sanctions had been imposed. These projects involve $2.6 billion of investment inflow through scheduled completion of Sirri in 2000 and South Pars in 2002, or about $500 million per year. Revenue inflows upon completion will run about $500 million and $1.5 billion per year, respectively, depending on the world price for natural gas. Of the other projects offered in 1996, most were small and some not very attractive to investors, but three of substantial size were influenced by the threat of ILSA sanctions. A $2 billion to $3 billion gas pipeline project to Pakistan was under negotiation with the Australian firm Broken Hill Proprietary (BHP), and the company backed off in 1996 after receiving protests from the United States. However, gas discoveries within Pakistan in early 1998 mean that this pipeline in any event may not be built any time soon, while BHP has recently announced it was opening an office in Tehran to explore new oil and gas ventures.

Another $2 billion offshore gas project in North Pars had been under serious consideration by Shell since 1993, but the company ruled out any further exploration projects in Iran in January 1997, with explicit reference to U.S. sanctions. North Pars was reopened to investors in June 1998, however, and in view of the May 1998 U.S. waiver on South Pars, Shell and others are now basically free to proceed. The third project was the $200 million Balal offshore oil offering to the Canadian Bow Valley Company, which has had difficulty financing the project, in part related to ILSA threats, although the pullout of its Indonesian partner was caused by the Asian financial crisis rather than ILSA. This project, too, will likely go forward in the wake of the South Pars waiver, perhaps with some Iranian financing. In sum, U.S. sanctions slowed down by a few years at least two substantial projects—North Pars and Balal— that might otherwise have gone forward, with a corresponding delay in the financial inflow on the order of $300 million to $500 million per year. After the May 1998 South Pars waiver, these projects, as well as all others related to oil and gas production, have become essentially open to non-U.S. investors.

The prevention of third-country investment in Iranian pipelines for Caspian Sea oil has been a high priority for U.S. sanctions policy, but the sanctions' impact is not yet clear because of delays in Caspian oil production and uncertainties about alternative East-West Transcaucasian pipelines. Cost estimates for construction of a pipeline from Baku to Ceyhan range from the government of Turkey's original figure of $2.3 billion to what could be a commercially unattractive $4 billion or more by private sector interests. A linking pipeline under the Caspian Sea is likely to be relatively high cost, subject to sovereignty claims by Russia and Iran, and runs the environmental risk of leaks in the Caspian seabed. An alternative and probably lower cost route is to pipe Caspian Sea oil to refineries in northern Iran, for domestic consumption, in a swap arrangement for Iranian oil exports from the Persian Gulf. Such a pipeline could later be extended to the Persian Gulf and Pakistan. In June 1998, following the South Pars waiver,

Iran asked for bids on a $400 million pipeline from its Caspian Sea port of Neka to the northern refineries, and reports indicate that there were several bidders by the September deadline. This pipeline offering will present another critical test case for ILSA sanctions because the United States and the EU disagree over the vague language on Caspian Sea pipelines in the May 18 Albright statement. In any event, U.S. sanctions have not yet blocked pipeline proposals related to Caspian Sea oil.

The future of foreign investment in the Iranian petroleum sector during the decade 2000–2010 holds enormous potential because Iran needs to rebuild its existing industry structure and to develop new oil and gas production. One estimate of Iranian needs for foreign capital is $50 billion from 1998 to 2010, or more than $4 billion per year, including upstream, refining, infrastructure, and pipeline investments.[20] On July 1, 1998, at a London conference attended by 450 oil company executives, Iranian officials presented 43 new projects valued at more than $5 billion, including onshore fields for the first time and longer-term "buyback" arrangements. Much still depends on the precise incentives offered to investors, but under current circumstances, ILSA will likely have little or no restraining effect on third-country investors. The extent to which the continued exclusion of U.S. firms will limit the quantity and quality of foreign investment offers is less clear. Many other companies—European, Japanese, Russian, Chinese, and other Asian, including majors such as Shell and BP-Amoco—are engaging with Iran and, year by year, as these others invest and establish themselves in the country, the absence of the once-dominant American companies will become less and less significant. In any event, it is almost certain that any reasonably attractive project offerings by the Iranian government will attract multiple non-U.S. bidders.

The foregoing elaborates the impact of U.S. unilateral trade and investment sanctions against Iran. Closely related in terms of impact on Iran have been U.S. pressures to curtail economic assistance to Iran, principally from the World Bank and bilateral aid donors. The World Bank earlier approved $400 million to $500 million per year of loans to Iran for economic infrastructure and social sector projects, but in the face of U.S. pressures no new loans have been approved since 1994. Similarly, Japanese economic aid projects, which could amount to $100 million to $300 million per year, have been suspended, and other potential aid donors have held back as well. Iran thus loses on the order of $500 million to $800 million per year in official development finance as a result of the U.S. policy to exert a financial squeeze on the Iranian economy. This figure represents the loss to the Iranian economy if alternative financing from commercial banks were not available, which almost certainly was the case for infrastructure and social sector projects in recent years.[21]

The overall impact on the Iranian economy of U.S. unilateral sanctions and related policies is summarized in table 1. The columns distinguish between the period 1995–1997, when sanctions were initially implemented and before the South Pars waiver, and the subsequent 1998–2000 period (although the 1995–1997 impact of ILSA in delaying investments shows up as a loss of disbursements in the 1998–2000 column). The total figures and the subtotal for sanctions on U.S. exports and investment are also calculated as a percentage of Iranian exports, as a measure of the relative degree to which Iranian hard currency inflows are curtailed. The total figures, $1.2 billion to $2.6 billion per year of adverse impact, are substantial, amounting to 6 to 13 percent of exports. The two largest categories, however, are the prohibition on U.S. imports from Iran and the curtailment of economic assistance. U.S. unilateral sanctions on U.S. exports and foreign investment, which have produced the most controversy, in contrast, caused relatively little damage to the Iranian economy—only $200 million to $800 million per year, or 1 percent to 4 percent of exports. Moreover, the largest portion of the export/investment subtotal, the $300 million to $500 million estimated loss in delayed investment disbursements during 1998–2000, will likely decline or disappear in light of the South Pars waiver.

On U.S. Commercial Interests

The impact of sanctions against Iran on U.S. commercial interests, inherently adverse for unilateral sanctions, can be addressed in terms of the same four categories as for the impact on the Iranian

Table 1
Adverse Impact of U.S. Sanctions and Related Policies on the Iranian Economy

	1995–1997 (per year)	1998–2000 (per year)
1. Prohibition on U.S. imports	$0.5–$1.0 billion	$0.5–$1.0 billion
2. Prohibition on U.S. exports	$100–$200 million	$100–$200 million
3. Prohibition on marketing oil to third countries	$100–$300 million	$100 million
4. Prohibition on U.S. investment and ILSA sanctions on third countries	0	$300–$500 million
5. U.S. pressures to limit economic assistance	$500–$800 million	$500–$800 million
6. Total (lines 1-5)	$1.2–$2.3 billion	$1.5–$2.6 billion
7. Subtotal for exports and investment (lines 2-4)	$200–$500 million	$500–$800 million
8. Total (line 6) as a percentage of Iranian exports*	6–12 percent	8–13 percent
9. Subtotal (line 7) as a percentage of Iranian exports	1–3 percent	3–4 percent

* Iranian exports of goods and services are estimated at roughly $20 billion per year. They were $19.3 billion in 1995, $23.8 billion in 1996, and substantially lower in 1997 and 1998 because of lower oil prices.

economy—imports from Iran, exports to Iran, marketing Iranian oil in third countries, and U.S. investment in Iran—plus one additional category of indirect adverse impact on investment in third countries, most importantly related to Caspian Sea oil and gas development.

1. Prohibition on U.S. imports from Iran. The effect of this prohibition on the United States is more a consumer than a commercial interest, a fact usually ignored and mentioned here only in general terms. The $0.5 billion to $1.0 billion per year of non-oil

Iranian exports that would be exported to the United States in the absence of the embargo is small compared with total U.S. imports and are for the most part easily replaced by imports from other sources. Product choice for the American consumer is limited, however, especially for Iranian carpets and the distinctive qualities of some agricultural products.

2. Prohibition on U.S. exports to Iran.   The estimated loss of U.S. exports from the sanctions policy depends on the baseline for the sanctions and also needs to take account of U.S. products that still reach Iran indirectly despite the embargo. In the 1970s, before the Iranian Revolution, 15 percent to 20 percent of Iranian imports came from the United States, but by the time of the May 1995 executive order banning remaining U.S. exports to Iran, the U.S. market share had dropped to 3 percent. This 3 percent share amounted to $330 million of merchandise exported in 1994, or $400 million including an estimate for services trade. These direct exports were lost, but taking account of indirect shipments, the net actual loss was less, probably on the order of $300 million. In addition, export restraints for "dual use" products were more stringent for U.S. exporters than was the case for European, Japanese, and other competitors, which can thus be considered a form of selective unilateral sanctions. There is no basis for a precise estimate of such losses to U.S. exports, but it would raise the $300 million figure significantly, perhaps to $500 million or more.

The broader and longer-term question concerns the impact on U.S. exports from the continuing hostile U.S.-Iranian relationship, particularly as relations between Iran and the rest of the world become more normalized under the changed circumstances since the election of President Khatami in May 1997. The earlier 15 percent to 20 percent U.S. share of the Iranian market would currently equate to about $3 billion to $4 billion of U.S. exports per year. This share may never be attained again in view of the history of the past 20 years, but a much larger share than the 3 percent in 1994 would surely result when relations are eventually normalized. A reasonable target figure of 10 percent of the Iranian market would equate to a $2 billion per year loss in U.S. exports from the overall hostile bilateral relationship, including the U.S. trade embargo.

3. Prohibition on American companies marketing Iranian oil in third countries. This again relates to the $4 billion of sales in 1994, and in terms of revenue losses to American companies, the marketing companies' share of export revenues is about 10 percent. This means an approximate $400 million per year transfer of business from U.S. to foreign companies from the prohibition in the May 1995 executive order.

4. Prohibition on U.S. investment in Iran. This is potentially the largest category of adverse impact on U.S. commercial interests over the coming three to five years, with even greater longer-term consequences. Conoco clearly lost the $600 million Sirri contract to Total in 1995 as a result of the unilateral U.S. sanction, an investment flow that would have been spent mostly on U.S. exports of goods and services over the ensuing four years, followed by a longer-term relationship in supplying support services and replacement parts. As for other projects moving forward, beginning with the $2 billion South Pars project and now others in the wake of the South Pars waiver, a benchmark for lost U.S. market share is that in neighboring Azerbaijan, where American companies obtained approximately 30 percent to 50 percent shares in six recent projects open to U.S. bidding. Applying this market share to an anticipated $1 billion to $4 billion per year in new investment in the Iranian petroleum sector over the coming decade equates to a projected annual loss for American companies of $300 million to $2 billion. Longer-term losses from follow-on servicing and replacement parts would be substantial in terms of direct sales and even greater in strategic business terms as non-U.S. technologies, equipment, and maintenance services progressively displace the earlier dominant U.S. position in this very large petroleum and gas sector. There are reports that the Iranian government is considering limiting the number of major foreign oil companies doing business in Iran to perhaps a dozen or so, as a practical matter of government management capacity. If this should proceed with all non-American companies, it will be even more difficult for American companies to reenter the Iranian market at a later date. U.S. unilateral sanctions have thus created an extraordinary mutual interest between the extreme anti-American elements in the Iranian government and non-U.S. oil companies to keep the sanctions in place as long as possible.

5. *Indirect adverse impact in third countries.* The most important indirect impact on U.S. commercial interests is in Caspian Sea oil and gas development and production. Caspian Sea oil production is projected to rise to 3 million barrels per day by 2010, and Azerbaijan alone, with about 35 percent of the projected production, has $26 billion of investment projects under way in just 8 out of 12 planned offshore production sharing contracts.[22] Thus far, again limited to Azerbaijan where project figures are available, American companies hold shares in six projects ranging from 28 percent to 56 percent. However, in two other projects— Shah Denis and Lenkoran-Talysh Deniz—Iranian companies participate and thus American companies are excluded. These two projects amount to $6 billion, and a benchmark 30 percent to 50 percent U.S. share indicates a loss to American companies of $1.8 billion to $3.0 billion. The largest shareholders in these two projects are France ($1.4 billion), Norway ($1 billion), and the United Kingdom ($1 billion). American companies could be excluded from other projects to the extent Iranian participation is extended, which could become more likely if pipelines are built through Iran, thus giving Iran leverage to insist on participation in the production projects. Another disadvantage to American companies would develop if pipelines are built through Iran that are lower cost than the East-West Transcaucasian pipelines being promoted by the United States—which is likely.[23] Under these circumstances, the U.S. share of production would have to be transported through the higher-cost pipelines with consequent lower rates of return on investment.[24]

Yet another problem for American companies could develop if a pipeline built under the Caspian Sea should require recognition by and payment to Iran on sovereignty grounds, which could exclude American companies from using the pipeline. Caspian Sea oil production has gotten off to a slow start and is only now taking shape in terms of actual production. The loss to American companies related to Iranian sanctions, however, is already substantial and could grow much higher in the years ahead, particularly to the extent Iran becomes an active participant through pipelines and production sharing.

The overall outlook for immediate adverse impact on U.S. commercial interests as a result of unilateral sanctions during the 1990s is thus roughly a $500 million per year loss in U.S. exports, $300 million–$2 billion per year in investment in Iran, and a less clear, but potentially substantial loss for Caspian Sea oil production. These figures do not take account of the loss in long-term market position in the country with the second largest gas and third largest petroleum reserves in the world. Once excluded from the Iranian market, it can take many years for American companies to reestablish a competitive market position vis-à-vis competitors. This was evident in the Vietnam case study, where American companies arrived only several years after European and Asian rivals. In Iran, the United States has now been largely excluded for 20 years and counting.

3. Net Assessment of U.S. Unilateral Sanctions Policy

A net assessment of U.S. unilateral sanctions policy against Iran needs to begin by defining which sanctions policy. U.S. policy at the end of 1998 was in a state of flux emanating from the May 18 South Pars waiver and the June 17 Albright speech. In this context, the presentation here consists first of an assessment of U.S. policy from 1993 through the South Pars waiver—characterized as the dual containment political strategy supported by comprehensive trade and investment sanctions, extended to third-country investors through ILSA. This assessment is then compared with three alternative policy courses in the following section. Current U.S. policy is somewhere between the heretofore dual containment approach and the second alternative of "step-by-step normalization."

To assess the dual containment/unilateral sanction experience from 1993 to May 1998 requires integrating the broad unilateral sanctions on trade and investment, particularly with respect to the executive orders of 1995 and the ILSA of 1996, and the narrowly targeted multilateral sanctions related to the development of weapons of mass destruction. The assessment must also distinguish three U.S. interests in Iran. The U.S. commercial interest, which inherently suffers from unilateral sanctions, has already been addressed in the previous section. The other two interests are closely related in terms of ultimate outcome, but are quite distinct in the immediate workings of sanctions policy. One concerns specific national security interests—international terrorism, weapons of mass destruction, and conventional arms related to regional peace and stability. These have been explicit from the outset and continue to be up front and vital. The other interest is to influence political change within Iran toward a more cooperative, market-oriented democracy, the post–Cold War paradigm being pursued throughout the world. In this latter context, the U.S. objective in Iran is in the process of shifting from the "rogue/outlaw state" target of the 1993 dual containment strategy, where a basic regime change was the implied solution, to the more hopeful and positive political assessment since May 1997. Each of these two interests is addressed in turn.

National Security Interests

The U.S. interest in curbing Iranian support for international terrorism, the development of weapons of mass destruction, and the buildup of conventional arms capability is where the targeted multilateral sanctions and the unilateral trade and investment sanctions tend to overlap, but unevenly:

1. International terrorism.   Neither the multilateral nor the unilateral sanctions have significantly affected Iranian support for international terrorism up to this point. Relatively small amounts of funds are involved, and the weapons used are readily obtainable. Progress on this front is more closely related to basic change in the political behavior of the Iranian government, as discussed in the following section, and progress in the Middle East peace process, which is beyond the scope of this study. The 1997 U.S. report on state-sponsored terrorism stated that "Iran remains the most active state sponsor of terrorism . . . [and that] Tehran conducted at least 13 assassinations in 1997, the majority of which were carried out in northern Iraq." A reference was also made to President Khatami, in a CNN interview, wherein he "agreed that terrorist attacks against non-combatants, including Israeli women and children, should be condemned." Of course, if and when international terrorism should move toward utilization of weapons of mass destruction, this issue becomes linked with the issues that follow.

2. *Chemical and biological weapons.* These national security threats are primarily addressed through multilateral sanctions and agreements, although with limited success. Commitments to abstain from producing or purchasing such weapons are extremely difficult to police, as evident in Iraq where on the ground UN inspection teams have been frustrated for eight years. In any event, the amount of financial resources involved is relatively small and affected little, if at all, by the limited economic impact of U.S. unilateral trade and investment sanctions imposed against Iran.

3. *Nuclear weapons.* Nuclear weapons could ultimately involve a considerable financial commitment by Iran, but the deterrents to such weapons development thus far have been related primarily to the importation of specific components or fuels and the availability of highly trained personnel, both of which are addressed by targeted multilateral, rather than U.S. unilateral, sanctions. Russia has reportedly violated its commitments to targeted multilateral sanctions, and the United States and Russia basically disagree about whether the completion of the Bushehr light-water nuclear power plants would provide the training base for Iranian nuclear weapons expertise and experience.[25] Iran has signed the Nonproliferation Treaty, but in view of the 1998 Indian and Pakistani nuclear tests and the widespread belief that Israel has a nuclear weapons arsenal, Iran is near or at the top of the list of future most likely nuclear proliferators. Once again, however, the limited impact of unilateral trade and investment sanctions was probably not a significant deterrent to whatever Iran has been doing related to nuclear weapons development.

4. *Launch missile capability.* This capability involves substantial up-front financial payments, and the initial economic squeeze from U.S. unilateral sanctions in 1995–1996, including the pending threat of ILSA sanctions against third-country investors, might have caused some postponement in planned

acquisition. The main constraints, however, were and are now even more the multilateral sanctions strategy, particularly with respect to China and Russia. The effectiveness of this multilateral strategy is open to severe criticism, and targeted sanctions against Russian firms that sell ballistic missile equipment and technology to Iran, as contained in legislation passed by Congress and vetoed by the president in 1998, could be a useful response. This does not change the fact, however, that U.S. unilateral sanctions on trade and investment with Iran are a relatively minor disincentive at best.

5. Buildup of conventional weapons.   This is the one clear area where the degree of impact from U.S. unilateral sanctions has been and probably continues to be a deterrent to earlier Iranian intentions. If U.S. sanctions and other economic measures reduce hard currency available to Iran by $1.2 billion to $2.6 billion per year, or 6 to 13 percent of export receipts, hard choices have to be made by the Iranian government, including delays in very large planned weapons purchases. The large majority of this sanctions-induced economic pain, however, is caused by the prohibition on U.S. imports from Iran and U.S. pressures to withhold economic assistance, while only a small to inconsequential share is caused by the sanctions on U.S. exports and investment. This area is also subject to targeted multilateral restrictions on arms shipments to Iran, but they are largely ineffective because of large earlier weapons orders still in the pipeline and thus exempted, especially from Russia.

The net assessment for the effectiveness of unilateral trade and investment sanctions to achieve U.S. national security objectives in Iran through 1998 is thus that they have not been effective, except to a limited extent in restraining a conventional arms buildup and perhaps a launch missile capability. In the future, even this impact will be weakened considerably in light of the South Pars waiver.

Political Change in Iran

The impact of U.S. unilateral sanctions policy on political change within Iran, as elsewhere, consists of two distinct effects—from the economic pain caused by the sanctions and from the disengagement of the U.S. private sector from contact with the Iranian government and general population. The point of departure for the 1993 dual containment strategy was that Iran was an outlaw state posing serious threats to U.S. national security and that any impact on underlying political change within Iran from U.S. sanctions policy was marginal, and certainly subsidiary to the principal objective of reducing financial resources available to the Iranian government.

This basic premise of U.S. policy is no longer sustainable for two reasons. First, as explained in the previous section, the economic pain inflicted by U.S. unilateral sanctions was relatively small from the outset—particularly with respect to the cutoff of U.S. exports and investment—and will be even less so in the wake of the South Pars waiver. And second, the electoral victory of President Khatami in May 1997 demonstrated that a process of political change toward a more open and just society is under way within Iran. Khatami's 70 percent overall electoral majority was even higher among the younger generation, women, and the better educated. Polls indicate that even a majority of the Revolutionary Guard, which enforces hard-line revolutionary disciplines, voted for Khatami. Although the political and police structures are still controlled by the hard-liners, a power struggle is clearly unfolding. Most experts foresee a process of gradual change over time, but events could turn violent. At the international level, and for the U.S.-Iranian relationship in particular, people-to-people contacts are more welcome, but official contacts, controlled by the predominantly hard-line leadership, remain minimal.

In this context, one question about sanctions policy is whether and how U.S. sanctions influenced Khatami's electoral victory. Did the modest economic pain and greater feeling of international isolation resulting from the sanctions induce younger Iranians to vote for Khatami? Or did the sanctions, with accompanying rhetoric about Iran as an outlaw state, play into the hands of the hard-liners in appealing to deeply felt Iranian nationalism? The impact probably worked a little in both directions, but experts are virtually unanimous that the Khatami victory was overwhelmingly decided by the internal disenchantment with 20 years of extremist clerical rule and that U.S. sanctions had minimal effect.

Far more important, what effect is the continuing U.S. sanctions policy, including the disengagement of the U.S. private sector from Iran, having on the process of political change under way in Iran? Again, the impact will be relatively small compared with internal forces at play, and not of the same order of magnitude, for example, as was projected in the Cuba case study. The policy is clearly more significant now in Iran than before May 1997, however. Indeed, the continued almost total disengagement of the U.S. private sector from Iran is a significant negative factor with respect to the process of change toward a more open, normal relationship with the United States. The rationale for this judgment is presented only briefly here and surely deserves greater recognition and attention as a factor influencing U.S.-Iran policy at this juncture. U.S. policymakers need to address the pros and cons of U.S. private sector engagement in Iran not only in terms of its impact on U.S. commercial interests but on political developments within Iran as well.

A detailed assessment of the positive results of U.S. private sector reengagement after two decades of isolation from U.S. unilateral sanctions is contained in the Vietnam case study. Many circumstances in Vietnam are very different from those in Iran, but the basic workings of U.S. private sector engagement in this period of ever-deepening economic globalization would be similar. Private sector engagement, especially for investment-related projects, means day-to-day contact between Americans and Iranians in both the public and private sectors, working together to create new, productive enterprises as well as new jobs for Iranians. American companies, with few exceptions, constitute a high visibility role model for U.S. values and corporate culture. National employees are treated with respect as individuals, in an atmosphere of openness, with compensation based on merit and performance, including opportunities for career advancement. American companies also stand out for maintaining high labor and environmental standards in their operations, up to national standards and then some. Especially noteworthy are their programs of training and technical assistance, not only for their own employees, but for customers and engaged government officials as well.

The foregoing paragraph draws heavily on the experience of about 300 American companies that have established resident operations in Vietnam since 1994 and are widely dispersed by sector. In Iran, initial reengagement by the U.S. private sector will likely be concentrated in the petroleum sector, but not nearly as much as it was two decades ago. If Iran is to succeed in the new world of economic globalization, including the development of non-oil exports, more productive industrial and agricultural sectors will have to be developed. In particular, a technologically advanced infrastructure for telecommunications, financial services, and transportation, where American companies tend to be at the forefront, will be needed, including for the training of local professionals. In Vietnam, Citicorp alone has trained more than 1,000 Vietnamese during the past four years, including a seminar for all state bankers on auditing procedures. Some Iranian nationalists may consider this example a good reason to keep foreign bankers out of Iran, but for most Iranians who see their future in terms of a modern, industrialized nation, the benefits of such training in financial services—starting with the capability to carry out credible auditing procedures—should be self-evident.

~ ~ ~

The overall net assessment of U.S. sanctions policy toward Iran since 1993 is thus predominantly negative. The adverse economic impact on Iran has been modest and more important for the U.S. embargo on imports from Iran than for the prohibition on U.S. exports to and investment in Iran, which can simply be replaced by third-country competitors, especially in light of the South Pars waiver. Important and continuing U.S. national security interests can and should be addressed primarily through targeted multilateral sanctions, pursued in a more forceful way, while broadly based unilateral sanctions on trade and investment have less and less relevance. With respect to political change within Iran toward a more open and less threatening relationship, the case for U.S. private sector engagement as a force for positive change is far more compelling with the election of President Khatami than it was before.

U.S. policy at the end of 1998 had been buffeted by recent events and was in a state of flux. The June 17 Albright speech offered to develop a "road map" toward normalization, but still retained some of the dual containment rationale: "The reality is that Iran's support for terrorism has not yet ceased; serious violations of human rights persist; and its efforts to develop long-range missiles and to acquire nuclear weapons continue." As for comprehensive unilateral sanctions, the Clinton administration is in broad retreat from the ILSA third-country sanctions. A major showdown on the Iran pipeline project for Caspian Sea oil looms, which, in turn, raises questions about U.S. geopolitical as well as commercial interests as Iran begins a massive program to rebuild and expand its petroleum sector based solely on non-American companies. In other words, the current U.S. policy toward Iran is in transition toward some alternative policy course.

4. Alternatives to Current Unilateral Sanctions Policy

There are three basic alternatives to the current state of unilateral sanctions policy toward Iran: (1) tighten and extend the sanctions to achieve the original intent of the dual containment policy; (2) normalize relations step-by-step, progressively relaxing the sanctions; and (3) lift the sanctions unilaterally. Although there can be some combination of these alternatives, especially between (2) and (3), there are important distinctions relating principally to the sequence of actions. In any event, each of the three alternatives is addressed in turn.

1. Tighten and extend the sanctions.   The reaction of some Republican members of the Congress to the South Pars waiver has been to consider legislation to restrict or remove the presidential waiver authority in ILSA so as to force the imposition of sanctions on third-country investors in the Iranian petroleum sector. They convincingly explain that the South Pars waiver vitiates the sanctions threat and negates the intent of the ILSA as signed by President Clinton in 1996. The rationale for such a course is that a tightening of sanctions against third countries would achieve the originally intended results of the dual containment strategy of isolating Iran and exerting substantial financial pressure on the Iranian government by preventing new foreign investment in the petroleum sector.

Although the intent in these case studies is to present the pros and cons for each policy alternative, the pros of this alternative, if implemented, at this juncture, are extremely difficult to understand. Putting forward legislative proposals to remove the president's waiver authority would convey a foreign policy message to President Clinton of Republican discontent with Iran policy, but the issue addressed here is what would happen if this alternative were actually adopted as law and implemented.

Such a legislative change would almost certainly have to be passed over a presidential veto, because by signing such legislation the president would be repudiating the carefully negotiated U.S.-EU agreement on both Iran and Cuba sanctions. He would also be undermining Secretary Albright's June 17 road map to normalization statement by agreeing to unconditionally impose sanctions on new third-country investments in Iran. Thus, in the unlikely event that Congress would override a presidential veto and force him to impose such sanctions against his will, U.S. unilateral sanctions policy toward Iran would reach the point of near total incoherence. In April 1995, President Clinton stated his opposition to extending sanctions to third countries on broad foreign policy grounds; in August 1996, he nevertheless signed the ILSA to do so, with much public fanfare as a presidential policy initiative; in May 1997, he effectively gutted the credibility of the ILSA with the South Pars waiver; and under this alternative, he would be forced to implement the same third-country sanctions against his will. Even for the world's preeminent military and economic power, there is a limit to inconsistent and unpredictable actions by the U.S. president. It is therefore almost inconceivable that this alternative will be realized during the final two years of the Clinton presidency, and to try to predict reactions by other governments if it were realized is left to others.

2. Normalize relations step-by-step. This is the general course the Clinton administration is apparently pursuing, which would include the phaseout of unilateral economic sanctions, but it is not clear what the sequence of actions on both sides would be, and how, in particular, the sanctions phaseout would fit in. The most specific proposal as to how such a step-by-step process could play out was made by Congressman Lee Hamilton in his April 15, 1998, speech at the Council on Foreign Relations. Such a process would move slowly, with the Iranian government extremely reluctant to undertake official contacts with the U.S. government pending some conciliatory actions on the U.S. side. First steps would be primarily through people-to-people contacts, such as sporting events and academic visits. U.S. private sector contracts remain precluded by U.S. sanctions, which, according to the Hamilton scenario, would only be addressed late in the process.

This approach was confirmed by the Albright proposal for a "road map," which was a clear reference, later confirmed by the State Department, to the U.S.-Vietnam experience in which the U.S. government presented a highly specific, four-phase road map in 1991 to restore normal relations. There are questions, however, about the appropriateness of the Vietnamese experience for the current U.S.-Iran context. The Vietnamese government proceeded on the basis of the U.S. road map, although it never formally agreed to it, because Vietnam was more eager than the United States to normalize relations, largely for geopolitical reasons. The principal U.S. objective, moreover, was to get full cooperation from Vietnam to account for Americans missing-in-action (MIAs), which did not involve broader foreign policy or national security commitments on the Vietnamese side, as would presumably be the case for a U.S.-Iran road map.

The prospect for this alternative policy course is thus to move forward more along the Hamilton than the U.S.-Vietnam road-map lines, at a cautious, slow pace largely determined by Iran. In fact, a closer analogy from the other case studies is not the Vietnam road map, but the "carefully calibrated" steps approach to normalization with Cuba contained in the 1992 Cuba Democracy Act, in which the United States would respond step-by-step to positive developments in Cuba.

A major problem with this step-by-step approach is that the lifting of sanctions on U.S. exports to and investment in Iran could be delayed for a number of years, while critical, long-term investment decisions, in the Iranian petroleum sector in particular, are being taken that exclude American companies. As noted earlier, there is an obvious mutual interest between the hard-line, anti-American elements within the Iranian power structure and non-U.S. petroleum companies to drag out the U.S. unilateral sanctions on American companies as long as possible. And a future U.S.-Iran relationship based on relatively small U.S. private sector participation in the Iranian petroleum sector would be largely devoid of geoeconomic and thus, to a considerable extent, geopolitical content.

3. *Lift the sanctions unilaterally.* The rationale for this alternative derives from several of the arguments developed in the net assessment of current sanctions policy:

- If unilateral sanctions on U.S. exports to and investment in Iran, post South Pars waiver, have little adverse impact on the Iranian economy; and

- If these sanctions cause substantial immediate and perhaps even greater longer-term damage to U.S. commercial interests; and

- If U.S. private sector engagement in Iran would support positive political change within the country; and

- If the lifting of these unilateral sanctions provides little bargaining leverage with the Iranian government in view of the mutual interest between the hard-liners within the Iranian power structure and non-U.S. oil companies to prolong the unilateral sanctions;

- Then the logical conclusion is that it is in the U.S. interest to lift these sanctions unilaterally.

These arguments can and should be debated as a rational process of policy formulation based on cause and effect. The reversal of policy course involved, however, would be an admission that the unilateral sanctions strategy for Iran over the past four years has been a failure, which would be difficult to accept for members of the administration and the Congress who have supported it.

Finally, the moral argument against such a policy course holds that even if U.S. foreign policy objectives were better served without than with the export and investment sanctions, it is still preferable on moral grounds to withhold business by American companies with a regime still classified as the foremost supporter of international terrorism and believed to be engaged in developing weapons of mass destruction. This is the "feeling good" versus "doing good" conundrum addressed throughout the case studies, and the consistent conclusion drawn here is that it is preferable to do good than to feel good in the conduct of U.S. foreign policy.

This alternative could, of course, be pursued in different ways. The most decisive move would be for the president simply to rescind the two executive orders of 1995 and permit American companies to resume exports to and investment in Iran. A more limited initiative would be to lift the embargo on U.S. exports, while limiting U.S. investment in the Iranian petroleum sector to $20 million a year per project, as freely permitted in ILSA. An even more limited first step would be to lift the export and investment embargo on consumer and other goods but not on petroleum sector–related commerce.

Any such unilateral steps by the United States would, of course, constitute the kind of action—as distinct from words—that the Khatami government has called for as a basis for the resumption of official engagement.

Finally, the embargo on U.S. imports from Iran does provide bargaining leverage for the United States because Iran has much to gain from its lifting and the United States suffers no significant adverse effects from its continuance. The relationship is similar to the remaining and most important unilateral sanction against Vietnam—the withholding of MFN from Vietnamese exports to the United States. The ongoing U.S.-Vietnamese negotiation over granting MFN and improved U.S. access to the Vietnamese market could be a precursor for what lies ahead for U.S.-Iranian trade. In the case of Iran, however, the opening of the U.S. market to Iranian companies could be linked, in addition to market access for U.S. exports to Iran, to the establishment of consular if not full diplomatic representation and assurances that Iranians engaged in commerce with the United States would not be associated in any way with international terrorism.

5. Conclusions and Recommendations

U.S. unilateral sanctions policy against Iran, as of early 1999, is having a substantial adverse impact on U.S. interests with little redeeming value. It is having only a small negative effect on Iran, principally from the embargo on U.S. imports from Iran. The sanctions against U.S. exports to and investment in Iran is having a substantial short-term and potentially much larger longer-term adverse impact on U.S. commercial interests and, through exclusion of U.S. firms from the Iranian petroleum sector, on the U.S. geopolitical position in central Asia as well. As a consequence, the rational policy response would be to phase out the unilateral sanctions as soon as possible, at least for U.S. exports and investment.

A tactical consideration for such a phaseout is how to use it to maximum bargaining advantage—to negotiate commitments by Iran in return. This concept underlies the Lee Hamilton step-by-step approach and the more structured road map proposal of Secretary of State Albright. Unfortunately, there is limited bargaining leverage at this point, largely because President Khatami, even if he wanted to pursue such a course, does not have sufficient power to do so and would be blocked by the unholy alliance of anti-American hard-liners within the Iranian power structure and non-American oil companies that benefit from the exclusion of Americans. Whereas in the Cuba case study much expert opinion concludes that Fidel Castro does not want to negotiate a step-by-step lifting of the embargo, for Iran the corresponding conclusion is that Khatami is unable to do so. Thus, the outlook is that, unless there is an unexpected sharp decline in the power position of the more radical Islamist clergy, there will be at best a very slow process of gradual opening between the United States and Iran, with trade and investment relations likely to remain in the deep freeze for several years or more.

The preferable route, therefore, is to take unilateral steps to lift the unilateral sanctions. At a minimum, the sanctions on U.S.

exports and investment, except for the petroleum sector, should be lifted by executive order. This would be a concrete first step from the U.S. side, which Khatami has stated repeatedly is necessary before he can take corresponding steps. Such unilateral action by the United States should allow official dialogue between the two nations to resume and offer the United States the opportunity, in particular, to press Khatami on the issue of international terrorism, where he has signaled his disavowal.

The bolder and preferred alternative would be a total lifting of the U.S. embargo on exports to and investment in Iran, with a licensing procedure for investment in the petroleum sector linked to the waiver procedure followed for ILSA until that act is amended or expires in 2001. The president would undertake these steps by executive order and would use the prospect for doing so to obtain closer collaboration with European and other allies on objectives in Iran related to the proliferation of weapons of mass destruction and international terrorism.

Finally, with respect to the embargo on U.S. imports from Iran, a corresponding offer to lift the sanction would be made, but in this case conditioned on certain actions by Iran. Official diplomatic and consular relations would have to be resumed first to deal appropriately with the related increase in travel by Iranians to the United States, and some reciprocal market-access commitments for U.S. exports to Iran would also be warranted.

Notes

1. The first official presentation of the dual containment policy was by NSC staffer Martin Indyk—later U.S. ambassador to Israel and assistant secretary of state for Near Eastern affairs—in a special report of the Washington Institute for Middle East Policy, May 21, 1993. The strategy was elaborated by NSC director and assistant to the president Anthony Lake in "Confronting Backlash States," *Foreign Affairs* 72 (March/April 1994), 45–55, from which the quotes are taken. Lake's use of the adjective "backlash" to describe Iranian behavior is less clear than his more widely cited adjectives "recalcitrant" and "outlaw."

2. White House Press Release, February 9, 1995. A widely cited February 25, 1995, edition of the *Economist* gave credence to the misleading German charges: "For the first time, America had overtaken Germany to

become Iran's biggest trading partner, responsible for some $4 billion of Iran's overseas business . . . the American government, say German diplomats in Teheran, is pushing Europe to break ties with Iran while American firms are sneaking in to snap up scarce contracts." As noted in the text, EU exports to Iran in 1994 were, in fact, more than 15 times larger than U.S. exports.

3.   President Rafsanjani later explained in an interview with Peter Jennings: "We invited an American firm and entered into a deal . . . this was a message to the United States, which was not correctly understood. We had a lot of difficulty in this country by inviting an American company to come here with such a project because of public opinion." *New York Times*, May 16, 1995.

4.   *New York Times*, March 7, 1995, and Kambiz Fordohar, "Big Oil versus Clinton," *The Middle East*, May 1, 1995.

5.   The quote is from the *New York Times*, March 10, 1995. For an account of the U.S. government reaction to the announced agreement, see Robert H. Pelletreau, "The United States, Iran, and the Total Deals," *Al-Hayat*, June 3, 1998. Ambassador Pelletreau was with Secretary Christopher in Tel Aviv and recalls that the secretary was "visibly angry at not knowing this deal was imminent."

6.   Edgar Bronfman and his two sons, board members who owned about a quarter of DuPont, publicly opposed the agreement, although Conoco management had earlier briefed the board on discussions with the Iranian government.

7.   AIPAC did not gear up its public campaign for comprehensive economic sanctions until after Senator D'Amato put forward his legislation in January 1995. The first of a series of AIPAC reports, the April 2 "Comprehensive U.S. Sanctions against Iran: A Plan for Action" was a detailed 74-page compendium that began with reference to the $4 billion oil marketing figure: "Iran is an 'outlaw nation' whose 'evil hand' we see throughout the Middle East and the world, in the words of Secretary of State Warren Christopher. Yet, in spite of cancellation of the Conoco deal, *United States companies have become Iran's largest trading partners*, recently surpassing Germany" [italics in original].

8.   *New York Times*, August 7, 1996.

9.   Among potential investors warned of possible sanctions by Senator D'Amato, and who did not go forward, were the Australian BHP company (pipeline project), the Japanese JGC construction company (gas project), and the UK Pell Frischmann and Canadian Bow Valley Energy companies (oil field development project). See AIPAC, "Recent Progress in Containing Iran," January 30, 1998. The Shell Company also announced publicly that it would not continue discussions about new contracts with Iran in view of the U.S. sanctions.

10. The potential adverse impact on relations with Malaysia from a decision to sanction were less clear. The Malaysian government did strongly protest the secondary boycott threat, and some American companies encountered greater difficulties, probably systematic, in obtaining appointments with government officials.

11. *New York Times*, May 30, 1997.

12. There had also been discussions since late 1996 for an Iran-Turkey natural gas pipeline, which would enable large Iranian gas exports to Turkey, but this project was not mentioned by Secretary Albright. In November 1998, the Turkish government announced that this pipeline was under construction, and again there was no clear reaction from the U.S. side.

13. See the *Journal of Commerce*, June 2, 1998.

14. AP press release, June 18, 1998.

15. The figures cited in this paragraph are from International Monetary Fund (IMF), "Islamic Republic of Iran: Recent Economic Developments," IMF Staff Country Report #98/27, April 1998. The figures are for Iranian years ending March 20 of the following year. Thus, "1996" in the text is Iranian year 1996/97, which involves a more than nine month overlap. A useful summary of the first five-year program and the first three years of the second program is contained in Jahangir Amuzegar, "Iran's Economy and the U.S. Sanctions," *Middle East Journal* 51, no. 2 (Spring 1997).

16. Social indicators also improved substantially. From 1986–1989 to 1996, the infant mortality rate dropped from 59 to 26, physicians per 10,000 people increased from 3.8 to 8.2, the number of students in secondary schools increased from 1.4 million to 3.4 million, and the number of university students increased from 250,000 to 1.2 million (including 600,000 in the new Islamic Azad University).

17. Considerable trade flows through the UAE to Iran, but there was only a small increase in the share of UAE imports from the United States after the May 1995 embargo on U.S. exports to Iran. The share of total UAE imports from the United States was 8.7 percent in 1994, 8.4 percent in 1995, 11.0 percent in 1996, and 9.3 percent in 1997.

18. Patrick Clawson, "Iran," in *Economic Sanctions and American Diplomacy*, Richard Haass, ed. (New York: Council on Foreign Relations, 1998), 93.

19. IMF, "Islamic Republic of Iran," 19.

20. The $50 billion estimate is from Julia Nanay, director of the Petroleum Finance Company, in a presentation at the Nixon Center, Washington, D.C., May 13, 1998. A higher $70 billion to $80 billion figure, attributed to unnamed economists, is contained in a July 2, 1998, story in the *Financial Times*.

21. If alternative commercial bank loans were available, the cost to the Iranian economy would be the interest rate differential between World Bank loans and what would have to be paid for the commercial bank loans, or considerably less than the $500 million to $800 million figure.

22. An assessment of Caspian Sea oil and gas development is contained in *Caspian Oil and Gas* (Paris: International Energy Agency, June 1998). The project description and figures for Azeri production-sharing contracts are from information provided by the Petroleum Finance Company. As of January 1999, however, these earlier projections may have to be scaled back in light of lower than anticipated initial production and lower world oil prices.

23. Ibid., 41.

24. "Swap" arrangements whereby Caspian Sea oil is delivered to an Iranian port in exchange for Iranian oil exports from the Persian Gulf is not subject to ILSA sanctions if already existing Iranian pipelines are used. An American company would still have to receive approval on a case-by-case basis from the U.S. government, and Mobil had such a request pending in 1998. A different and less clear case would arise, however, if the much larger Neka pipeline should go forward, which is then found "sanctionable" under ILSA even if the sanctions are then waived as for South Pars. Whether an American company oil could be swapped under such circumstances would present yet another interesting challenge for State Department lawyers.

25. The Russians argue that completing the Iranian nuclear power plants is similar to building such plants for North Korea as a tradeoff to forestall North Korean nuclear weapons development. The distinction, however, is that the North Korean plants are not being built by North Koreans—who in any event already have considerable weapons expertise—while the Merehr project would involve extensive training of Iranians who now lack such expertise.

4

Vietnam:
Phasing Out Sanctions in Asia

1. Narrative Account

U.S. UNILATERAL SANCTIONS ON TRADE and investment with all of Vietnam were imposed at the end of the Vietnam War in 1975, and a phased lifting of the sanctions began in 1992 and is still in progress. Thus U.S. sanctions policy toward Vietnam is moving in the opposite direction to policy in the other four country case studies where new sanctions have been imposed or threatened during the 1990s. The contrast is especially stark within Asia because the U.S. foreign policy objectives related to the use of sanctions—to support democratization and respect for basic human rights—are relevant to Vietnam much as they are to other target countries in the region such as Myanmar and China. How and why this change in sanctions policy direction came about for Vietnam is a central question of this narrative account.

U.S. economic sanctions were not seriously debated during the first dozen years because of the bitter feelings in the aftermath of the war and, more substantively, the lack of significant market opportunities for trade and investment in Vietnam even if the sanctions were lifted. The centrally planned Vietnamese economy was almost totally closed off to trade outside the communist bloc and was in a state of shambles sustained only in part by large amounts of Soviet economic aid on the order of $3 billion a year by the mid-1980s.[1] Food shortages and famine were severe in northern Vietnam while Soviet-style infrastructure and industrial projects produced disappointing results.

These dire circumstances forced an agonizing reappraisal on the Vietnamese communist leadership and led in 1986 to the new, more market-oriented economic strategy—*doi moi* or "renovation"—with emphasis on market-oriented incentives, rapid growth in trade, and high levels of foreign direct investment. The motivation was largely economic, following similar export-led growth models elsewhere in Asia, including in China, but also geopolitical. The Vietnamese leaders had become disillusioned with the dominant Soviet relationship while military clashes with China underlined the historic threat from the great power to the north. A strengthening of relationships elsewhere was thus imperative for strategic as well as economic reasons.

The international response to the Vietnamese economic reform initiative was broadly positive except for the United States. Japan was first and foremost in building commercial ties supported by a large bilateral economic aid program concentrated on infrastructure projects. ASEAN and some European countries were hesitant while Vietnam still had 140,000 troops in Cambodia (to hold the Khmer Rouge and, indirectly, China at bay), but they moved forward quickly in 1989 when the Vietnamese troops were brought home. In parallel, the World Bank provided policy advice on economic reforms during the years 1989–1992 and restored its lending program in October 1993 related to phase 1 of the U.S.-Vietnamese road map described below.

The United States thus became odd nation out in the rapidly opening Vietnamese economic relationship. The Vietnamese economy, benefiting from predictable large gains at the early stages of market-oriented economic reform, recorded annual GDP growth of 8 to 10 percent from 1988 to 1993. Imports (other than from the Soviet Union) rose from $600 million in 1986 to $2.6 billion in 1990 and to $3.9 billion in 1993. Vietnam became widely viewed as a potential new Asian tiger of sustained high economic growth and market opportunity, and American companies grew concerned about being left behind as Asian and European competitors rushed to establish themselves in the Vietnamese market.

Three foreign policy problems, however, initially blocked normalization of U.S.-Vietnamese relations and a lifting of the economic embargo. The first was the Soviet military presence in Vietnam, including the large Cam Ranh Bay naval facility directly across the South China Sea from the U.S. Subic Bay facility in the

Philippines. With the end of the Cold War, however, this problem faded away as Soviet forces were drawn down sharply beginning in 1989. The second problem—the Vietnamese military presence in Cambodia—was also resolved through the Cambodian Peace Accord and the Vietnamese withdrawal. The third and most important problem—accounting for the 2,300 Americans missing-in-action (MIAs) during the Vietnam War—became the central focus of bilateral negotiations for normalization of relations. Negotiations began in September 1990 when Secretary of State James Baker met with his Vietnamese counterpart, Nguyen Co Thach.

A step-by-step normalization of relations was presented to Vietnam by the Bush administration in April 1991 as a four-phase "road map," with specific undertakings on both sides during each phase. The road map involved Vietnamese commitments on MIA accountability, implementation of the Cambodian Peace Accord, and emigration to the United States of Vietnamese detainees previously affiliated with the United States. U.S. commitments began in phase 1 with some easing of travel restrictions for Americans and initial talks about normalizing diplomatic relations, but steps to lift the U.S. economic sanctions were drawn out over the later phases. U.S. firms could open commercial offices in Vietnam and sign contracts in phase 2, a lifting of the embargo on trade and investment would take place in phase 3, and the granting of MFN status would be "considered" but not necessarily granted in phase 4.

The road map was never officially agreed to by Vietnam, but it became the de facto program for normalizing relations based on mutual economic and geopolitical interests, the geopolitical interest more strongly felt by Vietnam to have a countervailing major power relationship to China. The substance of the normalization road map was narrowly drawn, however, and there were no commitments on the Vietnamese side related to democratization, human rights, or national security, as were central to U.S. unilateral sanctions objectives in the other four case studies. The policy context of lifting existing sanctions rather than threatening new sanctions also helped by providing a "positive sum" bargaining context.

In December 1992, President Bush, in the context of phase 2 of the road map, announced that progress had been made on the MIA issue as well as emigration for Vietnamese detainees, established a resident liaison office in Hanoi, and permitted American companies to sign contracts and do business in Vietnam (but not yet trade or invest). The Clinton administration continued the negotiating process in close consultation with MIA groups, and the president announced the phase 3 lifting of the embargo on U.S. trade with and investment in Vietnam in February 1994. Official diplomatic relations were restored in July 1995. The first postwar U.S. ambassador, former prisoner-of-war and Florida congressman Douglas "Pete" Peterson, arrived in Hanoi in May 1997 with a mandate to develop a positive political and economic relationship and actively seek an accounting for the MIAs. The normalization of economic relations, however, was still not complete. In particular, MFN treatment for Vietnamese exports to the U.S. market was withheld pending a presidential determination on the Jackson-Vanik amendment related to freedom of emigration and negotiation of a bilateral trade agreement. But the transition from almost total unilateral economic sanctions to normal commercial relations was well advanced and almost certainly irreversible.

A big question for this sanctions phaseout process is how U.S. democratization/human rights objectives, which were prominent in U.S. relations elsewhere in Asia during these same years, including China, Myanmar, and Indonesia, were handled in the U.S.-Vietnam negotiations. The short answer is that they were given low priority and not pressed as essential elements of the normalization process. Although a bilateral human rights dialogue was engaged in 1994, the road map contained no democratization/human rights provisions. Vietnam consistently reasserted its one-party communist political system and considered most human rights complaints as internal matters not subject to negotiation with the United States. A major concurrent problem—the matter of Vietnamese boat people who were applying for refugee status abroad—was mainly between Vietnam and third countries, principally the United Kingdom with 50,000 Vietnamese in Hong Kong detention camps. It was resolved when Vietnam satisfied the UN high commissioner for refugees that these people could be returned without fear of persecution. Earlier U.S. opposition to forcible repatriation was resolved through a program to permit repatriated Vietnamese to apply for emigration to the United States.

Two reasons why the United States did not press democratization/human rights objectives harder with Vietnam were the absence of high visibility negative events as occurred elsewhere in Asia and domestic political forces at play within the United States. In China, there was the Tiananmen Square massacre and continuing repression in Tibet. In Myanmar, there were the violent clashes in 1988, the annulled democratic election in 1990 by the military, and the courageous stand of democratic leader and Nobel Peace Prize laureate Aung San Suu Kyi. In Indonesia, there was the brutal repression in East Timor, also related to Nobel Peace Prize recipients. Each of these situations received wide and vivid news coverage and elicited strong outcries from human rights and prodemocracy groups in the United States and elsewhere. The situation in Vietnam, in contrast, was a less gripping authoritarian rule over an ethnically homogeneous Vietnamese people, almost fully out of reach of TV cameras. Imprisoned Tibetan Buddhist monks were more newsworthy than imprisoned Vietnamese Buddhist monks.

Relatively weak domestic political pressures in the United States to continue unilateral economic sanctions against Vietnam for democratization/human rights objectives reflected this more elusive target, as did two other factors. The first was that Vietnamese-Americans did not generally oppose normalization of relations and to a considerable extent supported it. They stood in sharp contrast to Cuban-Americans who played a central role in tightening U.S. sanctions against Cuba during the 1990s and to some prodemocracy Chinese-Americans, including survivors of Tiananmen Square and Chinese prisons, who were outspoken proponents of withdrawal of MFN status for China. The second factor was the higher priority emotional appeal of the MIA interests compared with human rights groups for the Vietnamese relationship. Once former prisoners-of-war Senator John McCain and Ambassador-designate Peterson, as well as the Veterans of Foreign Wars (although not the MIA family groups), came out in support of the Vietnamese government's commitment on MIA accounting, it was especially difficult for democratization/human rights groups to oppose the normalization process. The Human Rights Watch, for example, while continually insisting that human rights be raised with the Vietnamese government, did not propose conditioning normalization on specific human rights improvements.

There was finally the U.S. policy judgment as to whether U.S. private sector engagement would have a positive or negative impact on support for democratization and respect for basic human rights in Vietnam. This central question for unilateral sanctions policy was answered in the positive during the initial Bush administration negotiations, largely evaded in 1993–1994 when the Clinton administration was threatening withdrawal of MFN for China linked to democratization/human rights, and then reasserted more strongly in positive terms after economic sanctions were partially lifted in 1994. This key judgment for Vietnam nevertheless remained inconsistent with U.S. policy elsewhere as sanctions were adopted for Myanmar and strengthened against Cuba in 1996.

All of the foregoing complex of historical, geopolitical, economic, and emotional circumstances led the Clinton administration to take the decisive steps to phase out unilateral economic sanctions against Vietnam, and this policy continues to be broadly supported within Congress and by the American public, including human rights groups.[2] The process of sanctions phaseout, however, is incomplete, and a new, differently troubled phase of U.S.-Vietnam economic relations began in 1997. On the Vietnamese side, the economic reform program has stalled. Once the economic crisis of the late 1980s was alleviated, communist party hard-liners closed ranks to resist further market reforms, which they viewed as a threat to their political control. This reaction followed the familiar pattern whereby a market-oriented transition becomes more threatening to an authoritarian government as deregulation, privatization, and decentralization of economic power progress. Infrastructure project development has consequently fallen behind as a result of overregulation and bureaucratic inertia, and widespread corruption, inherent in a centrally planned economy, is becoming an increasing barrier to foreign trade and investment.[3] New foreign direct investment commitments fell precipitously from $9 billion in 1996 to $5 billion in 1997 and $1 billion in 1998. Moreover, this internally driven policy reform impasse/economic slowdown has been strongly reinforced by the Asian financial crisis. Seventy percent of Vietnamese foreign investment comes from Asia, and more than half of Vietnamese exports go to Asia, all of which have contracted due to the financial crisis. The selection of General Le Kha Phieu in late 1997 as the new secretary general of the communist party, an ideological hard-liner and the first military officer to hold the post, is ominous for the future course of the economic reform program, although Prime Minister Phan Van Kai is considered a reformer.

The United States, in turn, is still withholding MFN status for Vietnamese exports to the U.S. market, a key element of normal commercial relations. In 1997, less than 5 percent of Vietnamese exports went to the United States, compared with an average of 19 percent for other ASEAN countries.[4] With total Vietnamese exports of $8.7 billion, this represented a differential loss to Vietnam of more than $1 billion, much if not most of which can be attributable to the withholding of normal MFN access to the U.S. market.

To extend MFN to Vietnam, President Clinton must waive the Jackson-Vanik amendment, a 1974 Cold War relic related to emigration of Jews from the Soviet Union, and negotiate a bilateral trade agreement with Vietnam, subject to congressional approval.[5] The draft trade agreement proposed by the United States, under discussion for three years and the most comprehensive ever put forward in the MFN context, includes trade in services as well as goods, protection of intellectual property rights, and foreign investment policy commitments. The scope of the bilateral agreement, in fact, essentially equates, and then some, to what Vietnam will later have to do at the multilateral level to gain WTO membership. But although all of the provisions of the proposed agreement can be justified as in the Vietnamese self-interest, consistent with *doi moi*, they would require major steps forward that the Vietnamese government at this stage is ill-disposed to undertake. Meanwhile, the deepening economic problems in the Vietnamese economy, for both the internal and external reasons described above, make the MFN barrier to Vietnamese exports a more glaring asymmetry in the current state of partially normalized economic relations between the two countries.

In conclusion, the U.S. policy decision to phase out unilateral economic sanctions against Vietnam was taken for mutual geopolitical reasons and for the U.S. objectives of cooperation from the Vietnamese government in accounting for MIAs, emigration for detainees previously affiliated with the United States, and the pursuit of U.S. commercial interests. At the current stage of partial sanctions phaseout, however, U.S. policy has shifted from these predominantly foreign policy to almost solely trade policy objectives, through the required linkage of MFN status to the bilateral trade agreement. In organizational terms, the policy lead has correspondingly shifted from the State Department to the Office of the U.S. Trade Representative.

2. Economic Impact

On the Vietnamese Economy

The impact of unilateral U.S. sanctions on the Vietnamese economy is distinct among U.S. exports, foreign direct investment, and U.S. imports, both in the earlier almost total embargo phase until 1994 and, even more strikingly, in the current phase of partial sanctions phaseout. The adverse impact on Vietnam has been least important for sanctions against U.S. exports because other suppliers can readily substitute for most U.S. exporters. The principal constraint on the overall level of Vietnamese imports has been foreign exchange availability through Vietnamese exports, foreign direct investment, economic assistance, remittances, and other sources of finance. To the extent U.S. exports are of higher quality and lower price, purchases elsewhere exact a cost to Vietnam, but this effect can be offset somewhat through technology licensing and third-country sourcing of U.S. components. For example, a French company obtained an export contract for gas turbines in the early 1990s through licensing U.S. technology even though the American company, in the absence of the sanctions, would have preferred to export the entire turbines from the United States. Airbus negotiations for commercial aircraft leasing to Vietnam likewise utilized GE engines, as preferred by Vietnam, which was permitted under U.S. sanctions as long as U.S. value-added for the total aircraft did not exceed 25 percent. Overall, 12 to 20 percent of imports by other ASEAN countries come from the United

States, a benchmark for Vietnamese imports under normal commercial relations, but the large majority of these imports can be substituted by non-U.S. suppliers, at relatively small cost, which is what occurred in Vietnam up until 1994. Moreover, this substitution for U.S. suppliers carries over for a considerable time after the U.S. sanctions are lifted. In 1997, still only 3 percent of Vietnamese imports were from the United States, principally as a result of the lag effect from earlier U.S. sanctions.

The U.S. sanctions on foreign direct investment until 1994 had a more significant adverse impact on the Vietnamese economy because such investment was high risk and more limited in availability. Many investment projects require joint financing where in some cases access to well-financed U.S. partners can make a critical difference. American companies also tend to offer more advanced technology, superior management capability, and in some instances more creative financial packages than other investors. In some key sectors for longer-term modernization, such as financial services and telecommunications, American companies can quickly move in to play a major role, once permitted, which is happening to some extent in Vietnam, although telecommunications services and equipment are still mostly blocked out for U.S companies. The more significant impact on the Vietnamese economy from the earlier U.S. sanctions on investment is more difficult to quantify because data are more limited for foreign direct investment than for trade. The government of Vietnam provides figures for new investment commitments by country of origin, which indicates more than $1 billion of U.S. investment during the period 1995–1996, or about 10 percent of global commitments. These figures, however, understate U.S. corporate investment because commitments are recorded by country of immediate financing origin rather than by company origin. For example, the Coca-Cola investment is not listed as U.S. because it was financed out of the Coca-Cola/ASEAN regional headquarters. Actual disbursements, which are more directly relevant to economic performance, are only provided on a global basis and amount to about a third of commitments—$10 billion versus $28 billion from 1987 to 1996—reflecting the time lag for disbursement and the fact that many commitments never materialize as actual investments.

Overall, the best that can be said is that U.S. investors moved in quickly to make commitments once the U.S. sanction was lifted, but the level of disbursements to date is still small, probably on the order of $200 million to $300 million a year.

The continuing U.S. sanctions on U.S. imports from Vietnam through the withholding of MFN status and, related to this, tariff preferences under the generalized system of preferences, or GSP, have had the greatest negative impact by far on the Vietnamese economy. The much higher tariffs applying to Vietnam create an enormous competitive disadvantage vis-à-vis competing exporters to the U.S. market as well as more highly protected U.S. domestic producers. There has apparently been no attempt to calculate the MFN differential for Vietnamese exports to the United States, but for China the trade-weighted average tariff, if MFN status were withdrawn, would rise from 6 percent to 44 percent, a reasonable proxy estimate that would make most potential Vietnamese exports to the U.S market noncompetitive.[6] This lack of competitive access to the U.S. market adversely affects investment in export-oriented industries in Vietnam not only by U.S. firms but by all foreign investors. In any event, U.S. imports from Vietnam remain small, rising from $319 million in 1996 to $388 million in 1997, or less than 5 percent of total Vietnamese exports. Textile and apparel imports from Vietnam, especially hard hit by the lack of MFN status, are not yet large enough to be worthy of a U.S. import quota program! As noted earlier, compared with other ASEAN countries, Vietnamese exports to the United States for 1996–1997 are about $1 billion below the norm.

Recent difficulties in the Vietnamese economy from the stalled economic reform program and the Asian financial crisis further highlight the impact of the remaining U.S. sanction of non-MFN (or "abnormal trade relations" under the 1998 change in nomenclature) status on the Vietnamese economy. Total U.S. investment commitments declined from $1.3 billion in 1996 to $1.0 billion in 1997, and fell much lower in 1998, reflecting in part the termination of some previous commitments, such as by the Chrysler Company. The denial of MFN treatment for Vietnamese exports to the United States will clearly have an even more substantial damaging impact on Vietnamese economic prospects as exports to other

Asian economies slow and Asian export competitors to the U.S. market, already benefiting from lower MFN tariffs, become even more competitive through greatly depreciated currencies.

The net assessment is thus that the negative effect of U.S. unilateral sanctions on the Vietnamese economy was not noteworthy until 1986, then became significant for foreign direct investment until the basic sanction was lifted in 1994, and remains substantial for Vietnamese exports to the United States in the absence of MFN treatment. The sanctions against U.S. exports to Vietnam, in contrast, were of considerably less importance. Overall, U.S. sanctions have had relatively small impact on the course of the Vietnamese economy, which has been influenced primarily by economic reform decisions by the Vietnamese government and the preponderant trade, investment, and aid relationships with other Asian countries and the multilateral development banks. The growing financial squeeze on Vietnamese economic growth caused by the Asian financial crisis and the stalled economic reform process within Vietnam, however, have made the continued withholding of MFN treatment a more significant swing factor during 1998 and 1999.

On U.S. Commercial Interests

The impact of unilateral sanctions against Vietnam on U.S. commercial interests is likewise distinct among U.S. exports, foreign direct investment, and imports, but to opposite effect. The loss to U.S. exports was the most direct and substantial as Vietnamese imports grew rapidly beginning in 1988. In 1994, the year the U.S. export embargo was lifted, the U.S. market share in Vietnam was less than 1 percent of total merchandise imports of $6 billion. Compared with a U.S. market share of 12 to 20 percent in other ASEAN countries, this equates to a loss of $700 million to $1.2 billion in U.S. exports. By 1996, U.S. exports were still less than 5 percent of the $14 billion Vietnamese market, which implies an even greater loss of $1 billion to $2 billion. Adding an estimated loss of service sector exports (which were 27 percent of total U.S. exports globally, but which are not broken down by country) increases the implied total loss in U.S. exports in 1996 to $1.3 billion to $2.6 billion. Much of this continuing low market share is a transitional cost of catching up with competitors who established themselves in Vietnam earlier, but some loss could be more permanent, particularly where competitors have established their technologies and standards within the Vietnamese economy. For example, a European company won an early contract for supplying electric power transformers, including its distinct technology, which makes it more difficult for an American company to establish its competing technology later.

U.S. investment in Vietnam, once the embargo was lifted in 1994, moved in more quickly as noted earlier. Aggressive investment strategies and recognition by the Vietnamese government of the high technical standards and management competence of American companies were factors in this rapid growth. More recent disillusion with the investment climate in Vietnam and the departure or delay by prominent American investors, however, indicate that flexible investment strategies can operate in both directions. The overall impact of unilateral sanctions has been less severe for U.S. investment than for exports, in part because of the generally quicker response time displayed by U.S. investors.

The withholding of MFN status for imports from Vietnam has been of little significance to the U.S. economy. American consumers would benefit from lower-cost imports from Vietnam in some sectors, but these imports already enter in large quantities from other Asian suppliers, and the substitution of Vietnamese for some competing imports would have very limited effect on consumer prices. Likewise, competing domestic producers would face only small incremental import competition. The important textile and apparel sector is subject to extensive U.S. import quotas that would be quickly applied against Vietnam when and if imports rise substantially.

The net assessment for U.S. commercial interests is thus mixed and relatively small, in part because the time lag between the initial opening of the Vietnamese market and the lifting of the principal U.S. sanctions on exports and investments was limited to about seven years. If the sanctions had been continued, U.S. commercial interests would have suffered significantly more, including an even lengthier transition to normal market share once the restrictions were lifted.

3. Net Assessment of U.S. Unilateral Sanctions Policy

U.S. unilateral economic sanctions against Vietnam are assessed here for the period since 1986, when the Vietnamese market-oriented economic reform process got under way. U.S. policy has been to lift the preexisting unilateral sanctions and restore full diplomatic relations for three principal self-serving objectives: (1) geopolitical considerations related to regional peace and stability, (2) support for the economic reform process within Vietnam and, thereby over time, political reforms and democratization as well, through "constructive engagement" with the communist government in Hanoi, and (3) promotion of U.S. commercial interests. The lifting of the sanctions, while thus judged to be in the U.S. interest in and by itself, has also been used as bargaining leverage to negotiate specific commitments by the Vietnamese government, which has slowed the sanctions phaseout. The lifting of sanctions on U.S. exports and investment (as well as restoration of diplomatic relations) was linked to commitments on cooperation for MIA accounting, implementation of the Cambodian Peace Accord, and emigration for Vietnamese detainees, while the provision of MFN treatment for Vietnamese exports to the United States remains contingent on negotiation of a comprehensive bilateral trade agreement.

The assessment here of this constructive engagement policy, but with partial sanctions still conditionally in place, is presented, first, with respect to the impact on the longer-term objectives and then in terms of the degree of success in achieving the immediate negotiating objectives. The first longer-term objective, geopolitical considerations, is reasonably self-evident, and so the discussion is limited to the second and third objectives—support for economic reform/democratization and the promotion of U.S. commercial interests.

Support for Economic Reform/Democratization

This is a central policy consideration for unilateral economic sanctions in all "emerging market-oriented economies"—including all five country case studies here—where U.S. foreign policy interests are related to the evolving political/economic situation within the target country. Does constructive engagement between governments and through trade- and investment-related engagement by the U.S. private sector in particular help or hinder a process of market-oriented economic reform and related democratization? Vietnam is a particularly relevant case study because it is the one country where U.S. policy changed radically from near total economic embargo to considerable engagement during the post–Cold War 1990s, when even remaining communist countries (with the exception of North Korea) had shifted to some form of market-oriented, open trade economic strategy.

The assessment here is that this shift in U.S. policy away from unilateral sanctions to constructive private sector engagement has had a significant positive impact in hastening economic reforms within Vietnam and some first steps toward a more pluralistic political system as well. The influence of U.S. private sector engagement remains limited by the still low levels of trade and investment between the two countries, but it is relatively greater than market share figures alone in view of the unique way most American companies operate in projecting American values and related corporate culture, and of the synergy developing among an engaged private sector, an active group of American nongovernmental organizations that also moved into the country with the normalization of relations, and the active and well-staffed U.S. diplomatic presence in Vietnam. This important judgment is based on limited observation of relationships that have evolved during only five years and wherein the current economic problems within Vietnam and in East Asia more broadly raise uncertain prospects for the period ahead. Nevertheless, the initial positive effects are clearly evident.

U.S. private sector engagement as a force for economic and political change is heavily oriented to companies with resident operations, most evident in investment projects for in-country production and the provision of financial and other services, but it also includes export marketing, especially in technology-intensive industries that require continuing interaction with customers and government officials. More than 1,400 American companies have been registered to do business in Vietnam, and there are about 200 resident members of the American Chamber of Commerce (AMCHAM) in Hanoi and 300 members in Ho Chi Minh City. This resident U.S. corporate presence, with few exceptions, constitutes a high visibility role model for American values and corporate culture.[7] The very large majority of employees are Vietnamese, who are treated with respect as individuals, in an atmosphere of openness, with compensation based on merit and performance, including opportunities for career advancement. Employment with an American company is a mark of distinction and entails a somewhat greater degree of personal freedom within what is still an authoritarian society. American companies also stand out for maintaining high labor and environmental standards in their operations, up to national standards and beyond.

A positive contribution especially noteworthy for American companies are programs of training and technical assistance, not only for their own employees, but for customers and engaged government officials as well. In the financial services sector, Citicorp and American Insurance Group have provided extensive training programs. Citicorp alone has trained over 1,000 Vietnamese since 1995, including a seminar for all state bankers on auditing procedures. In 1997, General Electric had a three-week training course in the United States for 40 participants from ASEAN countries, including five from Vietnam—employees, customers, and government officials—where the Asian visitors learned GE corporate goals and management procedures together with American participants. American companies in Vietnam contribute to joint programs between U.S. and Vietnamese business schools as well as to the Business Alliance for Vietnamese Education. Vietnamese officials tend to seek technical advice from American firms based on their reputation for management and technical competence and their openness to frank discussion.

The current difficult period of declining foreign direct investment and pressing need to revise investment and other regulations, including an improved judicial process for contract disputes, increases the benefits of dialogue between the government and resident foreign firms. Periodic official consultations between governments and with international financial institutions do not have the in-depth impact of day-to-day contacts with resident private company representatives. More structured group meetings between Vietnamese government officials, up through the ministerial level, and the foreign private sector began in late 1997. It is a difficult learning process for a Vietnamese power structure that is habitually aloof and inaccessible. To experience first hand what works and does not work from resident private company managers is proving to be an effective, if painful, learning experience.

A central problem for Vietnam, as for other highly controlled economies under authoritarian governments, is the deeply embedded interrelationship between government regulation and corruption, and the American corporate presence stands out in pointing the direction out of this dilemma. American companies are constrained by U.S. law from making illicit payments, and implementation of the 1997 OECD anticorruption agreement by all OECD-country companies will push other companies in the same direction in their Vietnam operations—for example, toward enhanced transparency and disclosure procedures that will make corrupt officials more vulnerable to public exposure. This hopeful prospect, which goes to the core of political as well as economic change in Vietnam, would not exist without pervasive private sector engagement.

Finally, the rapid expansion of available information and knowledge, largely driven by telecommunications technology and fundamental to political change within a country such as Vietnam, is greatly accelerated by the presence of private multinational companies. American companies, in particular, are leaders in this information technology revolution with the added benefit of using the English language, the official international language of ASEAN countries. English language instruction is a rapid-growth service industry throughout Vietnamese society, and a dozen resident American companies provided financial support to the Ministry of Education to develop English-language textbooks for Vietnamese elementary schools. The opening of Vietnam to Internet connections in late 1997 provides another vehicle for the open exchange of information.

These are the highlights of how several hundred engaged American companies and nongovernmental organizations are a positive force for change within Vietnam. A broader role will evolve to the extent the Vietnamese government can weather current financial difficulties and move forward with its market-oriented economic reform program. Initial contacts between AMCHAM and the Vietnamese Chamber of Commerce and Industry—which has about 35,000 mostly small, "almost private" member companies—is one avenue for further development. Closer collaboration between AMCHAM and the large economic/commercial sections of the American Embassy in Hanoi and the Consulate General in Ho Chi Minh City, especially for training and technical assistance programs, is another.[8] Indeed, Vietnam could emerge over the coming decade as a classic case study of how the synergy among the host government, the official international community, and an engaged foreign private sector can make a positive contribution to the difficult transition from authoritarian government with an excessively regulated, centrally planned economy to an emerging market-oriented democracy.

Promotion of U.S. Commercial Interests

The lifting of the embargo on U.S. exports and investment has reduced somewhat the earlier adverse effects on U.S. commercial interests. The late arrival of U.S. exporters to the more open Vietnamese market and the delayed unavailability of Exim Bank facilities until 1998, however, continue to restrain the U.S. share of the Vietnamese market. U.S. exports to Vietnam, which were $253 million in 1995, rose to $616 million in 1996 related to commercial joint-venture aircraft sales, then fell to $278 million in 1997. These exports represent only 3 to 5 percent of the Vietnamese market compared with 12 to 20 percent in other ASEAN countries. As noted earlier, this 7 to 17 percent differential for a total Vietnamese market of $14 billion in 1996 equates to a shortfall of $1 billion to $2 billion in U.S. merchandise exports a year, or $1.3 billion to $2.6 billion including service exports, largely if not mainly attributable to the lag effects of the earlier embargo and the lack of Exim financing.[9]

The lifting of the embargo on U.S. direct investment in Vietnam has led to a faster and fuller entry of American companies compared with U.S. exports. The time lag between investment commitments and disbursements, together with the recent negative turn in the investment climate within Vietnam, has nevertheless produced limited results thus far. U.S. investment commitments account for only about 4 percent of the total accumulated commitments in Vietnam since 1989 ($1 billion out of $28 billion), but to the extent investment prospects improve within Vietnam, American companies are now well positioned to advance promptly to attain 10 percent or more of new investment commitments. The absence of MFN access to the U.S. market also discourages export-oriented investment in Vietnam for American investors as well as others.

Overall, U.S. commercial interests have benefited significantly from the lifting of the sanctions, although much catching up remains. One lesson learned is that regaining market share after a prolonged unilateral embargo, especially for exports, can take a considerable number of years even under favorable conditions.

Specific Negotiating Objectives

MIA accounting and emigration of Vietnamese detainees. U.S. satisfaction on this issue was clearly essential from the outset to normalizing bilateral relations, including the lifting of unilateral economic sanctions, and was achieved. This was an example where a narrowly defined objective could be accommodated by the other side without major policy change and where a mutual interest was established for a linked package of MIA accountability and normalization of relations. The opening position from the U.S. side of lifting preexisting sanctions rather than threatening new sanctions also put the negotiation in a more positive context.

MFN/bilateral trade agreement. In this major issue of negotiation for the principal remaining sanction, the outlook is unclear. The Vietnamese government considered the comprehensive draft trade agreement put forward by the United States, but indicated that the provisions go far beyond what can be agreed on immediately and responded with a very modest counterproposal. Meanwhile, the overall stalled economic reform program within

Vietnam and the effects of the Asian financial crisis raise further uncertainties about the likelihood of reaching a bilateral agreement any time soon.

On current course, the bilateral trade negotiations will likely drag on at least another year or more, and then the agreement, including the granting of MFN status, would have to be approved by Congress, which could take up to another year.[10] Thus, during the current critical juncture for the Vietnamese economic reform program and the related adverse impact on Vietnam from the Asian financial crisis, Vietnamese exports continue to be largely excluded from the U.S. market by the very high non-MFN tariffs. Indeed, Vietnam, Laos, and North Korea are the only Asian economies excluded from MFN access to the U.S. market during the Asian financial crisis.

The overall net assessment of U.S. policy since 1986 of negotiated sanctions phaseout is largely positive. The impact on the central foreign policy objective of supporting market-oriented economic reforms and related political change within Vietnam is clearly positive, with potential to broaden and strengthen over time. This ongoing case study experience, moreover, has implications beyond Vietnam for other countries where the United States continues to maintain or threaten unilateral sanctions. U.S. commercial interests have benefited somewhat from the Vietnam sanctions phaseout policy, although with a considerable time-lag effect. The linked negotiating objectives for agreeing to a sanctions phaseout were successful with respect to MIA accounting, but have still not been achieved for the MFN/bilateral trade agreement linkage, which continues to cloud the bilateral relationship both politically and economically.

4. Alternatives to Current Unilateral Sanctions Policy

The realistic alternatives to the current U.S. policy of negotiated sanctions phaseout are more limited for Vietnam than for the other case studies, given broad support for the current policy course and the lack of serious discussion under way for basic change. The full reimposition of unilateral sanctions on trade and investment is an alternative, but unless some unforeseen highly negative developments take place, few would advocate such a policy change, and the hypothetical circumstances for considering it are not pursued here.

The only serious policy alternative to consider at this point is an adjustment in the existing sanctions phaseout policy—namely, to accelerate the negotiation of MFN treatment through a scaling back of required Vietnamese commitments in the bilateral trade agreement. The rationale for such a change is that full normalization of commercial relations is in the U.S. interest during this period of financial stress in Asia, while the broader scope of trade policy commitments by Vietnam can be left for later WTO membership negotiations. This two-stage approach could, in fact, be explicit in the U.S.-Vietnam bilateral agreement.

Such an adjustment in U.S. policy could only be considered after consultation with the congressional trade committees and other congressional leaders who would later have to approve the bilateral agreement, including the granting of MFN. In this context, support by the U.S. private sector would be critical, and its position up to this point is not clear. American companies have particular interests in specific provisions of the draft bilateral trade agreement, and priorities among companies vary, as would become apparent in any scaling back of the comprehensive draft agreement. The USA*Engage organization is in general strongly opposed to unilateral economic sanctions, but it is not clear whether this also applies for granting MFN to Vietnam, which in turn relates to the U.S. strategy for a bilateral trade agreement. The same holds true for the U.S. Chamber of Commerce, including AMCHAM in Vietnam.

5. Conclusions and Recommendations

Two principal conclusions and one outstanding policy question emerge from the Vietnam experience with unilateral economic sanctions during the 1990s. The first conclusion is that the lifting of trade and investment sanctions was used effectively as bargaining leverage to obtain satisfactory commitments—for MIA accounting in particular—from the Vietnamese government, albeit at some cost to U.S. commercial interests. This rare exception to the frequent failure of unilateral sanctions to achieve their foreign policy objectives is nevertheless the exception that proves the rule because of the unique circumstances of the Vietnamese relationship. The principal U.S. objective of MIA accountability did not require the communist government to change its political behavior with respect to human rights and democratization. The Vietnamese willingness to allow the emigration to the United States of former supporters of the United States was also something that, if anything, made life easier for the communist regime through the emigration of potential dissidents. Meanwhile, a mutual geopolitical interest in normalizing relations was even stronger for Vietnam than for the United States, and of course, mutual economic benefits could be obtained from normalization, especially for American companies that had been shut out of a rapidly growing Vietnamese market.

The second conclusion is that the reengagement of the U.S. private sector in Vietnam clearly demonstrates how such engagement can motivate positive political and economic change in a nation still under harsh authoritarian rule with a highly corrupt, for the most part centrally planned economy. This demonstration effect, in turn, highlights the contradictory U.S. policy with respect to private sector engagement. Why support it in Vietnam as the U.S. government does with conviction, while taking the opposite view for Cuba and Myanmar? This policy inconsistency on a central issue with respect to economic sanctions—multilateral as well as unilateral—is addressed more fully in the concluding chapters, but an important test case during the 1990s for U.S. private sector engagement as a positive force for change has been provided by the Vietnam experience.

The important policy question concerns the continued withholding of MFN status for Vietnam, subject to a far-reaching bilateral trade agreement to be approved by Congress. The United States provides MFN treatment for nations that together account for more than 99 percent of world trade. To withhold it from Vietnam, especially during this extremely difficult period of financial crisis, cannot be justified for a nation with which the United States otherwise has normal and reasonably good relations.

Withholding MFN treatment for Vietnamese exports to the U.S. market is a critical disincentive for foreign direct investment from any source in Vietnamese export-oriented industry, which is what Vietnam needs to help avoid a disruptive financial crisis and the familiar IMF rescue package, as has happened elsewhere in Asia and in other regions.

The United States should thus shift its strategy toward a two-stage approach, accepting a scaled-back bilateral agreement of trade policy commitments now, and leaving the rest, explicitly, for later negotiation of WTO membership. Such a policy change will require the Clinton administration, at a high level, to consult with congressional leaders, particularly in the trade and foreign policy committees, to explain the U.S. interest in an early phaseout of the major remaining unilateral sanction against Vietnam. A barrier to such a policy change is that once the MIA accountability issue was resolved, interest in Vietnam policy plummeted within the U.S. government and the Washington foreign policy establishment. Interest thus needs to be revived to deal with this important remaining issue from the earlier total embargo policy.

Notes

1. The $3 billion figure includes direct aid payments and subsidized trade through below-market prices and soft loans, as for Soviet oil exports to Vietnam. The figure is based on stories in the *New York Times*, April 6, 1990, and January 5, 1992.

2. Recommendations in recent reports by the Human Rights Watch/Asia—"The Suppression of the United Buddhist Church" (March 1995), "Human Rights in a Season of Transition" (August 1995), and "Rural Unrest in Vietnam" (December 1997)—call for the international community to urge change by the government of Vietnam and in some respects to place conditions on economic assistance. The reports do not advocate sanctions on trade and investment for human rights objectives. It is not clear, however, whether the human rights groups will seek human rights conditions for a bilateral trade agreement including MFN treatment for Vietnam.

3. An interesting comparison that emerged during the course of the country case studies in this project is that all American businessmen interviewed who have had recent experience with both Vietnam and Myanmar said that corruption was a bigger problem in Vietnam than in Myanmar.

4. The Association of Southeast Asian Nations (ASEAN) country shares of total exports going to the United States are Malaysia 19 percent, Indonesia 14 percent, Singapore 18 percent, Thailand 19 percent, and the Philippines 34 percent.

5. In the spring of 1998, President Clinton waived Jackson-Vanik as a preliminary step to opening the Overseas Private Investment Corporation and Exim Bank facilities to Vietnam.

6. For the China figures, see Hugh M. Arce and Christopher T. Taylor, "The Effects of Changing U.S. MFN Status for China," *Weltwirtschaftliches Archiv* 4 (1997), 737–753. Their results are discussed in chapter 6.

7. The most newsworthy exception was the Nike shoe company, whose coverage included extensive treatment in *Doonesbury*. Nike, however, contracted production through a South Korean firm, and Korean companies have the worst reputation for labor standards among foreign investors. Nike's lack of resident representation in Vietnam has been duly criticized. More recently, improved working conditions have been reported, and Vietnamese still find Nike jobs attractive compared with the available alternatives.

8. In late 1997, the American Embassy and Consulate General in Vietnam had about 10 American economic/commercial officers plus numerous Vietnamese employees. This is exceptionally large for any country and compares with one American officer and one national employee in Yangon, Myanmar.

9. The U.S. share of Vietnamese imports is also adversely affected by large economic aid project assistance by other industrialized countries, especially Japan, wherein project procurement, explicitly or de facto, is tied to procurement in the donor country. This same situation, however, prevails in other ASEAN countries where U.S. economic project assistance is almost nil compared with other large aid programs, and so the Vietnam/ASEAN market share comparison in the text remains valid.

10. Congress is required to vote on an MFN-related trade agreement within 90 days after the agreement is submitted by the president, but a lengthy presubmission consultation period would also likely transpire.

5

Myanmar:
Phasing In Sanctions in Asia

1. Narrative Account

U.S. UNILATERAL ECONOMIC SANCTIONS POLICY against the military government of Myanmar evolved through defensive actions by the Clinton administration in the face of pressures from members of Congress and prodemocracy groups. It was predicated largely on the faulty U.S. assessment that Myanmar is a faraway country of little importance to American foreign policy. There is broad support among all interested groups in the United States for the central U.S. foreign policy objective of peaceful democratic change in Myanmar, including support for the National League for Democracy (NLD) and its courageous leader, Aung San Suu Kyi, but how unilateral economic sanctions should work toward this end is largely undefined by the federal government. Meanwhile, state and municipal governments, as well as what is referred to here as Web-site diplomacy, have moved to the forefront in advocating and implementing wide-ranging sanctions beyond what exists at the federal level, and for objectives that are at odds, or so it appears, with U.S. government sanctions policy. This unfocused and in some respects confused course of events could contribute to potentially tragic consequences for a deeply troubled nation struggling to make a transition from an isolated and highly repressive military regime toward the beginnings of a market-oriented democracy.

This harsh judgment requires first an extended note of historical and political context. Burma—as the country was officially named until 1989[1]—achieved independence from British colonial rule in 1948, and the colonial seeds of democratic government initially took hold. The hero of the independence movement, General

Aung San, was assassinated several months before independence, and for ten years the less-distinguished civilian political leader U Nu headed an elected parliamentary government whose abuses of power were constrained by a resolute and independent judiciary. A split in the governing coalition between the U Nu faction and a more militant grouping supported by key military leaders led to a two-year political impasse and a basically free election in 1960—again won by the U Nu faction. But in 1962 the military moved decisively to usurp the democratic government and establish the Socialist Republic of the Union of Burma under a Revolutionary Council comprising 17 senior military officers. The council was headed by Ne Win, who had been one of Aung San's famed "Thirty Comrades" during the struggle for independence.

The downfall of the initial Burmese democracy and the subsequent repressive rule of the Ne Win military government was caused by internal security threats and failed economic policies, compounded by U Nu's indecisive leadership. Burma, a product of imperial demarcation, lacks ethnic identity and national cohesion. The Burman two-thirds majority of the population generally occupies the fertile central plain while the other one-third comprises diverse ethnic groups—principally the Karen, Mon, Shan, Arkanese, and Kachin—who inhabit the mountainous border regions. The British gave favored treatment and considerable autonomy to the "hill tribes," the familiar divide-and-conquer strategy. Kachin and Karen troops formed the bulk of the colonial army and fought alongside the British during World War II, while their Burman counterparts—including Generals Aung San and Ne Win—were schooled by the Japanese and collaborated with Japan against British rule until the final days of the war. After independence, fighting between the ethnic minorities and the Burmese military posed a continual threat to government control of the country, as did the insurgency movement of the Burmese Communist Party, which received logistical support and safe haven from communist China. Debate over how to deal with these internal security threats was central to the split between U Nu and Ne Win, with the Ne Win military regime responding more aggressively than its democratic predecessor. As for economic strategy, the U Nu socialist program of land reform, nationalization, and industrial planning failed to produce economic growth and jobs, and the deteriorating economy became more and more dependent on foreign aid. In this case, however, the Ne Win military government merely intensified the U Nu socialist experiment, turning inward and becoming more xenophobic in the process.

The Ne Win government, which lasted 26 years, is now acknowledged by almost everyone as a tragic failure. Considerable success was achieved in suppressing revolt by the ethnic minorities and the Communist Party, but as these opposition groups were pushed back into impoverished border regions, they turned increasingly to covert illicit drug production as an economic lifeline that propelled Burma to become the largest opium and heroin producer in the world. Economic circumstances in the country went from bad to worse. Quasi-socialist dogma, crony capitalism, corruption, and black market activities thrived while the population at large suffered a continual decline in per capita income and social services. International trade dropped sharply along with other economic contacts with the outside world. Incompetent military officers took charge of newly created state enterprises with disastrous financial results.

This quarter-century of repressive military rule, failed socialism, and isolation from the world economy collapsed during demonstrations and confrontations that occurred from March until September 1988. The military brutally suppressed wide-ranging protest groups—including political activists, students, and Buddhist clergy—and as many as 3,000 people were killed. In July, Ne Win resigned, and in September a new State Law and Order Restoration Council (SLORC) was established, still dominated by the military, but with the expressed objectives of moving toward a private sector, market-oriented economy and a multiparty democratic system of government. The name of the country was changed from Burma to Myanmar, and the capital city from Rangoon to Yangon.

The abrupt change in political and economic direction in terms of stated objectives has since bogged down in implementation, particularly with regard to a democratic political transition. A first round of economic reforms did go forward. Some state enterprises were privatized, trade barriers were lowered, and foreign direct investment was encouraged through tax and other incentives. As a result, economic growth surged from the negative figures of the late 1980s into the 4 to 7 percent range in 1991–1995. As in other emerging market economies, however, the first stage of market-oriented reforms can be the easy part, and the next stage of creating more open and effective competition through, in particular, a transparent banking system, is far more difficult. The military rulers of Myanmar (just as their communist counterparts in neighboring Vietnam) are loath to relinquish the pervasive regulations and controls over economic activity that go to the core of their authoritarian political culture and yet are a critical barrier to a sustained path of market-oriented growth and job creation. Budget resources are disproportionately devoted to the military while public spending on economic infrastructure and education languishes.

The impasse over democratization was triggered by a gross miscalculation of the SLORC. They held free and open parliamentary elections in 1990, believing their National Unity Party (NUP) would win, when in fact the principal opposition party, the NLD, won more than 60 percent of the vote and 392 of 485 assembly seats (with only 10 for the NUP). The NLD victory emanated from the inspired, tough-minded leadership of Aung San Suu Kyi, daughter of the revered General Aung San, who became the rallying point for antimilitary, prodemocracy forces. The SLORC attempted to discredit Aung San Suu Kyi for having lived abroad for many years, with an English husband, and placed her under house arrest prior to the elections, but her continued physical presence decisively carried the day for the NLD.

The military leadership, faced with the loss of political power and both licit and illicit financial resources, together with deep concern among at least some of the generals that an NLD government would foster political instability and increased ethnic conflict, ignored the election results for several months and then announced that the elections had been for a constituent assembly to draft a new constitution rather than for a government. The SLORC waited until 1993 to establish a national convention to draft the constitution. Those elected in 1990 composed less than 10 percent of an assembly dominated by appointees of the military. The constitution-drafting process has since been sidetracked by attempts to negotiate support from the minority ethnic groups, who seek considerable autonomy, if not outright independence, and have advanced in parallel with stepped-up military campaigns to gain physical control of the mountainous border areas. These bloody conflicts have included use of forced labor by the army for support services, relocation of villagers in disputed areas, and cross-border flight of threatened minority populations—all subject to sharp criticism by human rights groups. By the end of 1998, the political and military campaigns achieved a basic cease-fire except for continuing negotiations with the Karen minority on the Thai border. But the government still does not have physical control in the countryside, and bitter distrust between the army and the ethnic minorities remains a threatening political fact of life for the nation.

As for the NLD, the government has accepted the party's official existence while trying to suppress it through widespread and sustained arrests and violence, including some deaths.[2] The marginal role in the constitutional assembly was rejected by the NLD, and periodic attempts at government/NLD dialogue during 1997 and 1998 got nowhere. Aung San Suu Kyi remained under house arrest until mid-1995 and has since had her movements and political activities tightly controlled. A series of initiatives by the NLD to hold meetings, from May until October 1998, related to the tenth anniversary of the 1988 demonstrations, met with renewed military suppression in which more than 1,000 NLD activists were arrested and Aung San Suu Kyi's travel was blocked in a highly publicized military confrontation.

The SLORC was reconstituted in November 1997 as the State Peace and Development Council (SPDC). A number of the older, more corrupt members of the SLORC were removed from office, but the new SPDC still entirely comprises senior military officers. A cabinet reshuffle in December 1997 put a couple of the more able generals into key economic positions, but no significant economic initiatives were forthcoming during 1998. The long-promised transition to a multiparty democracy, moreover, remains undefined and is officially characterized as a gradual process, with the military maintaining a dominant role at least in the early years. Provisions in the draft constitution for the president to have a "military background" and for only part of the parliament to be popularly elected support this approach. The generals long made reference to the "Indonesian model," where the slow transition from military to civilian democratic rule was under way for more than 30 years. The rapid pace of change in the post–Cold War, economic globalization world of the 1990s, however, now makes such a leisurely timetable unrealistic, and the Asian financial turbulence that struck Indonesia decisively in January 1998, leading to the downfall of the Suharto regime, discredits further talk of an Indonesian military–dominated model for Myanmar, as explained in the policy assessment sections below.

This is a brief summary of the extraordinary course of events during the first 50 years of Burma/Myanmar independence, officially celebrated on January 9, 1998, with the NLD holding a separate event. The country has moved from a 15-year period of initial democratic rule through a quarter-century of self-imposed isolation under an authoritarian socialist regime to the past decade of impasse over how to make the transition to a market-oriented democracy. The current phase, beginning in 1988, was precipitated by the internal political and economic crisis, but it has also been increasingly influenced by external events, in particular the concurrent collapse of the Soviet Union, the end of the Cold War, and the shift in economic strategy by its still communist neighbors, China and Vietnam, toward an open, market-oriented economy.

The response of the international community to the unfolding course of events in Myanmar, and of the United States in particular, changed dramatically with the end of the Cold War. Throughout the 26-year rule of General Ne Win, Burma was one of many nonaligned countries benefiting from the East-West rivalry. The deeply troubled socialist economy of the Ne Win Revolutionary Council was sustained to a large extent by foreign economic aid from Japan (with more than $2 billion as war reparation payments), the United States, the Soviet Union, and the multilateral development banks. Ne Win was invited to a state visit to Washington in 1966, after visits to Beijing and Moscow the year before. Democratization, human rights, and market-oriented economic reforms were never matters of serious discussion.

The international response to the military crackdown of 1988, the ensuing failed elections, and the continuing political impasse has been more forceful, for the most part punitive, but also highly diverse, reflecting the greatly changed geopolitical and economic circumstances of post–Cold War relationships. Three distinct relationships dominate the international response to the internal Myanmar conflict.

The first relationship is with the Western democracies— Europe and North America, with the United States in the lead— who exert strong overt pressures on the Myanmar military government to democratize and respect basic human rights. Their most severe measure has been the cutoff of almost all economic aid and financial support from the World Bank, the Asian Development Bank, and bilateral aid donors, which deprives Myanmar of up to a billion dollars per year in project assistance. In 1991, Aung San Suu Kyi was awarded the Nobel Peace Prize, which galvanized public support throughout the Western democracies for her gallant struggle for democracy. Strong diplomatic pressures are brought to bear to isolate and repudiate the military government, and military shipments of any kind are banned. The United States continues diplomatic relations with the Myanmar government, but through a chargé d'affaires rather than an accredited ambassador, and follows the unusual and insulting procedure of officially calling the country Burma instead of Myanmar. Normal trade, investment, and other commercial relations with Western countries, however, basically continued until 1997 when the United States imposed unilateral investment sanctions as described below.

The second relationship is with the ASEAN countries—until 1996 consisting of Brunei, Indonesia, Malaysia, the Philippines, Singapore, and Thailand—accompanied by largely tacit support from Japan. These nations have pursued a policy of "constructive engagement" with the Myanmar government in support of a gradual process of democratization, but with greater emphasis on economic reforms that over time will presumably foster democratic political change as well. Japan did halt its bilateral economic aid to Myanmar—the largest bilateral program potentially on the order of

$200 million to $300 million per year—under pressure from the United States, but would like to resume the program for foreign policy and commercial reasons. In mid-1997, in the face of public U.S. disapproval, ASEAN admitted Myanmar—along with Vietnam and Laos—to membership, which involves frequent high-level meetings and the beginning of economic steps toward regional free trade. In July 1998, after the collapse of the Suharto regime in Indonesia, the democratic members of ASEAN, particularly the Philippines and Thailand, called for a more activist prodemocracy, "flexible engagement" dialogue with the Myanmar government, although other ASEAN members resist such a change. All ASEAN members, however, remain critical of U.S.-led sanctions policy against Myanmar, arguing that such sanctions could help precipitate economic collapse and political violence in Myanmar, after which the United States would withdraw and let ASEAN pick up the pieces. Probably the most important ASEAN concern, although communicated in more muted terms, is that the current sanctions approach opens Myanmar to growing Chinese influence—the third relationship. A principal political reason for creating ASEAN was to form a cohesive Southeast Asian grouping of more than 500 million people as a counterweight to Chinese power and influence, and the longest China-Southeast Asia border by far is with Myanmar—more than 1,350 miles.[3]

The Chinese relationship with Myanmar over the past 10 years has been growing in relative and absolute terms. An uncontrolled flow of Chinese into the northern area, particularly into the number two city of Mandalay, is visibly evident, and unrecorded cross-border trade, already large, grew rapidly through 1996. A military cooperation agreement between the two countries, signed in 1996, included the training of Myanmar officers, exchange of military intelligence, and likely arms shipments to Yangon at "friendship prices." The communist government in Beijing evidently sees advantages in dealing with the current authoritarian government in Yangon compared with a democratically elected and presumably anticommunist successor.

China, in fact, has a historic interest in penetrating Myanmar as a route to the sea for its southwest provinces, as is now being achieved through a bilateral agreement reported in October 1997 to build a road, rail, river, and port network through to the deep-water Myanmar port of Kyaukpyu on the Bay of Bengal. One likely provision of this agreement would be to provide access to Kyaukpyu for the emerging Chinese blue water fleet, which is a concern to India as well as to ASEAN members. In October 1998, a Chinese $250 million, 10-year export credit to the Myanmar Power Ministry was reported, for the purchase of equipment and technical assistance to construct the largest hydroelectric power plant in the country, which would increase Myanmar's total generating capacity by 30 percent.[4]

All of the foregoing set the stage for the U.S. move to unilateral economic sanctions, which is the focus here. In 1993, the Clinton administration inherited the grim situation in Myanmar of a totally stalled process of democratization and widespread abuse of human rights. The image of an embattled Aung San Suu Kyi under house arrest was riveting and received outspoken official as well as public support. Then UN representative Madeleine Albright broke off from First Lady Hillary Clinton's delegation to the International Women's Conference in Beijing in September 1995 for a visit with Aung San Suu Kyi in Yangon. Strident calls by prodemocracy groups for unilateral U.S. trade sanctions, however, were resisted by the administration, and official policy was to stay the course of strong diplomatic pressures, together with the cutoff of multilateral and bilateral aid, to pressure the military regime to move forward with democratization. The market-oriented economic reforms of the military government were viewed favorably, as was U.S. private sector engagement in the long-closed Myanmar economy, despite criticism from Aung San Suu Kyi and prodemocracy groups that such engagement benefited the military rulers.

In any event, Myanmar had a low priority in Asia policy at the outset of the Clinton administration, and overall Asia policy quickly became troubled. A controversial trade initiative based on sectoral targets was proposed to Japan, and Japan said "no." Economic sanctions policy was even more conflicted. A lifting of sanctions against Vietnam was agreed after satisfactory cooperation was obtained for MIA investigations, but without linkage to human rights and democratization. Pressures to impose sanctions against Indonesia over human rights abuses in East Timor were resisted.

And President Clinton had to reverse himself in 1994 on China policy and oppose withdrawal of most-favored-nation treatment after having committed in 1993 to impose such a sanction unless there was improvement on a number of human rights objectives. Although official policy was to oppose unilateral economic sanctions in Myanmar as well, the administration was unprepared to resist pressures for sanctions as strongly as it had for Indonesia and China, not to mention reversing direction by the lifting of sanctions against Vietnam.

The initiative that led to the imposition of unilateral sanctions in 1997 came from prodemocracy groups opposed to the military regime in Yangon working through individual members of Congress.[5] Public frustration over the unresponsiveness of the military government in Yangon to diplomatic pressures and highly provocative reports of human rights abuses brought outcries for action from some members of Congress. Military action was out of the question, and so sanctions on trade and investment became a convenient alternative, but with little consideration of what the impact of such actions would actually be. For members of Congress, it was an apparent win-win initiative, domestically popular with constituents and without perceived significant foreign policy interests at stake such as for China and Indonesia. As far back as 1992, Senators Jesse Helms, Patrick Moynihan, and Paul Simon had proposed a nonbinding resolution to ban U.S. trade with Myanmar, but the definitive initiative came from Senator Mitch McConnell in 1995. His Burma Freedom and Democracy Act called for a mandatory prohibition on U.S. investment in that country until the president certifies that "an elected government of Burma has been allowed to take power."

The bill was referred to the Senate Committee on Banking, Housing, and Urban Affairs, an unusual move in view of the foreign policy content of the legislation, although Senate Foreign Relations Committee chairman Jesse Helms did not object. A brief hearing of less than an hour was held in May 1996. Three outside witnesses testified—a costume designer who had played Aung San Suu Kyi in the movie about the 1988 violent upheaval in Rangoon, her husband, who was a musician and artist, and an NLD-elected representative from Myanmar. Statements were later submitted for the record by the State Department, the U.S.-ASEAN Business Council, and the Unocal Corporation, but their representatives did not appear before the committee.[6] The hearing centered on human rights conditions in Myanmar, and there was little discussion of the likely impact of the proposed sanctions on the Myanmar economy or U.S. commercial interests.[7] The only reference to the growing Chinese influence in Myanmar was by Senator McConnell: "I believe Asian nations can be persuaded it is in their long term interest to join in a strong, sustained initiative because of their deep concerns about the rapidly expanding political, economic, and military ties between China and Burma. Over the past few years, the region has witnessed what amounts to the colonization of Burma." Senator Christopher Bond asked a key question that went unanswered: "If we were to implement sanctions unilaterally in a country where U.S. investment is relatively insignificant and would quickly be taken up by our competitors, what would be accomplished?"

The McConnell bill was never voted out of committee, but was inserted instead as an amendment to the annual appropriations bill before the Appropriations Subcommittee on Foreign Operations, which McConnell chaired, and its approval appeared likely. At that point, opponents of the McConnell bill, in the Congress and in the State Department, worked together to develop a weaker and more discretionary alternative sanctions measure. In parallel, the Unocal energy company of California, a participant in a billion-dollar joint-venture contract to develop natural gas off the coast of Myanmar, appealed to Senator Diane Feinstein to head off the McConnell prohibition on foreign U.S. investment. In July 1996, Feinstein, together with Senator William Cohen (later secretary of defense), introduced an alternative Burma sanctions amendment as a replacement for the McConnell amendment in the Foreign Operations appropriations bill, which was adopted without hearings or significant discussion and subsequently signed into law by the president as part of the overall appropriations bill.

The Cohen/Feinstein "Policy toward Burma" amendment is a confusing and somewhat contradictory piece of legislation that reflects its hurried drafting and limited input from the executive branch. The first section (a) reaffirms the existing cutoff of bilateral and multilateral economic assistance, but grants discretion to the president to resume aid if he determines there has been "substantial progress in improving human rights practices and implementing democratic government," a much weaker test than the McConnell requirement for an empowered elected government. U.S. humanitarian and counternarcotics assistance, previously suspended, are explicitly permitted, although in the latter case subject to certification of full Burmese cooperation and consistency with U.S. human rights concerns. The second section (b) contains prohibitions on new U.S. investments, but permits investments that take place before the sanction is implemented. Implementation is conditioned on a later presidential finding of either specified acts against the person of Aung San Suu Kyi or "large scale repression of or violence against the democratic opposition." Such specific findings are asymmetrical, however. Once the sanction is implemented, there are no specific conditions or authority for the president to lift the sanction unless he determines the investment sanction contrary to "U.S. national security interest," an implausible if flexible provision under foreseeable circumstances in Myanmar. The term "new investment," moreover, is elaborated as "a contract that includes the economical development of resources located in Burma, or the entry into a contract for the general supervision and guarantee of another person's performance of such a contract," which could be interpreted broadly to include much trade as well as investment, although this meaning would appear to conflict with another provision that the investment sanction should not restrict trade. Finally, and most extraordinary, the drafters of the amendment omitted specific authority for the president to implement the sanction, and State Department lawyers later disagreed as to whether such authority was implied. Thus, when the sanction was actually invoked in May 1997, as explained below, the president, in part for this reason, took recourse to the entirely separate International Economic Emergency Powers Act, or IEEPA, which, in effect, delinked the sanction from any legal requirements of the Cohen/ Feinstein amendment.

The State Department, or at least the East Asia and Pacific Bureau, was pleased with the outcome on the grounds that investment sanctions would probably not be implemented because the

Myanmar government had released Aung San Suu Kyi from house arrest, was making conciliatory gestures, and would therefore not engage in "large-scale repression," but the State Department was wrong. With the threat of U.S. sanctions, Aung San Suu Kyi and the NLD pressed for more open meetings and participation in the political process, and the government reacted with arrests and tighter restrictions. In December 1996, largely independent student demonstrations at the university in Yangon led to some violence, many arrests, and a shutdown of the university that continued through 1998. By the spring of 1997, congressional and other pressures were building on President Clinton to invoke the investment prohibition, including for the first time from Aung San Suu Kyi.[8] A finding of "large scale repression and violence" in the spring of 1997 was not, however, convincing because the repression of the previous fall had subsided (aside from the legal question of whether the Cohen/Feinstein amendment was inoperable in the first place), and it was the new foreign policy team of the second Clinton administration—Secretary of State Madeleine Albright, National Security adviser Sandy Berger, and UN representative Bill Richardson—all outspoken critics of the military regime in Yangon and strong supporters of Aung San Suu Kyi, that was decisive in recommending that the investment sanction be implemented. Thus on May 20, President Clinton declared a national emergency, as required by the IEEPA, on the grounds that Myanmar policy constituted "an unusual and extraordinary threat to the national security of the United States," and issued an executive order to invoke the sanction. The rules and regulations for implementation, however, including questions about the definition of investment, were left to the secretary of the Treasury in consultation with the secretary of state and were not issued until a year later in May 1998.

The Cohen/Feinstein investment restrictions in any event were being rapidly overtaken by events elsewhere in the United States even before they were imposed. Prodemocracy, Burman exile, and other groups opposed to the military government in Yangon turned to state and municipal governments and pressed for sanctions against any companies doing business in Myanmar, whether through investment or trade, usually linked to eligibility to bid on public procurement contracts. By mid-1998, such sanctions had been enacted in one state (Massachusetts) and 21 municipalities and were pending in a dozen others. These sanctions were possibly unconstitutional in that they are directed at influencing the conduct of foreign governments, often in conflict with U.S. foreign policy at the federal level, but the Clinton administration did not challenge or seriously examine this constitutional issue, presumably for reasons of domestic politics. The state and municipal sanctions also generally applied to foreign companies, and Japan and the EU challenged the Massachusetts sanctions against Burma as in conflict with U.S. commitments in the WTO. A Massachusetts legislator went so far as to hold informal discussions with officials of the EU to formulate a more forceful coordinated approach of pressures against the Myanmar government—in other words, direct foreign policy formulation with foreign governments. In response to these state and municipal sanctions, the U.S. private sector organization, the National Foreign Trade Council, brought suit against the government of Massachusetts before the federal district court in April 1998, and in November the district court judge found the Massachusetts sanction unconstitutional on the grounds that foreign policy is the exclusive domain of the federal government. This ruling was appealed, with an appeals court decision pending in early 1999. (The issue of sanctions and the Constitution, including this case, is described in detail in appendix A to this study.)

Prodemocracy and other groups have also proceeded actively, through the Internet and other media, with a deluge of often one-sided and at times erroneous Web-site information about events in Myanmar, targeting companies doing business there and threatening demonstrations against their facilities in the United States if they do not cease such business. A particular target of unfair criticism has been the natural gas pipeline project led by the French company, Total, with participation by Unocal and Thai and Myanmar energy companies. The only one of three contracted pipeline projects actually built, the pipeline runs through southern Myanmar to the border, carrying gas for export to Thailand. Antigovernment activists have reported the use of forced labor to build the pipeline and suffering by villagers in the pipeline locale in general. In fact, the pipeline jobs were the highest paid and most sought-after jobs in the highly impoverished region, and the project budget included several million dollars for local development projects including schools, health clinics, and agricultural support activities. When the pipeline came into operation in the summer of 1998, several hundred permanent jobs, largely for skilled workers, were created, mainly to operate the offshore rigs. Training for these workers began in 1997.[9]

Almost all foreign companies have far greater interests in the U.S. market than in Myanmar, and many are vulnerable to such threats. For example, the three U.S. energy companies—Unocal, Texaco, and ARCO—that had joint-venture projects under way in Myanmar were permitted to continue based on the Cohen/Feinstein federal sanctions and the related executive order by the president limited to new investments. Under targeted Web-site attack and threatened demonstrations at U.S. gas stations, however, Texaco sold out its Myanmar national gas project share to the UK firm Premier in late 1997. ARCO was the next priority for Web-site attacks, and it announced its pullout from the Myanmar consortium in October 1998, although in this case disappointing commercial considerations, related in part to the Asian financial crisis, also influenced the decision. This leaves Unocal, with the pipeline noted above already in operation, subject to concentrated, continuing attacks.[10]

U.S. unilateral economic sanctions against Myanmar in early 1999 are thus in a state of considerable confusion and largely out of the control of the federal government. The actual federal sanction is limited to new U.S. investments in Myanmar, which, as explained in the following section, has had no significant adverse impact on Myanmar. The conditions to be met for lifting the sanction are not contained in the Cohen/Feinstein amendment (as they were in the original McConnell proposed legislation or in other sanctions legislation, such as the Libertad Act against Cuba), and in any event the amendment is irrelevant in legal terms because the president ended up using IEEPA to implement the sanction. Even more important, as discussed in the later policy assessment sections, the Clinton administration has not stated what the Myanmar government needs to do for the president to terminate the sanction (presumably by executive order related to

IEEPA). Does Myanmar first have to have a democratically elected government in place, as in the McConnell proposed legislation, or are first steps, including a positive dialogue between the military and the NLD, adequate?

Meanwhile, sanctions against U.S. and other companies doing business in Myanmar are being imposed by municipal governments, mostly in conflict with the limited sanctions approach of the federal government. Finally, what is referred to as Web-site diplomacy, while perfectly legal and part of a free democratic society in the emerging information age, appears to be having an impact on American and non-American companies doing business in Myanmar that is comparable to sanctions by the federal, state, and municipal governments combined.

2. Economic Impact

On Myanmar

Geographically, Myanmar is the second largest country in ASEAN after Indonesia, more than twice the size of Vietnam, with a population of almost 50 million. It is rich in fertile land and natural resources, including substantial offshore natural gas. Myanmar is relatively unpopulated—three times the size of neighboring Bangladesh and only one-third the population[11]—with enormous areas of pristine natural beauty. It is also the second poorest member of ASEAN (after Laos) as a result of the violent political conflict and wrongheaded economic policies of the past 50 years. The hopeful economic movement in the early 1990s away from state-controlled isolation has now been overtaken by stagnation in the countryside, where 70 percent of the population live, and deepening financial crisis in urban Yangon.

The question addressed here is how recent U.S. unilateral sanctions are contributing to this economic stagnation and financial crisis, given that such sanctions are chiefly intended to inflict sufficient economic pain to cause the targeted authoritarian government to change its behavior. In the case of Myanmar, this unilateral U.S. sanctions effect is of a second- or third-order magnitude, but mutually reinforcing to three other forces that are driving down the national economy:

1. Government mismanagement. This somewhat euphemistic term involves the lack of follow-through on the initial market-oriented reforms, an excessive military budget, a pervasive lack of technocratic skills and administrative structure for implementing government programs and policies, and corruption. Much of this is an institutional carryover from the earlier period of state control and isolation. The predominant military composition of the government invites excesses in military budget expenditures (including growth in the armed forces from 175,000 in 1989 to 320,000 in 1997) and is a major factor inhibiting the selection of experienced technocrats and private sector leaders for senior management positions in government.[12] Widespread corruption, as evident in the surge in recent years of luxury automobiles and apartment buildings in Yangon, results from all of the other government shortcomings in the context of expanding crony capitalist relationships, including substantial drug trafficking money. Yet another reason for government mismanagement is the absence of foreign technical assistance and training related to the aid cutoff.

2. The foreign aid cutoff. The cutoff of almost all multilateral and bilateral aid is having a major impact on the Myanmar economy, in terms of both financial and technical support.[13] If development assistance agencies were fully engaged, the World Bank, the Asian Development Bank, and Japan would each be offering on the order of $300 million per year in project commitments to this largest of the least-developed countries in Southeast Asia, and total assistance commitments from all sources would probably exceed $1 billion per year. This compares with about $1.2 billion of exports in 1995, an estimated $550 million inflow from narcotics trafficking, and $350 million in remittances from workers abroad.[14] The financial assistance would be concentrated in infrastructure, agriculture, health, and education projects, which would necessitate extensive technical training and related institutional building in order for projects to move forward. In fact, when development assistance is resumed, there will be a time lag of some years before the Myanmar government would have the capability to absorb the levels of assistance estimated here, and actual disbursement of project money would rise only gradually.

3. The Asian financial crisis.   The regional financial crisis that began in the second half of 1997 is having a somewhat delayed, but nevertheless substantial, negative effect on what was already a deeply troubled Myanmar economy. Myanmar's exports, roughly two-thirds of which go to Asia (in 1995, 44 percent to ASEAN, 11 percent to China, and 8 percent to Japan and South Korea), declined in 1997 and dropped even more sharply in 1998. About one-third of the $234 million of foreign direct investment disbursements in 1995 came from ASEAN, concentrated in hotels for tourism, office buildings, and luxury apartments, now mostly financially vulnerable if not already bankrupt. Further such high-risk investment from ASEAN countries have been small if not negative through sell-off of existing assets. Remittances are also down because most overseas workers are in Asia as well.

These three driving forces are principally responsible for the deteriorating rural economy, which was further damaged by major flooding of rice production areas in 1997, and the deepening financial crisis in the Yangon urban economy through accelerating inflation and a corresponding rapid depreciation of the national currency. The currency depreciation particularly threatens banks and real estate investments with outstanding hard currency loans, while wage levels in Yangon lag far behind the rise in consumer prices. The American Embassy estimated a 50 percent inflation rate in 1997, a rate that was probably higher in 1998.

In these already deeply troubled circumstances, the recent imposition of U.S. unilateral economic sanctions, writ large to include federal sanctions on new investment and more broadly based sanctions at the state, municipal, and Web-site levels, are having some but relatively small additional adverse impact. The federal investment sanctions alone, limited to a prohibition on new investment, are having no significant effect on the Myanmar economy. The three existing natural gas projects with U.S. participation were exempted, and European and Asian companies can easily replace American companies in bidding on future concessions in this sector. Likewise, in the case of a U.S. engineering company that had worked up specs on the Yangon port development project and then decided not to pursue bidding on the project because of the federal sanctions, a Chinese company won the contract, making this also an example of increased Chinese penetration into the Myanmar economy that might not have happened absent the U.S. investment sanctions. An American company reportedly backed away from bidding on components for an electric power project, pending clarification of the U.S. Treasury definition of the sanction, but again other bidders were readily available. No other potential U.S. investors of significant size were uncovered that were blocked by the federal government sanction.

The more important impact of U.S. sanctions comes from the cumulative effect of state, municipal, and Web-site actions on top of and, to a large extent, legitimized by the federal sanctions, a sanction synergy effect, particularly in the area of export-oriented investments where the investor has a substantial U.S. market exposure. Garment assembly is the fastest growing Myanmar export industry, with two-thirds of its products destined for the U.S. market. Under pressure from the various U.S. sanction activities, name-brand U.S. companies—such as Liz Claiborne, Eddie Bauer, and Levi Strauss—terminated contracts with Myanmar producers, and some of the approximately 30 apparel operations reduced production or shut down. Myanmar textile and apparel exports to the United States nevertheless continued to grow, although at a subdued rate, from $65 million in 1995 to $85 million in 1996 and to $92 million in 1997.

The adverse effects on the Myanmar economy of U.S. sanctions in the aggregate are thus small, principally in the area of export-oriented investment in manufacturing unrelated to the federal sanctions. The overall outlook for the Myanmar economy, however, influenced principally by the three driving forces described above, is exceedingly negative, and thus any additional effects from U.S. sanctions could play a significant role in the ability of the military government to weather the current economic difficulties and maintain effective political control over the country.

On U.S. Commercial Interests

U.S. commercial interests in Myanmar have been relatively small, although they grew rapidly from 1989 to 1996, with direct investment flows more prominent than exports. These investment and export interests will now likely drop off sharply as a result of U.S. sanctions and the depressed state of the Myanmar economy, although the potential market, if the Myanmar government can get its political and economic acts together, could again be one of rapid growth in view of the wealth of untapped natural resources and population size. For example, total Myanmar imports quadrupled from 1989 to 1995, from less than $600 million to $2.4 billion, and a substantial renewed growth should take place, given the right incentives, including restoration of foreign assistance programs.

Total foreign direct investment into Myanmar from 1990 to 1995 was $1.2 billion, of which about $850 million was in oil and gas, almost all offshore natural gas development, $170 million in hotels and tourism, $80 million in manufactures, mostly apparel, $60 million in real estate, and $40 million in mining. The United States was the largest source of this investment, with $281 million, or 23 percent of the total, but this amount was concentrated in 1990–1992 and has since dropped off. In 1995, U.S. investment was $31 million, only fifth largest after the investments of the United Kingdom, France, Singapore, and Thailand. U.S. direct investment has been overwhelmingly concentrated in the three large offshore natural gas projects in which Unocal, ARCO, and Texaco were participants, with much smaller interests identified in mining and apparel production.

U.S. exports to Myanmar are more difficult to quantify because most are trans-shipped through third countries, such as Singapore, and are not recorded as U.S. exports in either Myanmar or U.S. trade statistics. Recorded figures show an increase from about $10 million per year in 1993–1994 to $30 million in 1996, or only 1 percent of total Myanmar imports, but actual imports of U.S. origin are probably at least double that level, or in the range of $60 million to $90 million for 1996.[15] Machinery and transport equipment accounted for two-thirds of recorded U.S. exports, and other manufactured goods and chemicals made up nearly all of the rest. Consumer goods are likely to be more prominent in the indirect, unrecorded U.S. exports.

An assessment of the impact of U.S. sanctions on U.S. investment in and exports to Myanmar needs to distinguish the immediate and longer-term effects, as well as the federal versus the state, municipal, and Web-site sanctions impact. The immediate effects are more adverse on investment than on exports, although both will in any event be reduced as a result of the depressed Myanmar economy. The three offshore natural gas projects were exempted from the federal restrictions on new investment, but other consid-erations, including state and municipal sanctions, have forced Texaco and ARCO to pull out. Unocal is more secure because it has relatively few U.S. domestic facilities vulnerable to demonstra-tions and boycott. Other shutdowns of Myanmar-based operations of U.S. companies, from PepsiCo to Apple Computer to apparel producers, were likewise caused by nonfederal sanctions. The deci-sion of the U.S. engineering company not to bid on the Yangon port project and a similar decision on the electric power project are the only investments identified as possible direct victims of the fed-eral sanctions, although other smaller opportunities may also have been lost.

The immediate impact on U.S. exports is even more difficult to identify in view of the indirect flow of much of the bilateral trade, although the lack of a physical presence by American compa-nies in Myanmar has to be a significant disadvantage for export development. Membership in the American Business Council (ABC) in Yangon was down from about 30 in 1995 to less than 20 in 1997, and most of what remains are small business interests, including individual consultants and lawyers, some of whom are dual nationals of Myanmar origin. This compares with the 200 to 300 members of the American Chamber of Commerce in Vietnam. It is also noteworthy that the American Embassy Economic/ Commercial Section in Yangon, normally tasked with promoting U.S. exports, is greatly constrained by a highly unusual directive:

> In accordance with U.S. Government policy of neither pro-moting nor prohibiting trade with Burma by U.S. firms and nationals, the Embassy does not actively collect and declines to publish information on marketing U.S. products and services. However, the Embassy Economic and Commercial Unit will provide to U.S. firms and nationals upon request such infor-mation as is readily available on the subject.[16]

The minimal service upon request only is reflected in the fact that the embassy has only one American economic/commercial officer assisted by one full-time national analyst, compared with about 10 Americans and numerous national employees in Vietnam. It is therefore not surprising that U.S. exports, even taking account of the indirect exports, comprise only 2 to 3 percent of Myanmar imports, compared with about 15 percent in other ASEAN countries where the United States has normal commercial relationships.

The longer-term impact on U.S. commercial interests in the Myanmar market will likely be much larger than the immediate effects. U.S. companies are precluded from bidding on future offshore natural gas concessions, as well as on mining and other natural resource projects. They are also unable to participate as joint-venture investors in infrastructure projects in the transportation, communications, and electric power sectors (except one planned Yangon power facility that is part of the Unocal joint venture). Infrastructure projects are currently constrained by the lack of financial resources, but some are going forward, contracted principally with Japanese, ASEAN, and Chinese companies.

The broadest and most serious adverse impact on U.S. commercial interests in Myanmar over the longer term is the almost total disengagement of the U.S. private sector from a physical presence in the Myanmar market. Asian and European companies are doing some business and in the process positioning themselves, their technologies, and their people in-country to take immediate advantage of future growth prospects, while American companies will have to start from scratch when unilateral sanctions are eventually lifted. The transitional and in some cases permanent losses to U.S. commercial interests from delayed market entry are examined in the Vietnam case study, where unilateral sanctions have recently been phased down. The post-market opening time lag for American companies in Myanmar could be even longer than it was in Vietnam in view of the number of years Myanmar has already been open to foreign investment and trade, and thus the relative adverse impact on U.S. commercial interests could be greater.

The loss of U.S. investment and exports from the unilateral Myanmar sanctions is difficult to specify in quantitative terms. In the short run, the $30 million to $50 million per year level of U.S.

direct investment will decline sharply, and to zero except perhaps for the remaining Unocal natural gas project, but the overall level of foreign direct investment into Myanmar, which was about $200 million per year over the period 1990–1996, has also declined sharply. As for U.S. exports, the sanction constraints are a major reason why the U.S. share of Myanmar imports is only 2 percent to 3 percent rather than the 15 percent level elsewhere in ASEAN markets. This would translate to more than $300 million per year in U.S. exports compared with the recent $60 million to $90 million of estimated actual exports, although again all trade figures are headed downward, at least during 1998. Over the longer term, to the extent the government of Myanmar improves its economic performance and economic aid is restored, losses to U.S. investment and exports, including the lagged market-entry effects, would be larger—probably much larger.

3. Net Assessment of U.S. Unilateral Sanctions Policy

A net assessment of recent experience with unilateral sanctions against Myanmar needs to include all significant U.S. interests in the country, of which there are four: (1) supporting democratization and respect for human rights; (2) strengthening geopolitical relationships in Asia; (3) reducing heroin production and trafficking; and (4) promoting commercial interests. Principal attention here is given to the first—the democratization/human rights objective—because it has been given top priority by the Clinton administration and by involved members of Congress and is the most complex and controversial. The other three interests are more clearcut and are thus treated more briefly, but this does not necessarily mean that they are of lesser importance to overall U.S. interests in Myanmar.

1. Democratization and respect for human rights. This has been the overriding U.S. and European foreign policy objective in Myanmar for 10 years, as exercised through strong diplomatic pressures and the cutoff of multilateral and bilateral economic assistance. The specific issue addressed here is how the more recent U.S. unilateral sanctions on investment and trade have affected the overall pursuit of this objective. The summary assessment is that while initial unilateral actions at the state and municipal levels and the threat of federal sanctions in 1996 may have created some additional pressures on the military government to make conciliatory gestures to the NLD, and to the person of Aung San Suu Kyi in particular, the actual imposition of the federal sanctions in 1997, together with the proliferation of sanctions at other levels effectively out of the control of the federal government, have ended up reducing the U.S. government's ability to influence political developments within Myanmar.

A central problem in using the legislated unilateral sanctions as leverage against the military government is the absence of specific objectives, or criteria, for lifting the sanctions. The State Department has not stated what needs to happen before the president would lift the prohibition on new investment. The immediate objective is to begin a process of "dialogue" between the generals and Aung San Suu Kyi and the NLD, but this presumably would not be enough. When pressed, executive branch officials indicate that the administration would be unlikely to lift the investment sanction unless Aung San Suu Kyi publicly supports such a move, but this is a disturbing policy corner to be painted into. It makes one protagonist in the political struggle within Myanmar the decision maker for U.S. policy toward the country and also puts her in a difficult tactical position. To call for a lifting of U.S. sanctions before a fully specified political transition is agreed upon would weaken her bargaining position.

The failure of the U.S. executive branch to define the criteria for lifting the federal sanctions is complicated further by its unwillingness to restrain or even criticize state- and municipal-level sanctions whose conditions for lifting the sanctions can be more sweeping, although not necessarily precise, in terms of democratization and respect for human rights. There is thus conflict among the objectives for imposing or lifting the sanctions, with reluctance by the president to challenge what are essentially foreign policy activities of state and municipal governments.

Another related problem is the relatively minor economic impact of the U.S. unilateral sanctions once imposed. The outspoken view of the generals in Yangon is that U.S. market share, relatively small to begin with, is simply taken up by other countries, and Premier's quick buyout of Texaco's share in one of the offshore natural gas projects provides the clearest example. The replacement of Apple computers by Japanese competitors is another cited case in point. Even textile and apparel exports to the United States continue to grow, although at a slower pace. The unilateral investment and trade sanctions, once imposed, have now been accepted as a fait accompli of relatively minor impact.

The net result of the departure of the U.S. private sector from Myanmar and the reality of unilateral sanctions as a spent force is that the United States has become a largely disengaged player as the political impasse and economic crisis within Myanmar approach what could be a decisive phase. The American chargé, who does not even refer to the country by its official name, operates in a decidedly cool and somewhat distant relationship with the generals, and high-level U.S. official visits to Yangon or contacts with the Myanmar embassy in Washington are rare. In April 1998, when UN representative Bill Richardson sought to visit Yangon to discuss a democratic transition, the Myanmar government refused to grant him a visa because cabinet-level members of the Myanmar government are refused visas to visit the United States. Nonofficial visitors to Yangon are dutifully received by members of the government as well as by Aung San Suu Kyi and her NLD colleagues, but this is very different from an engaged official relationship in which U.S. diplomacy would communicate directly and forcefully with a still closed and largely xenophobic military government.

Thus the U.S. unilateral economic sanctions imposed in 1997, as an adjunct to the multilateral diplomatic pressures and aid cutoff of prior years, are having little or no significant benefit in fostering democratic change, while inducing the military government to shunt aside the U.S. relationship and become more deeply engaged with the Chinese, ASEAN, and other Asian governments. The impact on human rights violations could be even more negative because the overriding concern of the U.S. government with the political impasse between the military and Aung San Suu Kyi has led to a reduced ability to deal directly with human rights abuses that are mostly in the countryside, unrelated to the military/Aung San Suu Kyi impasse. Last but not least, any economic sanction effects, by definition, cause economic pain for the people, often the poorest people, through loss of jobs and a reduced ability to import basic consumer goods.

2. Geopolitical relationships in Asia.   This issue received little attention during the course of debate in the United States at all levels about economic sanctions against Myanmar, but it is clearly high in the thinking within the Myanmar and other Asian governments and should receive greater attention in the U.S. government as well. Myanmar, like other smaller countries in Asia, has had a long and at times bloody history of trying to balance geopolitical, and now geoeconomic, relationships with larger powers. During World War II and its aftermath, it was Japan versus the United Kingdom. The Cold War period enabled Burma to balance the Soviet Union against the United States, and both those superpowers against the ever-present threat of Chinese penetration. Since 1989, ASEAN and Japan have replaced the West as countervailing forces to China, but the financial crisis of 1997–1998, including the revealed inner problems of government–private sector relationships in these countries, makes ASEAN and Japan a far less secure pillar for Myanmar resistance to Chinese influence. Indeed, even the most nationalistic leaders in Myanmar, be they within the military government or the democratic opposition, should see a distinct advantage in a firmly rooted political and economic relationship with the United States and other industrialized democracies of the West to balance the growing influence of Chinese political and Southeast Asian financial interests within Myanmar.

The U.S. interest would likewise be served by a strengthened and more engaged relationship with Myanmar, as with other ASEAN countries, for "preventing the dominance of any one power in Asia," which is the official U.S. way of expressing concern about growing Chinese influence. And in this context, the debilitating impact on Myanmar over the past 10 years from the full range of sanctions and aid cutoff has presented China with a historic opportunity, which it is seizing with apparent alacrity, to move into Myanmar.

3. Heroin production and trafficking.   The major U.S. interest in curtailing Myanmar production and export of heroin to the United States has clearly been hampered by economic sanctions, which have prevented U.S. support for antinarcotics efforts by the Myanmar government. The Myanmar government has attempted to shut down some drug activities in connection with military campaigns and political negotiations with the border minority groups. In 1996, heroin seizures by Myanmar authorities, while relatively small, were at least comparable to those in neighboring Thailand.[17] The U.S. Drug Enforcement Agency (DEA) believes cooperative programs with Myanmar drug enforcement units could produce better results, and the Myanmar government would be receptive to such cooperative programs. The unilateral sanctions policy, however, has precluded serious consideration of such an initiative, which is assessed here as another adverse consequence of the sanctions policy.

4. U.S. commercial interests. The inherent adverse impact on U.S. commercial interests from the unilateral sanctions has been assessed in the previous section for U.S. investment in and exports to Myanmar. Another trade policy problem relates to state- and municipal-level sanctions that Japan and the EU have challenged in the WTO as violating U.S. commitments, especially related to the Uruguay Round services agreement. The dispute is technically complex, and the U.S. Trade Representative is placed in the position of having to defend the sanctions even though their foreign policy intent may be at odds with the president's foreign policy and their legal basis unconstitutional in the first place. The net effect is further bad publicity in the United States for the WTO, as outspoken proponents of sanctions decry commitments in the WTO as undermining U.S. sovereignty.

The net assessment of unilateral sanctions policy against Myanmar is thus negative on all four counts, and unreservedly so with respect to geopolitical, drug trafficking, and commercial interests. Meanwhile, events within Myanmar are turning worse and worse in economic terms while the democratization impasse deepens and comes closer to violent confrontation. The U.S. role in influencing the outcome is currently small, some would say marginal, and consideration of alternatives to the unilateral sanctions approach is therefore clearly in order.

4. Alternatives to Current Unilateral Sanctions Policy

There are three basic alternatives to the current partial U.S. unilateral sanctions for responding to the prolonged political impasse over democratization, including human rights abuses, and the deepening economic crisis in Myanmar: a further tightening of the sanctions, the unilateral lifting of the sanctions, and a negotiated phaseout of the sanctions, referred to here as proactive flexible engagement.

Alternative 1: A Further Tightening of the Sanctions

Early in 1998, it appeared as though the military government and the NLD were moving toward a dialogue on political transition. On March 27, a top general made a particularly conciliatory statement: "Whichever parties or organizations above ground are our citizens, our nation, though our beliefs and commitments may not be the same, there is no reason to bear a grudge. . . .Conditions may not permit today, but we must at one time strive for unity of our nation's political groups." The NLD responded, "We can attain our goal through the path of talks." Prospects turned sharply negative for the rest of the year, however, including the massive arrests and threatening confrontations noted earlier. Western governments have consequently stepped up diplomatic pressure on the military regime in Yangon. In September, the UK government announced that it might seek to expel Myanmar from the International Labor Organization (ILO) in 1999. The EU, in October, expelled military personnel attached to Myanmar diplomatic missions in the EU, but decided not to place any ban on EU investment or other commercial activities in Myanmar. Under these circumstances, the United States could move to restrict further U.S. investment in and trade with Myanmar, in keeping with actions taken at the state and municipal levels. A ban on U.S. imports from Myanmar, for example, which President Clinton could presumably impose by invoking the IEEPA again, would deal a substantial blow to the already desperate Myanmar economy, in the hope of forcing the military leaders to yield power.

The downsides of such a move, however, could also be severe. Thousands of Myanmar workers, especially in the textile and apparel sector, would be thrown out of work and suffer greatly from a U.S. import sanction. The military leaders, even more desperate than before, could react with a decisive violent crackdown against the NLD and Aung San Suu Kyi, or at a minimum simply expel her from the country. Aung San Suu Kyi herself would be put in a difficult position over whether to support or oppose such a tightening of U.S. sanctions with its economic pain inflicted on workers in Myanmar. Moreover, if a violent confrontation followed a tightening of U.S. sanctions, the United States would be blamed for igniting the violence through a unilateral sanction approach that has been almost universally condemned elsewhere, such as against Cuba and Iran.

Alternative 2: A Unilateral Lifting of Existing Sanctions

This move in the opposite direction would be based on the assessment that the U.S. unilateral sanction on new investment is ineffective in economic terms while having no positive and some adverse consequences on the ability of the United States to change the attitudes and behavior of the military leadership in Myanmar. Such a lifting of the sanctions would be done in the context of increased multilateral diplomatic and other pressures against the Myanmar government. Closer collaboration with ASEAN governments toward a "flexible engagement," in particular, should result from such a change in U.S. policy.

There are reasons, however, not to pursue this alternative. It could be misperceived by the military regime at this critical juncture as a weakening of U.S. support for democratization within Myanmar. Another reason is that it would provoke strong protests from members of Congress and prodemocracy groups within the United States that could lead to more rather than fewer sanctions. The president could lift the embargo by executive order, using IEEPA, but it could well be counteracted by congressional initiative to legislate mandatory new and enhanced sanctions. Such a move would likely be reinforced by protests from Aung San Suu Kyi, even though some other prodemocracy activists in Myanmar oppose the U.S. sanctions approach on the grounds that it increases the suffering of the people.

Alternative 3: A Proactive Flexible Engagement

This alternative would begin with the United States specifying what needs to happen before President Clinton would issue an executive order to lift the unilateral sanction on new investment. The conditions would be limited to first steps such as a dialogue to develop a specific schedule for the transition to democracy and assurances for the safety of Aung San Suu Kyi and other NLD members. The administration would also take a clear stand against state and municipal sanctions that conflict with the objectives of such a calibrated approach. Web-site diplomacy against the military regime in Yangon and support for sanctions would, of course, be free to continue unhindered, but supporters of a "flexible engagement" strategy would enter more actively in the Internet debate.

In parallel, there would be high-level diplomatic engagement with the Myanmar government. Ministerial or other high-level meetings would be offered. Some of the generals have been almost totally isolated from contacts with Western democratic leaders, which only tends to strengthen deep-seated anti-Western nationalism and historic xenophobia. Bilateral ministerial meetings in another ASEAN capital, perhaps in the Philippines, would be appropriate. In view of the special cultural bonds among military institutions throughout the world, a distinguished U.S. military leader, such as General Colin Powell or John Shalikashvili, might play a catalytic role in establishing the dialogue. Under these circumstances of high-level official dialogue, the United States could also exercise stronger leadership for multilateral initiatives with Europe, Japan, and ASEAN governments to press reforms on the military regime in Yangon.

On the substantive level, other specific proposals, contingent on the first steps linked to lifting the investment sanction, would include the following:

1. Multilateral development bank project assistance. The United States would support limited World and Asian Development Bank project assistance targeted on alleviating poverty and human rights problems, and in late 1998 World Bank management was in fact considering such a renewed program in Myanmar. A principal human rights concern is the widespread, centuries-old practice of conscripting unpaid, forced labor for road construction and maintenance and other infrastructure work in rural areas. Under criticism from human rights groups, the military has reduced such forced labor somewhat in recent years, to some extent replacing forced peasant labor with military cadres, but this is the wrong way to go. Far better is to begin to build a technically competent civilian structure for this critical infrastructure support work, which the World Bank is well positioned to help organize and support financially. Other humanitarian-related aid projects would likewise be given positive consideration by the development banks and the international donor community.

2. Antinarcotics enforcement. The United States would offer an antinarcotics enforcement support program as has been advocated by the DEA and for which the Myanmar government has indicated receptivity. The Cohen/Feinstein amendment permits such assistance subject to the finding of full cooperation by the Myanmar government and consistency with U.S. human rights concerns. This is a judgment call that has been swayed decisively, up to this point, by the U.S. unilateral sanctions policy, but a case for making such a certification, consistent with standards for other countries, appears reasonable.

3. U.S. bilateral aid for democratization infrastructure. An almost total lack of organizational support structure for the functioning of democratic government exists both for the military and the NLD and other opposition parties. The U.S. Agency for International Development (USAID) has widespread recent experience to support such democratic infrastructure building, and an offer to do so in Myanmar would be a highly visible sign of constructive engagement. Initial projects could be very modest in size and consist of the least controversial forms of training and administrative support, but the symbolic effect of any AID program in Myanmar would be significant.

Finally, and heavily contingent on progress along the foregoing lines, the United States would be prepared to assume a mediator role in bringing the military leadership and the NLD together at the bargaining table for serious negotiations. Such a major step, of course, depends on both sides' wanting to do so, and such an interest was clearly not evident in late 1998, especially by the military. As political and economic circumstances continue to deteriorate, however, a willingness to resolve the long-standing impasse may materialize, and in view of the deep distrust between the parties, a resolute mediator could play a critical role.

The United States is not the only potential mediator if such circumstances should materialize. UN assistant secretary general Alvaro De Soto, who visited Yangon in January and October 1998 to try to get the two sides talking to one another, is scheduled to return in early 1999. The United Nations, however, has generally been more adept at peacekeeping than at peacemaking, and a UN mediator could find it difficult to take the specific initiatives involved in shaping what would be a highly politically charged compromise. An ASEAN mediator might also be appropriate, although ASEAN as a subregional political grouping has become weakened by the financial crisis and political upheaval in Indonesia. The United States, in contrast, has an impressive track record for proactive mediation that includes recent efforts in Bosnia, Northern Ireland, Kosovo, and the Middle East. If an agreement were ultimately to be reached in Myanmar, the United States is also best situated to mobilize maximum international economic and other support for the implementation.

5. Conclusions and Recommendations

The central conclusion is that U.S. unilateral economic sanctions against Myanmar have had no significant success in fostering democratization and respect for human rights in that country. The initial threat of sanctions may have helped elicit some conciliatory moves by the military regime, but during 1998 the situation has worsened in both political and economic terms. The United States, while claiming the moral high ground through unilateral sanctions, has almost entirely disengaged from contacts with the Myanmar government and private sector. A close relationship is maintained with Aung San Suu Kyi and opposition leaders, but it is not clear how this contact has helped their cause.

Another conclusion is that other U.S. interests in Myanmar—namely, the geopolitical interest of limiting Chinese penetration into the country, the suppression of illicit drug production and trafficking, and U.S. commercial interests—have all clearly suffered as a result of the unilateral sanctions policy.

Meanwhile, conditions continue to deteriorate within Myanmar, and the threat of violent confrontation grows. The deepening economic crisis—the result of gross mismanagement by the military government, the Asian financial crisis, and the 10-year cutoff of multilateral and bilateral economic assistance—could at some point cause a near total economic collapse that would bring people out into the streets. In 1998, moreover, the Myanmar military is larger, better equipped, and better prepared than it was in 1988, and a violent confrontation could result in a devastating setback for prodemocracy forces within the country.

A final conclusion of particular relevance to assessing the most appropriate U.S. policy response is that the United States is and will remain only a secondary player in terms of Myanmar interests and relationships. Myanmar membership in ASEAN and relationships elsewhere in Asia are of primary political and economic importance. The United States can play a significant, perhaps decisive role at this critical juncture, but it can only do so in close collaboration with ASEAN members, Japan, and other industrialized democracies. Acting alone through a policy of unilateral economic sanctions and almost total disengagement from the Myanmar government and private sector conflicts with such a collaborative approach.

The recommendation here for the U.S. policy response is therefore alternative 3 as outlined above, a proactive flexible engagement strategy. This would indeed be a collaborative approach with other Asian nations and Western democracies, but within a framework of U.S. leadership and renewed U.S. public–private sector engagement with Myanmar. It may not succeed, but it would at least force the recalcitrant generals to respond more fully to what they mean by a goal of multiparty democracy. It may also help them to decide how to extricate themselves from the political dead-end in which they find themselves. Myanmar has now become the last military government in Asia, whose minister/generals have recently begun wearing civilian clothes to ASEAN meetings to mask this anachronism. They now need to be convinced that an orderly, definitive withdrawal to the barracks is their only longer-term option for the good of their country and themselves.

Notes

1. Standard international procedure is to accept the legitimacy of a government—and its name for the country—if it effectively controls the national territory (governments in exile do not count), even if there is no formal recognition through diplomatic relations and fundamental disputes exist, which can even include a declaration of war. In this context, the country is referred to in this study as Myanmar, which implies no value judgment. The substantive significance of the different names is a complex matter. The British named their colony "Burma," while the Burmese called the country "Bamah Pyi" in speaking and "Myanmah Pyi" in writing. The capital city name Rangoon is uniquely British, derived from the national versions Yankon, Yangon, and Dagon, the latter as in the revered and magnificent Shwe Dagon Pagoda in the center of the city. See Mya Maung, *Totalitarianism in Burma: Prospects for Economic Development* (New York: Paragon House, 1992), XII–XIV. Whether "Burmese" or "Burman" should be used for all nationals of the country (and the other adjective as members of the "Burmah" ethnic group) is not clearly established, and "Myanmarese" is seldom heard.

2. Since 1988, at least six NLD members have died while imprisoned where, at a minimum, health facilities are inadequate. Many others were conscripted into support services to the military in the conflicts with ethnic minorities where at least four died under unclear circumstances during 1997. See U.S. Department of State, *Human Rights Reports*, 1996–1997.

3. The other China-ASEAN borders are with Vietnam (790 miles) and Laos (260 miles).

4. *Vietnam Business Journal* (October 1998): 54.

5. It is noteworthy that the major human rights groups, as distinct from smaller groups opposed to the military regime in Yangon, did not support the McConnell or Cohen/Feinstein sanctions legislation. Amnesty International has never taken a position on sanctions in Myanmar or in any other country. The Human Rights Watch is not opposed to the military Myanmar government, per se, but believes that international investors should not operate in

the country because of human rights abuses, particularly the widespread use of forced labor. Similarly, neither Amnesty International nor the Human Rights Watch has supported the state and municipal sanctions against companies doing business in Myanmar, although testimony on human rights abuses in Myanmar has been provided. Thus, in the text, the term "prodemocracy" groups is used rather than "human rights" groups, although some human rights groups are included within the "prodemocracy" label and indeed the objectives of democratization and respect for basic human rights are inherently interrelated.

6. The three-page official State Department submission by Deputy Assistant Secretary Kent Wiedemann (later the American chargé d'affaires in Yangon) was principally devoted to an assessment of recent developments within Myanmar. The only reference to the likely impact of the proposed sanctions was as follows: "We note that unilateral sanctions would have limited economic impact on the regime." Wiedemann opposed the mandatory sanctions contained in the McConnell bill while expressing willingness to explore legislation for discretionary sanctions.

7. The only specific figure mentioned at the hearing about the economic impact of cutting off U.S. investment, by Ms. Adell Lutz, the costume designer, was wrong and misleading: "The SLORC . . . through these deals that they've recently made in the past year for the pipeline, they're bringing in from that 400 million (dollars) annually." In fact, the first Total/Unocal pipeline did not begin operations until the summer of 1998, and the Myanmar government will receive little income during the first three or more years because payments from its share of the approximately $400 million annual *gross* revenue will be withheld to pay for its equity share in the project.

8. Aung San Suu Kyi continues to support the U.S. investment sanction, as explained in an interview in *Business Week* (March 30, 1998). She has also been criticized for being ill-disposed to market-oriented reforms in general and multinational corporate investment in particular, but this is not borne out by her statements, such as contained in her book *Letters from Burma* (London: Penguin Books, 1997), 43–45. These views were confirmed in an interview with the author in November 1997.

9. Pipeline project critics also cite the use of forced labor—"army porters"—in support of expanded Myanmar Army units in the region to protect the pipeline construction against attacks by ethnic minority insurgents. This is part of the much broader, legitimate human rights concern throughout the country of military use of unpaid forced labor. In this case, however, the pipeline consortium argued against the practice and began to pay some army porters, and the army, in response to that and other international criticism, apparently reduced or stopped the practice in the vicinity of the pipeline.

10. See, for example, the *Los Angeles Times*, October 23, 1998. This article reports a Department of Labor report of allegations that forced labor was used in the early stages of the Unocal pipeline project, and may still continue, but specific allegations are related to the army units in the region, not the pipeline construction itself.

11. A credible concern expressed in Myanmar is that once the country is embarked on a sustained path of economic growth, it will face a problem of large-scale illegal migration from Bangladesh into Myanmar. At present, however, in addition to the impoverished economy, anti-Moslem oppression acts to deter such migration.

12. The Myanmar armed forces total 320,000, the second largest in ASEAN after Vietnam with 572,000. Indonesia has the next largest armed forces of 299,000, while the democratic Philippines has 108,000. See International Institute for Strategic Studies, *The Military Balance 1996/97* (London: Oxford University Press, 1997).

13. A small UN aid program of $10 million to $15 million per year is engaged in rural development, but this amount is minuscule compared with the billion-dollar cutoff from the principal aid donors. The controversy over this essentially token UN program, with Aung San Suu Kyi and some groups in the United States questioning their continuance because they constitute a show of support for the military regime, amounts to little more than a minor rearrangement of the Titanic's deckchairs for the sinking Myanmar economy.

14. Trade figures for Myanmar, approximate at best, derive from three widely variant sources. First are the official Myanmar statistics based on the official exchange rate, which greatly overstate the dollar figures. Second is a set of statistics based on the Myanmar government figures but using a market-oriented dollar exchange rate, prepared by the American Embassy. And third is a set of reverse trade figures prepared by UNCTAD in which the figures of Myanmar's trading partners are used, reversing exports to imports, etc. The UNCTAD figures are used here. Other problems, such as the exclusion of much border trade with China and indirect U.S. exports, exist for all three sets of trade figures, as explained in the text. The estimates for dollar inflows from narcotics and remittances are from the American Embassy Rangoon's excellent *Foreign Economic Trends Report* (1997): 72–73.

15. See the *American Embassy Country Commercial Guide: Burma*, Fiscal Year 1998, pp. 34–35.

16. Ibid., 38.

17. In 1996, heroin seizures in Myanmar were 0.505 metric tons for the full year compared with 0.370 in Thailand for January-September. See U.S. Department of State, *International Narcotics Strategy Report*, 1997.

6

China:
Where It All Comes Together

1. Narrative Account

THE U.S.-CHINA RELATIONSHIP during the 1990s brings together all of the major issues posed by the use of unilateral economic sanctions as an instrument of foreign policy. National security, as well as human rights/democratization foreign policy objectives, is engaged. Comprehensive and targeted sanctions have been applied or threatened. Important U.S. commercial interests are at stake, and the related issue of private sector engagement as a force for positive change within the target country faces its most critical test. Geopolitical considerations for U.S. relations with Asia today, and possibly on a global scale in a decade or two, pervade everything else. And last but not least, domestic politics in the United States have played a major and at times decisive role in U.S. policy decisions.

This narrative account—as for succeeding sections on economic impact and policy assessment—is divided into two very different parts. The first deals with the troubled course of linking MFN treatment for U.S. imports from China to improved respect for human rights, and thus a more democratic political system, within China. This defining example of broadly based or comprehensive unilateral sanctions as a means for forcing political change on an authoritarian government is a central theme throughout all five of the case studies. The second part addresses the more elusive yet currently more important issue of other, mostly targeted U.S. export sanctions, primarily related to U.S. national security interests.

The MFN Debate

The United States granted MFN trading status to China in 1980 as a key component for building a strategic relationship with China against the Soviet Union during the Cold War. The two relevant characteristics of such trading status for U.S.-China policy are the geographical scope of MFN versus non-MFN treatment and the annual process for renewal. MFN treatment means that U.S. imports pay relatively low tariffs as have been negotiated down over 50 years of multilateral trade negotiations, most recently in the Uruguay Round concluded in 1993. Those countries not receiving MFN, in contrast, have to pay the very high tariffs established in 1930 under the Smoot-Hawley Act. For imports from China, this amounts to an average 6 percent tariff with MFN compared with a largely prohibitive 44 percent average under Smoot-Hawley rates, as explained in the following section on economic impact. Moreover, MFN is now granted to almost all countries, and many countries receive even lower rates or duty-free entry as developing countries or as members of a free trade agreement such as NAFTA. The only countries that do not receive at least MFN status today are Afghanistan, Cuba, Laos, North Korea, Yugoslavia (that is, Montenegro and Serbia), and Vietnam, which together account for less than one-half of 1 percent of world exports. A more appropriate nomenclature, recently enacted into law but not yet fully into policy discussion, is "normal trade status," or NTS, rather than "most-favored-nation," or MFN.

The review process for MFN treatment for China is a Cold War legacy from the 1974 Jackson-Vanik amendment, which was adopted to pressure the Soviet government to allow Jews to emigrate freely from the Soviet Union. For communist countries, Congress must first approve application of MFN rates, and then the president has to conduct an annual review and make a positive determination about freedom of emigration or waive the freedom of emigration provisions in order to renew MFN treatment. For China, the president has used the waiver route since 1980, in which case he needs to announce the determination to do so to Congress by June 3. Congress then has 90 days (or more precisely 60 days from the July 3 expiration date) to review the waiver and possibly vote on it. If both houses vote against renewal, the president can still veto the congressional vote, subject to a two-thirds congressional override.

The annual MFN renewal process for China progressed routinely from 1980 through 1988, but became highly controversial, starting in 1989, as a result of the Tiananmen Square massacre and the collapse of the Berlin Wall marking the beginning of the end of the Cold War U.S.-China strategic relationship. The ensuing MFN debate has pitted the supporters of an engaged relationship with China, based on U.S. geopolitical and economic interests, against an alliance of liberal human rights and conservative anticommunist advocates of a more confrontational approach on moral and ideological grounds. Renewal of MFN has been debated, year after year, almost entirely in such broad foreign policy terms, and there has been little serious analysis of what actually would happen to the U.S.-China economic relationship if MFN were withdrawn.

The first full analysis of the consequent trade impact on China was not produced until 1994, almost at the end of the principal MFN debates. Opponents of MFN, in particular, never explained in detail how the withdrawal of MFN would serve to promote human rights and other U.S. foreign policy objectives in China. Moreover, the U.S. domestic political dynamic for the annual decision on China policy went through two highly distinct phases, during the Bush and Clinton presidencies, respectively, which can be characterized as the threat of irrational behavior and capitulation/delinkage.[1]

The threat of irrational behavior: 1989–1992. The immediate reaction to the June 1989 Tiananmen Square massacre was a wide-ranging set of diplomatic protests and economic sanctions against China, mostly on a multilateral basis. A subcommission of the UN Human Rights Commission voted in September 1989 for a full commission examination of the massacre and subsequent repression, and high-level visits and meetings with Chinese officials were sharply curtailed. The principal economic sanctions involved a halt in arms sales, a suspension of World Bank and Asian Development Bank loans, except for humanitarian-related assistance, and a similar suspension in bilateral economic aid, especially the very large Japanese aid program. Normal commercial relations continued except for the United States, which closed down operations of the Overseas Private Investment Corporation, or OPIC, and the Trade and Development Program, or TDP (currently the Trade and Development Agency, or TDA), which provide private investment guarantees and grants for feasibility studies, and suspended U.S. Exim Bank loans. Export licensing on U.S. advanced technology exports to China was also tightened.

These initial reactions, however, had little impact on the Chinese government, which repudiated any outside interference in what it considered an internal matter and cracked down brutally on Tiananmen Square prodemocracy demonstrators through dozens of executions and thousands of arrests and imprisonment under extremely harsh conditions. In the national security field, reports indicated that China continued its sales of ballistic missile technology to Iran and Pakistan and its nuclear weapons development assistance to Pakistan. Moreover, as the post–Tiananmen Square repression ran its course, the initial multilateral reactions dissipated as well. In February 1990, the World Bank selectively resumed consideration of loans to China, as did the U.S. Exim Bank. In March, the full UN Human Rights Commission refused to criticize China, and in August, after obtaining the concurrence of the United States and other Western leaders at the annual G-7 summit, Japan announced the resumption of its bilateral aid program for China.

President Bush, committed to constructive engagement with China since his tour as head of the U.S. interests section in Beijing in 1972–1974, pressed the Chinese government to cease the repression of prodemocracy dissidents and, in the national security field, to join in the Nuclear Nonproliferation Treaty and the Missile Technology Control Regime (MTCR). But he stopped short of threatening unilateral sanctions beyond the initial legislated package of sanctions on military sales, OPIC, and TDP. He publicly joined in the boycott of senior-level contacts with Chinese leaders, but in July 1989, only a month after Tiananmen Square, his national security adviser, Brent Scowcroft, and Deputy Secretary of State Lawrence Eagleburger, traveled secretly to China. They tried to negotiate an easing of the repression and other concessions so as to get U.S.-China relations back on a more positive track, but their initiative produced only modest results, such as the suspension of martial law and the release of some prisoners, partly because of divisions in the Chinese leadership. When the secret mission became public after an open second visit in December, the Bush administration was severely criticized by congressional leaders of both parties for deceit about the secret visit and a weak, ineffective overall U.S. response to the Tiananmen Square massacre.

The Bush administration campaign for MFN renewal in early 1990 thus faced far more active and concerted opposition in Congress than it had the previous year, when the president had announced renewal shortly before the massacre and Congress, in the immediate aftermath, allowed the 90-day period to lapse without a vote. By mid-1990, the rest of the world was largely back to normal relations with China, and the Chinese economy, which had faced considerable difficulties during the 12 months after Tiananmen Square, was beginning to recover from the relatively low average GDP growth of 4 percent in 1989 and 1990 to 10 percent in 1991. Withdrawal of MFN access to the U.S. market would have dealt a significant blow to Chinese exports—as described in the following section—but overall economic vulnerability, and thus U.S. leverage from the threat of MFN withdrawal, was receding rapidly from the 1989 high point. Nevertheless, continuing moral outrage over Chinese repression and criticism of Bush administration pusillanimity in the face of such repression was widely popular in the United States, and resistance to economic sanctions against China was politically unappealing to members of Congress. The president was committed to MFN renewal,[2] but the ultimate threat of what could be considered an irrational congressional override of a presidential veto became credible. The president was able to avoid a negative congressional vote and thus the need to sustain a presidential veto in 1990, but in 1991 anti-MFN political pressures continued to grow. Congresswoman Nancy Pelosi (D-Calif.) introduced legislation linking human rights objectives to continued MFN treatment, which passed the House in October by 409 to 21.[3]

The showdown in the Senate came in early 1992, with Majority Leader George Mitchell heading the campaign for a human rights linkage to MFN treatment. Bush administration appeals to the Chinese government, buttressed by the threat of a congressional veto override, produced only a few token releases of political prisoners. The January State Department human rights report on China stated that during 1991 China was a repressive regime, "falling far short of internationally accepted norms." In February, however, President Bush rallied a veto-sustaining 39 votes in the Senate, thanks in part to support from five Democratic farm-state senators led by Senator Max Baucus of Montana. Farmers remembered the futile unilateral sanctions on U.S. grain exports to the Soviet Union in 1981 when the Soviets simply shifted their grain purchases to Australia, Canada, and other suppliers.

The defeat of the Pelosi/Mitchell legislation ended the Bush administration phase of the debate over linking MFN renewal to human rights objectives in China. The threatened congressional override of the president's stand against such a linkage did not materialize, but neither was the president willing or able to use a rather credible threat forcefully to obtain a substantial easing of Chinese repression against prodemocracy dissidents. The entire balance of political forces within the United States for and against an MFN linkage to human rights, however, was about to change. Democratic congressional leaders forced President Bush to exercise his veto of human rights conditions on MFN renewal on September 18, just before the presidential elections, on the grounds that an unpopular veto would add to his electoral defeat. The Democratic challenger, Bill Clinton, who had denounced Bush for having "let his friendships in China obscure what those kids did in Tiananmen Square," stated in his campaign manifesto: "We believe that the Bush administration erred by extending most-favored-nation trade status to the Peoples' Republic of China before it achieved documented progress on human rights. We should not reward China with improved trade status when it has continued to trade goods made by prison labor and has failed to make sufficient progress on human rights since the Tiananmen Square massacre."[4]

Capitulation and delinkage: 1993–1994.   Candidate Bill Clinton's definitive statement on China policy, in an October foreign policy speech, criticized Bush in general for his "ambivalence about supporting democracy" and then specified that "there is no more striking example of President Bush's indifference to democracy than his policy toward China . . . I do not want to isolate China. . . . but I believe our nation has a higher purpose than to coddle dictators and stand aside from the global movement toward democracy."[5] Together with his commitment to link MFN renewal to human rights, Clinton had thrown down the gauntlet for a renewed and more direct confrontation with China over democratization and human rights. Circumstances in China, however, had evolved considerably in the more than three years since Tiananmen Square. The Chinese economy with its booming 14 to 15 percent annual growth during 1992–1993 could much better withstand the reduced access to the U.S. market from MFN withdrawal. In parallel, U.S. direct investment in China had grown from $400 million in 1989 to $900 million in 1993, and corresponding U.S. exports were up from $5.8 billion to $8.8 billion. These increases would galvanize strong opposition in the U.S. business community to an MFN withdrawal that would inevitably lead to retaliation against U.S. investments in and exports to China. The United States, by this time, no longer had any support from friends and allies for economic sanctions against China, and all others opposed MFN withdrawal. The January 1993 State Department human rights report on China, moreover, was mixed, reiterating that China's human rights practices fell far short of accepted norms, including show trials of dissidents, arbitrary arrests, and torture of prisoners, but also noting the "more positive" development that 80 percent of prodemocracy advocates imprisoned after Tiananmen Square had been released. For China policy, the big question facing the new president was thus what to do about his campaign commitment for an MFN/human rights linkage.

After his electoral victory, President Clinton toned down the rhetoric and placed greater emphasis on the need to work toward a more cooperative relationship with China, but he remained firm in his commitment to condition MFN renewal on Chinese human rights performance. The new foreign policy team sought to develop a specific MFN/human rights proposal that could produce results in negotiations with the Chinese government while obtaining the support of Congress, including Congresswoman Pelosi and

Senator Mitchell. Debate within the administration intensified as the June 3 deadline for a presidential MFN renewal decision approached, with some senior members, including Secretary of the Treasury Lloyd Bentsen, Secretary of Commerce Ronald Brown, and head of the newly established National Economic Council Robert Rubin, concerned about the adverse economic consequences of a withdrawal of MFN and preferring to delink MFN from human rights objectives. Secretary of State Warren Christopher and National Security Council director Anthony Lake, however, had the lead in formulating China policy, and Assistant Secretary of State for Asian Affairs Winston Lord, the former U.S. ambassador in Beijing until shortly before Tiananmen Square and a preelection public advocate of an MFN/human rights linkage, was tasked with developing specific proposals. Lord held a series of meetings in Beijing in May without making significant headway on human rights objectives or other outstanding issues, but he still believed that a carefully drawn, modest MFN/human rights linkage could produce positive results. He was also constrained by the fact that Clinton's foreign policy had gotten off to an appalling start elsewhere in its reversing or backing off from campaign commitments for Haiti, Somalia, and Bosnia. Maintaining the MFN/human rights linkage for China, with support from Democratic congressional leaders, was considered essential.

The Clinton decision to officially link MFN to human rights took the form of a May 28 executive order proclaiming that the president would renew MFN for another year, but that a further renewal in 1994 was conditioned on seven specific improvements in Chinese human rights performance. Two conditions—freedom of emigration related to Jackson-Vanik and Chinese compliance with a 1992 bilateral agreement on prison labor—required definitive resolution. But the other five conditions—concerning adherence to the Universal Declaration of Human Rights, the treatment of Tiananmen Square–related prisoners, access to prisons by international humanitarian and human rights organizations, protection of Tibet's distinctive religious and cultural heritage, and access for Voice of America broadcasts into China—were subject to an assessment by Secretary of State Christopher that "overall significant progress" had taken place. These were indeed modest conditions. The two mandatory ones required nothing new from China while "significant progress" on some but not necessarily all of the other five could be assessed flexibly.

This relatively weak package of linkages nevertheless received the support of Pelosi and Mitchell, who then withdrew their legislative proposals for much tougher conditions, and no attempt was made by Congress to contest the president's renewal decision. Even some private sector leaders were relieved at the relatively modest package of demands that could form the basis for a negotiated solution. The Chinese government was reportedly pleased in private that MFN treatment would continue for another year, but publicly denounced the link with human rights: "The Chinese government hereby expresses its strong opposition to the U.S. move and lodges a protest with the U.S. government. . . . Any attempt to impose one's way on others will go nowhere. We hope that the U.S. government will size up the situation, change its course, and correct its erroneous practice on the MFN issue."[6]

The following 12 months was a period of gathering momentum toward a showdown between the United States and China over the MFN/human rights linkage. The U.S. strategy was to engage an intensive dialogue through cabinet-level and other high-level visits to Beijing, and some elements of progress initially emerged—for example, on the prison labor agreement and Red Cross inspections. By the beginning of 1994, however, the Chinese position hardened, and a few token releases of political prisoners was more than offset by a general tightening of repression against prodemocracy dissidents. The reasons for this change in Chinese attitude are not clear. There were divisions within the Chinese leadership, and the hard-liners may simply have carried the day. The Chinese surely understood that even modest concessions to a human rights/MFN linkage in 1994 could have led to greater U.S. demands the following year. The U.S. side also, however, made a tactical blunder by not holding together in support of the linkage. The economic agencies, faced with a mounting campaign from U.S. business leaders for unconditional MFN renewal, became more outspoken against linkage, which leaked into the press.

Most important, the president appeared indecisive by not publicly supporting Secretary of State Christopher's determined negotiations with the Chinese. The critical point was Christopher's visit to Beijing in March. Chinese officials flatly rejected U.S. demands for human rights commitments, and Prime Minister Li Peng informed Christopher: "China will never accept the U.S. human rights concept. History has already proven that it is futile to apply pressure on China."[7] This rebuff threw the Clinton administration into a state of confusion as the June 3 deadline for decision approached. Secretary Christopher made his assessment that "overall significant progress" had not been achieved. A last-minute attempt to formulate a partial withdrawal of MFN to products made by the Chinese state sector, or by the hundreds of companies run by the Chinese military, was rejected on the grounds that it would create a legal and administrative nightmare. On May 27, with unusual bluntness, President Clinton announced that China's economic and strategic importance had grown so great that he would renew MFN without conditions: "I am moving, therefore, to delink human rights from the annual extension of most-favored-nation trading status for China. . . . We have reached the end of the usefulness of that policy."[8]

The president was duly criticized for his humiliating capitulation with references to his having adopted the Bush policy of coddling dictators. An exasperated Winston Lord, informing the Chinese ambassador of the president's decision, commented: "You said this way was going to be more productive . . . now prove it."[9] The Chinese government, however, proved otherwise by tightening antidemocracy repression further in subsequent months. Thus the threatened use of broad unilateral economic sanctions through MFN withdrawal against China as a means for promoting U.S. human rights objectives came to an inglorious end. The annual review process and congressional debate continue, but President Clinton has remained firm in delinking human rights from MFN renewal, and there has been no further significant threat of congressional override of a presidential veto of a negative vote. In 1997, a majority House vote supported unconditional MFN renewal, and in 1998 the majority grew larger, to 264–166.

Other Mostly Unilateral Economic Sanctions

Parallel with the debate over withholding of MFN status—a comprehensive unilateral sanction whereby the high duties on all U.S. imports from China would inevitably lead to broadly based Chinese retaliation against U.S. exports and investment—a wide range of other economic sanctions, mostly targeted on particular goods or services, have been imposed or threatened against China. They vary greatly as to content and objective, and to a large extent they are linked to multilateral commitments in the national security field. But the economic sanction itself can be unilateral or in some cases applied more stringently by the United States than it is by other trading nations, which by the definition adopted in this study would make the differential a form of unilateral sanction. In the aggregate, these mostly unilateral sanctions have had a significant adverse impact on U.S. exports to and investment in China, but with mixed results in terms of the foreign policy objectives. The experience can be summarized in terms of five groupings.

1. The Tiananmen sanctions. In the aftermath of Tiananmen Square, Congress unanimously adopted a package of selected sanctions that halted the OPIC and TDA programs and banned the export of arms and military-related equipment.[10] The arms sanctions are multilateral because they are applied together with NATO and other allies, but the OPIC and TDA sanctions are unilateral—that is, other industrialized country governments have continued to provide their companies investment insurance and preproject technical assistance—and have significant adverse effects on U.S. investment in China. Moreover, the OPIC and TDA sanctions are no longer linked to any particular foreign policy objective, and because the president has the authority to waive them if it serves the national interest, they will probably be lifted at some convenient point.

2. Nuclear nonproliferation and peaceful nuclear cooperation. This comes closest to being an example of how a targeted unilateral sanction on U.S. exports helped to achieve a U.S. foreign policy objective—namely, strengthened Chinese commitments on nuclear nonproliferation—although at significant cost to U.S. commercial interests.[11] The Atomic Energy Act of 1954 requires the United States to negotiate a bilateral agreement for nuclear cooperation with each nation before permitting the export of nuclear power plants and related fuel and services. By the early 1980s, China indicated that it would oppose nuclear weapons proliferation, which led to the 1985 bilateral agreement with the United States on peaceful nuclear cooperation. The United States did not implement the agreement, however, because of reports that China was providing weapons-related nuclear assistance to nations such as Pakistan and Iran, and U.S. export restrictions in the nuclear sector were in fact tightened after Tiananmen Square. The mutual interest in nonproliferation and peaceful nuclear cooperation nevertheless increased during the 1990s. China acceded to the Nuclear Nonproliferation Treaty in 1992 as well as to its extension in 1995, worked closely with the United States to halt North Korea's nuclear weapons program, and signed the Comprehensive Nuclear Test Ban in 1996. In parallel, China contracted 8 joint ventures with foreign companies to build electric power nuclear reactors—4 French, 2 Canadian, and 2 Russian—with plans for about 20 more reactor projects over the coming 20 years. A key early decision for such an ambitious peaceful nuclear program is standardization of reactor design for reasons of safety and effective management. China expressed interest in the U.S. technologies, purported to be safer, more reliable, and more cost competitive than other existing technologies, but could not take bids on them until the U.S. government lifted the export restrictions.

This growing mutual interest in nonproliferation and peaceful nuclear cooperation set the stage for the October 1997 agreement during the U.S. visit of Chinese president Jiang Zemin. China undertook additional commitments to prevent the transfer of nuclear weapons technology to third countries, including full membership in the Zangger Committee, the nuclear exporters group of the Nuclear Nonproliferation Treaty. President Clinton, in turn, certified he had "clear and unequivocal" assurances from China on nonproliferation and requested congressional approval of the bilateral agreement that would, inter alia, lift the export restrictions on nuclear power reactors. Congress approved the agreement in March

1998. Thus the negotiations over lifting the targeted export sanctions appeared to have been a significant incentive for Chinese nonproliferation commitments, although some observers believe that evolving Chinese geopolitical interests in restraining the proliferation of nuclear weapons to South Asia and elsewhere was the overriding reason why China agreed to the 1997 commitments. In any event, the linkage of U.S. commercial nuclear exports to Chinese nonproliferation commitments took place under unique circumstances. The U.S. export ban on light-water reactors was unrelated to the already advanced Chinese nuclear weapons program, but the entire package was limited to the nuclear technology sector. China wanted access to superior U.S. technology, design, and services for electric power reactors, while the United States faced being shut out of a prospective large export market if non-U.S. technologies became the Chinese standard. In effect, there was a window of mutual commercial opportunity in the mid-1990s, and both sides moved to take advantage of it in the context of enhanced Chinese commitments with respect to nuclear nonproliferation.

   3. Ballistic missile proliferation. Targeted sanctions on U.S. advanced technology exports to China, particularly in the commercial satellite sector, have been used as a deterrent to Chinese shipments of ballistic missile technology and equipment to third countries such as Pakistan and Iran, although implementation has been irregular with limited if any positive foreign policy results. Sanctions on the use of Chinese launch services for U.S.-produced and marketed commercial satellites figure prominently in this experience, as in the following section on Chinese military modernization, and a technical note of explanation is thus in order. Such launch services are available primarily in four countries—the United States, France, Kazakhstan (Russian facilities), and China—and are in short supply. In 1998, there was a waiting line of two to three years for launching a commercial satellite, and U.S. satellite producers, who hold 60 to 70 percent of the world market (including Hughes, Motorola, and Loral), depend on launch availability to make sales. If scheduled Chinese launch services are sanctioned, the U.S. company can face stiff penalties for any delay or higher costs for shifting to alternative launch services. The Chinese launch company, in contrast, can easily replace U.S. company launches with European or other commercial satellite producers eager to obtain an earlier and generally lower-cost place in the Chinese waiting line. A similar disadvantage faces U.S. suppliers of components for European-built satellites if the components could be sanctioned, which is an incentive for non-U.S. producers to avoid U.S. components if the alternative cost is not excessive.

In 1989, after Tiananmen Square, President Bush banned exports of U.S. commercial satellites and satellite components for launch in China, and this sanction was codified in the February 1990 Foreign Relations Authorization Act, subject to presidential waiver. However, President Bush had already begun a policy of waiving the sanctions in December 1989, when he approved waivers for three satellite projects, including one to be launched by a Chinese end-user. Additional sanctions-related legislation passed in 1990, the Arms Export Control Act and Export Administration Act, which required the United States to apply sanctions against proliferating companies, including those that provide ballistic missile technology or equipment to third countries in violation of the multilateral MTCR. Because no other MTCR member threatens or applies such actions, the U.S. sanctions experience in this area has been strictly unilateral.

In May 1991, two Chinese companies—including the China Great Wall Industry Corporation, which launches commercial satellites—were found to have sold missile technology to Pakistan, and the Bush administration restricted waivers for U.S. satellite launches as well as the sale of U.S. satellite components for use in Chinese communications satellites. In March 1992, after the Chinese government had promised to observe MTCR guidelines, but not to officially join the regime, President Bush again lifted the related sanctions on exports of components for communications satellites and subsequently approved waivers for six satellite projects in September of that year. President Clinton initially continued the policy of routinely approving waivers for satellite projects until August 1993, when China was found to have transferred M-11 missile technology to Pakistan. The president imposed sanctions on 11 Chinese companies, affecting up to $1 billion of annual advanced technology exports to China, including $500 million in the commercial satellite sector, and banned the use of Chinese launch services for U.S. commercial satellites. By November 1993, however, in the face of strong complaints from American companies threatened by European competitors, the Clinton administration reversed its earlier position of insisting on formal Chinese accession to the MTCR and resumed the approval of export licenses for commercial satellites. In November 1994, with new Chinese assurances to observe MTCR guidelines, but still not join the regime, the Clinton administration lifted the 1993 sanctions and followed a prompt and basically routine waiver procedure through the middle of 1998 for commercial satellite launches.

This whole experience of on-again, off-again U.S. unilateral sanctions, especially on the use of Chinese commercial satellite launch services, achieved little in terms of restraining Chinese ballistic missile-related sales to third countries, while incurring adverse impact on the U.S. commercial satellite industry, at least in terms of contract delay and reduced reliability as a supplier. As for Chinese disciplines on third-country exports, the July 1998 Rumsfeld Commission report on the ballistic missile threat to the United States concluded that it is unlikely that China "will soon reduce its . . . sizable transfer of critical technologies, exports, or expertise to the emerging missile powers."[12] This overall discouraging sanctions experience was complicated further in the summer of 1998 by a failed Chinese satellite launch and its possible impact on Chinese ballistic missile capability, as explained below.

4. Chinese military modernization.   Slowing the Chinese program of military modernization is an important U.S. foreign policy objective for which unilateral sanctions have played a relatively small role. Most U.S. export restrictions related to Chinese military modernization are part of multilateral arrangements and are thus not unilateral sanctions as defined in this study. Restrictions on technology and goods useful to the production of conventional weapons are coordinated within the 1996 Wassenaar Arrangement, the successor of the Coordinating Committee for Multilateral Export Controls (CoCom), and those useful to the production of weapons of mass destruction and ballistic missiles are coordinated by members of the Nuclear Suppliers Group (NSG), the Australia Group, and the MTCR. These multilateral arrangements exercise some restraint on Chinese military modernization, but they are largely undercut by Russian sales to China of advanced weapons systems and technical assistance, including supersonic antiship cruise missiles, submarines with wake-honing torpedoes, and advanced jet fighters.

The unilateral sanctions dimension of this issue pertains to where U.S. export restrictions go beyond those imposed by other members of the multilateral groups. A ban on the export of commercial satellites and related equipment, for example, is clearly in this category because they are not included in any of the multilateral arrangements. Far more complicated are "dual-use" goods and services acknowledged in the multilateral arrangements to have both civilian and military uses. For them the scope and process for export license restrictions vary greatly, and a more restrictive U.S. implementation would involve a degree of unilateral sanction.

The experience during the 1990s has been that U.S. export licensing of dual-use goods and services has been progressively liberalized to the point where the product definitions appear to be roughly comparable to those of other industrialized country members of the multilateral arrangements, although these definitions, which evolve over time, can vary to some extent by sector. For example, the United States prohibits the export to China of semiconductor equipment used in the production of wafers with lining width at or below 0.7 microns, while the Japanese Nippon Electric Company won a joint-venture contract to process wafers with lining width of 0.5 microns, later to be reduced to 0.35.[13] For export licenses for the high performance or supercomputer sector, the United States has been out in front of its allies in liberalizing standards, reflecting the dominant position of American companies in this market. In terms of million theoretical operations per second, or MTOPS, the earlier CoCom limit of 195 MTOPS was raised by the United States first to 2,000 and then to 7,000, with an estimated 100 to 150 of such U.S. computers sold to China during 1996–1997.[14]

In the late 1990s, the policy of dual-use export-licensing restrictions, for China and other nonmembers of the multilateral arrangements, has become more complex with respect to both definition of products and end-use monitoring. The definition problem is caused by the rapid advances in technology whereby a wider and wider range of basic components and services for advanced technology industries also have potential military application. An important element of the U.S. defense modernization program, or the "Revolution in Military Affairs," is to use "commercial, off-the-shelf technologies," or COTS, which can be the same technologies exported on a major scale to commercial markets abroad, including China. End-use monitoring is becoming correspondingly more difficult, if not impossible, and is therefore only feasible for a limited number of the most sensitive goods.

Growing concerns within Congress over the effectiveness of U.S. controls on dual-use exports came to a head in the summer of 1998 over a failed Chinese satellite launch. The reported post-launch technical analysis shared with the Chinese by the American commercial satellite supplier, Loral, may have helped the Chinese military improve the accuracy of its long-range ballistic missiles. One result was a legislative change in the National Defense Authorization Act for FY 1999 that transferred satellites previously controlled under the Commerce Department's Commerce Control List back to the State Department's Munitions List, thereby shifting export-licensing authority to State. This new procedure will at least slow down the process of export license review, although the legislation includes funds to institute a faster application process.

In August, another result of congressional concern was the establishment of the Select Committee on U.S. National Security and Military/Commercial Concerns with the People's Republic of China, chaired by Congressman Christopher Cox (R-Calif.), with a broad mandate focused on missiles and rockets, manufacturing, and supercomputers. The 700-page committee report was completed in December 1998, but was classified secret, and only excerpts of its conclusions and recommendations were made public. The recommendations apparently concentrate on the "urgent priority" to implement a U.S. counterintelligence program against Chinese espionage to obtain U.S. technologies. There are also recommendations, however, to tighten export licensing and end-use monitoring for U.S. exports to China, particularly in the commercial satellite sector.

The first significant result of the new export-licensing procedures, influenced by the concerns expressed in the Cox Committee
report, was the administration's rejection in February 1999 of an
export license request by the Hughes Company for a $450 million
commercial satellite to be launched in China, which could involve
some Chinese military participation. Hughes reportedly has to pay
China $100 million in penalties for not fulfilling the contract.

The U.S. interest in Chinese military modernization ranges
well beyond the scope of this study, which is limited to the impact
of the unilateral economic sanction dimension of export-licensing
restrictions. Such restrictions can have some restraining impact on
military modernization, although at significant cost to U.S.
commercial interests, as in the case for restrictions on commercial
satellite exports or more generally for the more costly and time-
consuming U.S. requirements for export licensing and end-use
monitoring compared with European, Japanese, and other competitors. As for the broader challenge to U.S. foreign policy, however, which has been defined in terms of an "effective American
deterrence of the use of force by China, whether the use of force is
the result of malign intent or just exuberant miscalculation,"[15]
export sanctions, multilateral as well as unilateral, can only be one
relatively small part of the response.

5. Miscellaneous sanctions unrelated to national security.
Various other targeted economic sanctions against China have been
proposed, mostly unrelated to U.S. national security interests as in
the previous three categories, and each of which has to be judged
on its own merits. One is the recurring proposal to sanction
Chinese exports by the more than 1,500 companies controlled or
operated by the Chinese military. The purpose would be to punish
the military suppression at Tiananmen Square or to restrain profits
and thus financial resources available to the military. The overriding technical problem, as noted earlier in the context of the MFN
debate, is that such restrictions would create a legal and administrative nightmare, including the fact that thousands of other nonmili-
tary Chinese companies are suppliers to or purchasers from the
military companies. In any event, in July 1998, President Jiang
ordered the army to dismantle its commercial firms, which, if and
when implemented, would terminate the U.S. concerns.[16]

Another example—the Freedom from Religious Persecution Act signed by President Clinton in October 1998—takes selective actions against governments that practice religious persecution, which will prominently include China. The Clinton administration strongly opposed earlier versions of this legislation on the grounds that it would be overly rigid in application and potentially counterproductive. It is not clear whether the final, much watered-down version will actually lead to the imposition of significant economic sanctions.

Yet another example are proposals to prohibit U.S. imports from China of goods made with prison labor, related to the 1992 bilateral agreement with China that has not been satisfactorily implemented. The United States has a strong case for unilateral sanctions in this instance, and indeed such sanctions would be permitted under WTO commitments and procedures. One U.S. option, once China joins the WTO, would thus be to bring a complaint within the WTO dispute process under threat of WTO-sponsored sanctions if China did not convincingly cease such practices.

~ ~ ~

The foregoing summarizes the recent and ongoing U.S. policy process for unilateral economic sanctions against China. There are important differences between the experience with comprehensive sanctions as threatened by withdrawal of MFN status and other sanctions, mostly targeted on advanced-technology goods and services related to U.S. national security interests. The economic impact of these threatened or actual sanctions, both on the Chinese economy and on U.S. commercial interests, is addressed in the next section, followed by an overall assessment of U.S. unilateral sanctions policy toward China.

A final note here concerns the distinction between unilateral sanctions for foreign policy objectives, which is the subject of this study, and sanctions threatened or applied within the context of the international trading system. The threat of unilateral trade sanctions is an integral part of the multilateral WTO trading system as a discipline for maintaining mutually open markets, and even though China is not yet a member of the WTO, the same conceptual framework applies. Thus, U.S. threats in 1996 to restrict specified imports from China unless China reduced violations of U.S. intellectual property rights was a highly credible threat that led to a negotiated resolution of the immediate problem. The point highlighted here is that such use of trade sanctions within the trade relationship is not addressed in this study of foreign policy–directed sanctions and should be considered in the quite different policy framework of the international trading system, notwithstanding occasional relatively small overlapping issues such as prison labor.

2. Economic Impact

On the Chinese Economy

As in the preceding narrative summary, the economic impact of U.S. unilateral sanctions against China is assessed first for MFN withdrawal and then for the other targeted sanctions on U.S. exports. The distinction is made partly because MFN withdrawal was threatened but never imposed—thus the impact has to be projected rather than observed—and partly because the analytic framework for assessing the economic impact is very different between MFN withdrawal and targeted sanctions.

MFN withdrawal. The withdrawal of MFN status for imports from China would raise the trade-weighted U.S. tariff level from 6 percent on an MFN basis to a very high 44 percent with non-MFN Smoot-Hawley rates, resulting in a significant loss for Chinese exports and consequent adverse impact on overall Chinese economic performance. Because the purpose of MFN withdrawal, as for any other foreign policy–motivated economic sanction, is to inflict economic pain on the target country to the point where the government changes its political behavior—in the case of China, an improved human rights performance, in particular—key analytic questions must be asked to assess whether MFN withdrawal would achieve its foreign policy objectives. How much would Chinese exports actually decline if MFN status were withdrawn, and what would be the impact of such a decline in exports on the overall performance of the Chinese economy, such as the level of GDP? A second order of more speculative questions involves the anticipated retaliation by China against U.S. exports and investment that, while designed principally to punish U.S. commercial interests, would also cause some additional negative impact on the Chinese economy.

Surprisingly, to say the least, no such analysis was conducted in a systematic way within the U.S. government during the years of intensive debate over MFN withdrawal. In February 1994, only three months before President Clinton's decision to delink MFN from human rights, the World Bank first produced an estimate of the impact of MFN withdrawal on Chinese exports, based on a partial equilibrium model for 15 core products and sectors covering a little more than half of total Chinese exports to the United States, which was then extrapolated to estimate the total impact on Chinese exports.[17] A more comprehensive assessment was published in 1997 by two economists at the U.S. International Trade Commission, Hugh Arce and Christopher Taylor, using a multi-country "applied general equilibrium" model and detailed data covering virtually all U.S. imports from China.[18] This latter study, incidentally, was not requested by the executive branch or members of Congress, but was done at the initiative of the two economists on an independent basis.

The World Bank study estimated a decline in Chinese exports from U.S. withdrawal of MFN status of $7 billion to $15 billion, based on 1990 trade, which is roughly consistent with the more definitive $11 billion estimated decline, based on 1992 trade, by Arce and Taylor. Two-thirds of the $11 billion was in four product categories—toys, apparel and clothing, footwear, and telecommunications and sound equipment—and in these categories the average tariff increase from MFN withdrawal is especially large (from 12 to 68 percent for apparel, and from 3 to 60 percent for "other manufactures," which includes the other three categories). The $11 billion represents slightly more than half of total U.S. imports from China and 13 percent of total Chinese exports. The net impact on Chinese exports would be lower, however, because some of the lost Chinese exports to the U.S. market would be diverted to other markets, although such diversion would occur over a considerably longer time period compared with the immediate decline in Chinese exports to the United States from the imposition of very high, non-MFN tariff rates. Arce and Taylor estimate a net drop in Chinese exports of only $2 billion to $3 billion, but this represents the longer-term equilibrium result. Finally, Arce and Taylor estimate a decline of $6 billion, or 0.4 percent, in Chinese GDP from MFN withdrawal, but again the immediate short-term decline, before export diversion, would be greater—on the order of 1 to 2 percent.

The Arce/Taylor estimates based on 1992 trade coincide with the first MFN confrontation in Washington—the Bush veto and the threatened congressional override of legislation linking MFN status to human rights objectives. Moving forward to 1994, the time of President Clinton's threatened withdrawal of MFN if China did not undertake human rights commitments, a larger loss in Chinese exports to the United States would have occurred in view of the rapid growth in exports from 1992 to 1994. The $11 billion figure would rise to about $16 billion, although still representing 13 percent of total Chinese exports. The loss of Chinese GDP would also be slightly higher because exports had grown faster than GDP.

The additional adverse impact on the Chinese economy from retaliation against U.S. exports and investment would probably be small because China would be selective in choosing products and industries that could be most readily and efficiently substituted by third-country suppliers—Airbus for Boeing, French or other suppliers for GE electric generators, Japanese for American suppliers of less-than-super computers, and, of course, non-American suppliers of grains and other basic agricultural commodities. If total U.S. exports to China of $7 billion in 1992 and $9 billion in 1994 were cut back by half, the additional cost to China from buying such imports from alternative sources would probably be no more than several hundred million dollars per year. The impact from retaliation against U.S. direct investment in China is more difficult to assess. The total flow of U.S. investment to China in these years was about $1 billion per year, with the cumulative total of U.S. investment rising to $600 million in 1992 and $2.8 billion in 1995. This U.S. direct investment flow, however, represented only 3 percent of total foreign direct investment into China, with most investment coming from Taiwan, Hong Kong, Japan, and Europe. China, again, would selectively punish existing and potential U.S. investors so as to minimize negative effects on the Chinese economy.

The overall impact of U.S. MFN withdrawal on the Chinese economy in 1992 and 1994 would thus have been significant but relatively small. Chinese exports would be down a maximum of 13 percent, and probably considerably less over time. Similarly, Chinese GDP would have been down initially on the order of 1 to 2 percent, including the likely small impact from retaliation against U.S. exports and investment. This assessment is less harsh than most media and other comments that came out during the course of the annual MFN debate in Washington would indicate, with a corresponding misperception of the economic leverage wielded by the United States in threatening MFN withdrawal.

Other mostly targeted unilateral sanctions.   The critical judgments for this assessment are the degree to which the sanctions are applied unilaterally—as distinct from multilateral sanctions—and how the unilateral sanctions affect the Chinese economy. The ban on U.S. military exports to China, for example, is generally adhered to by other industrialized countries and thus is not addressed in this assessment, although this sanction falls short of being fully multilateral in view of Chinese military purchases from Russia. In a few instances, however, targeted sanctions have been clearly unilateral while the important category of dual-use sanctions is not well defined.

U.S. sanctions on light-water nuclear reactors, which were clearly unilateral, did require China to look elsewhere for its first eight joint-venture projects in the nuclear power field and presumably to pay a higher price in the absence of competitive U.S. bidding. It is doubtful, however, that the cost to the Chinese economy was more than a few billion dollars spread over 10 years. This unilateral sanction in any event ended with the October 1997 bilateral agreement, subsequently approved by Congress.

The on-again, off-again ban on U.S. use of Chinese launch services for American-made commercial satellites in response to alleged Chinese MTCR violations has had little if any impact on China because non-U.S. commercial satellite suppliers stand ready to replace U.S. suppliers in the waiting line for such services. The relatively briefly enforced restraints on other advanced technology exports, especially related to telecommunications satellites and components for Chinese end-users and manufacturers, presumably had some adverse effect on the Chinese economy, although it was probably small because of the short periods of time involved.

The impact of U.S. export restrictions on Chinese military modernization is the most difficult to assess, and no overall judgment is offered here, although the unilateral sanction dimension of such restrictions is in any event relatively small. The Cox Committee report and follow-up review should shed further light on this subject, but the U.S. policy response, as addressed more fully in the section below on alternatives to current sanctions policy, lies principally in policy areas other than unilateral sanctions.

A final sanction that is clearly unilateral but not targeted on particular products is the closing down of OPIC and TDA programs as part of the "Tiananmen sanctions." The exclusion of China from these normal support programs for U.S. investment in developing countries has been a constraint on U.S. investment in China, but probably to a small degree. U.S. investment in any event comprises only 2 to 3 percent of total foreign investment in China. If China wants to attract a particular U.S. investment because of superior technology or other reasons, incentives can be offered to offset the absence of the investment insurance and feasibility studies support provided by OPIC and TDA. The negative investment climate engendered by the Asian financial crisis increases the potential benefits of OPIC and TDA programs, but such programs, if reopened in China, would still have only a small effect on total foreign direct investment in China.

Overall, then, U.S. targeted and other unilateral sanctions did have some significant adverse impact on the Chinese economy up through the early 1990s—particularly for nuclear power reactors and advanced technology goods and services in general—but such impact was largely phased out by early 1998. The basic review and reformulation of U.S. export licensing for dual-use and sensitive technology products begun in mid-1998, however, including the

Cox Committee findings, could lead to a more restrictive approach that would have some negative effect on the Chinese economy.

On U.S. Commercial Interests

An assessment of the negative impact on U.S. commercial interests and the U.S. economy from unilateral sanctions against China also must distinguish the threatened withdrawal of MFN status from the actual, mostly targeted sanctions.

MFN withdrawal. The Arce/Taylor study estimates a drop in 1992 U.S. real income of $422 million, or 0.04 percent of GDP, from MFN withdrawal, caused by the shift to higher-cost alternative sources for imports from China. The direct cost to consumers, although considerably higher, would be largely offset by the increased tax revenues from the higher duties levied on remaining imports from China. This relatively small impact reflects the fact that China represented only 6 to 7 percent of total U.S. imports in 1992–1994 and that the third-country substitution effect would work against Chinese exports in this case as it does for U.S. exports in the other direction.

The more important consequences for U.S. commercial interests would result from the anticipated retaliation by China against U.S. exports to and investment in China. If China had cut back imports from the United States by 50 percent (comparable to the estimated effect on Chinese exports to the United States), it would have meant a loss of up to $4 billion of U.S. exports in 1992 and $5 billion in 1994. This can again be considered a maximum loss because some U.S. exports would also be redirected to other markets, although such a shift is less likely for technology-intensive U.S. exports where project-related markets are relatively finite. It would certainly be the case for commercial jet aircraft, where Boeing and Airbus compete directly in each country market, and would likely be generally applicable in other sectors such as telecommunications equipment, electric power generators, and agricultural machinery.

The adverse impact on U.S. investment in China is even more difficult to predict, beginning with difficulties in measuring the value of existing investment. The only U.S. figures on foreign direct investment, by country, are on a "historical basis," which indicates cumulative U.S. investment in China of $600 million in 1992 and $5 billion in 1997. Alternative measures, which are probably a more accurate reflection of actual value—that is, "market value" and "replacement cost"—roughly double the historical basis amount on a global level, although the differential would probably be smaller for China because all investments are relatively recent or, in other words, closer to the historical base.[19] How China would react to such existing as well as potential new U.S. investment if MFN were withdrawn is highly speculative. New non-American investors would certainly receive preference if their price and technology/management quality were close to U.S. bidders. Existing U.S. investment in China would also face major difficulties on a discriminatory basis.

The adverse consequences for U.S. exporters and investors would therefore likely be substantial, at least several billion dollars per year in exports, and a cumulative impact over time of billions of dollars in investment. The figures are nevertheless relatively small, again because the Chinese market, despite China's overall size and dynamic economic character, represented only a small share of total U.S. exports and direct investment in 1992–1994, the time of serious MFN debate within the U.S. government.

Finally, two important yet nonquantifiable considerations for U.S. commercial interests are the uncertainties of doing business in China in the context of an annual political debate in Washington over MFN withdrawal and the longer-term market implications for American companies if MFN were actually withdrawn. Uncertainty over possible MFN withdrawal has been a disincentive for joint-venture participants to seek American partners as compared with more secure non-U.S. partners, although this uncertainty has greatly diminished since 1994. As for longer-term market implications if MFN were, in fact, withdrawn, much would depend on what happens next and on how long MFN status is withheld, which is difficult to predict. There would have been a greater likelihood of a relatively quick negotiated settlement if Congress had overridden President Bush's veto and withdrawn MFN in 1992, as compared with a conscious decision by President Clinton to do so in 1994.

Other mostly targeted unilateral sanctions. These sanctions have or would have more substantial impact on U.S. commercial interests than on the Chinese economy because of their unilateral application and thus the ability of China to shift to other suppliers at the expense of American companies. The clearest case of adverse impact was the nuclear reactor sanctions linked to Chinese commitments on nuclear nonproliferation. American companies were unable to bid on the first eight Chinese light-water reactors, while in the absence of the sanctions Westinghouse and perhaps others would have been highly competitive bidders. For example, if American companies had won four of the eight contracts, approximately $5 billion of initial investment would have ensued, mainly to purchase U.S. exports of goods and services, while maintenance and spare parts contracts over 30 or more years of plant operations would have amounted to further multibillion dollar revenues. No new joint-venture contracts have gone forward since American companies became eligible to participate in the spring of 1998. It is not clear to what extent non-American companies will have a competitive edge for future projects. Chinese plant managers and government officials have become accustomed to the technologies of the non-American companies, whose significant advantage grows year by year in the absence of American companies in the Chinese nuclear power sector.

Export-licensing restrictions and other sanctions related to ballistic missile proliferation and Chinese military modernization are more difficult to quantify. The on-again, off-again ban on the use of Chinese launch services for commercial satellites have had and continue to have adverse impact on U.S. commercial satellite producers through penalties related to launch delay or the inability to conclude contracts. Satellite equipment suppliers to European and other non-American satellite producers have also suffered. Over the whole range of dual-use export licensing, the more costly U.S. license application procedures and end-use monitoring requirements constitute a significant competitive disadvantage for American companies compared with European, Japanese, and other exporters to China. Moreover, although most of these negative effects on U.S. exports were progressively reduced or eliminated from the early 1990s through mid-1998, this trend could be reversed, as evident in the October 1998 legislation to tighten controls on U.S. commercial satellite exports.

Finally, the shutting down of OPIC and TDA programs in China since 1989 places American companies at a competitive disadvantage. Other industrialized nations have official programs for foreign direct investment insurance, and most provide some grant assistance for such preproject activities as feasibility studies. The Japanese programs are especially generous and flexible. How much U.S. firms are disadvantaged is not clear. The OPIC and TDA experience in ASEAN provides something of a proxy for China. U.S. investment in ASEAN in 1996 was $4.5 billion compared with $1.2 billion in China, while during the same year OPIC provided $1.0 billion of investment guarantees and other facilities in ASEAN nations, and TDA provided $8 million of grant assistance, mostly for investment-related feasibility studies.

3. Net Assessment of U.S. Unilateral Sanctions Policy

This net assessment of the extent to which U.S. unilateral sanctions policy against China achieved their intended foreign policy objectives is divided, after the pattern of previous sections, into three principal and distinct components: MFN renewal linked to human rights/democratization objectives, targeted sanctions related to national security interests, and OPIC/TDA program suspension, which currently is not conditioned on any specific foreign policy objective. Indeed, it is convenient to dispose of OPIC/TDA first because it is relatively simple to assess.

OPIC/TDA.   These programs were suspended in 1989 as part of the initial "Tiananmen sanctions" package, and suspension continues after all other Tiananmen-related unilateral sanctions have been lifted. The immediate post-Tiananmen sanctions included a suspension of Exim Bank loans and were linked to other bilateral and multilateral actions to restrain Chinese persecution of prodemocracy demonstrators, but the overall sanctions policy had limited impact at best in restraining the persecution. By mid-1990, economic relations with China, including economic aid programs, were more or less back to normal, and debate in the United States focused on MFN renewal, with OPIC/TDA suspension largely ignored. With the delinking of MFN renewal from human rights objectives by President Clinton in 1994, the continued OPIC/TDA sanction was essentially cast adrift in terms of a specific foreign policy purpose. The opening of TDA and OPIC programs in Vietnam, announced in the spring of 1998, raised a further question about their continued nonoperation in China. In any event, the assessment here is that suspension of OPIC/TDA programs in China since 1989, except perhaps during the first year after Tiananmen, has produced no positive results for U.S. foreign policy.

MFN renewal linked to human rights/democratization objectives.   The experience during the 1990s of using MFN renewal as leverage to obtain improved human rights conditions that in turn support democratization leads to two conclusions and one interpretive comment. The first conclusion is that initiatives taken to link MFN renewal to human rights objectives, by Congress in 1991–1992 and by the Clinton administration in 1993–1994, were unproductive and, in some respects, had negative consequences for U.S. interests. The second conclusion is that whatever the possibilities might have been for such a linkage during those years, by 1998, with Tiananmen Square fading further back into history, the threat of MFN withdrawal has lost almost all credibility as a viable instrument of U.S. human rights/democratization policy. The interpretive comment relates to various reports and recollections about the 1991–1992 and 1993–1994 experiences: perhaps something positive could have been achieved if the United States had played the MFN economic sanctions card differently.

The unproductive and in some respects negative results of the 1991–1992 and 1993–1994 periods are explained in the foregoing narrative account. The Bush administration suffered from three years of fundamental discord over MFN and over China policy more broadly within the U.S. government. President Bush strongly opposed conditioning MFN renewal on human rights performance on the grounds that overriding geopolitical and commercial interests would have been threatened by such a high-risk confrontation.

A large bipartisan majority of Congress disagreed, however, and voted for the MFN/human rights linkage. The president did sustain his veto of congressional votes in favor of the linkage, but at considerable cost to a potentially more productive, strong bipartisan U.S. response to the Tiananmen massacre and post-Tiananmen reprisals.

President Clinton, in contrast to Bush, began by obtaining support from Congress for linking MFN renewal to human rights objectives, but was unable to negotiate significant human rights commitments from China. When in the end his bluff was called, he had to capitulate by delinking MFN renewal from human rights objectives. The net assessment is thus a clearly failed policy, including a loss in U.S. great power credibility in the eyes of the power-sensitive Chinese leadership. The failure may, as a consequence, have led to more confrontational Chinese positions on other issues. One initial shortcoming leading to this result was that candidate Bill Clinton made the commitment to link MFN renewal to human rights objectives in the context of the domestic electoral campaign, largely to attack the Bush China policy and before having thought through the issue or assembled his foreign policy team. His first meeting with Winston Lord, who would play a key role in formulating and implementing the policy, did not take place until September 1992, well after the commitment to a human rights linkage had been made.

In any event, the substantive circumstances for linkage were far less favorable in 1993 than they were in 1989–1990. Tiananmen was four years past, and there was no support elsewhere for new trade sanctions. The Chinese government was consequently more resistant to any international negotiation over human rights conditions within China. The Chinese economy, also much stronger than it was in 1989–1990, would not have suffered inordinately from MFN withdrawal, although the assessment in support of this point presented in the previous section had not been done at the time of President Clinton's official linkage in May 1993, not to mention at the time of his personal commitment as a presidential candidate a year earlier. Yet another unfavorable circumstance in 1993 that was less clear on the surface and greatly underestimated by the Clinton administration was the relatively shallow congressional support for human rights objectives compared with commercial interests in China. It was easy to take the moral high ground for human rights in 1992 in the knowledge that President Bush would veto the MFN linkage, but this changed with candidate Clinton's commitment to the linkage. U.S. trade and investment in China were growing rapidly, and members of Congress listened to their corporate constituents.

Finally, to complete the record, an interpretive comment is offered on various press reports, expert analysis, and recollections by participants in the policy process, including a number of interviews undertaken during this study, as to whether the United States might have used the threat of MFN withdrawal to more positive effect if handled differently. Once again, the circumstances were greatly different for the Bush and Clinton administrations. A key factor for the Bush administration was that the greatest vulnerability for the Chinese government, when the introduction of a credible threat of MFN withdrawal could have made a significant difference, was the 6 to 12 months immediately following the Tiananmen Square massacre. If President Bush had mobilized bipartisan congressional support for an overall tougher U.S. response, including MFN status in some threatening way, together with more sustained multilateral sanctions, perhaps a significant easing of reprisals against Tiananmen Square demonstrators could have been achieved. No conclusion is offered here on what involves a judgment of how a divided and threatened Chinese communist regime would have reacted. The Bush administration, including its senior China experts, clearly concluded that such a high-risk strategy was unlikely to succeed and was not warranted in view of overall U.S. interests in the China relationship. In any event, however, there is no doubt that the immediate post–Tiananmen Square period was the most promising time for using the threat of MFN withdrawal as a foreign policy instrument and that its potential utility declined sharply thereafter.

The speculative reports and recollections about the Clinton experience are of a different character, as described in the narrative account. The seven specific human rights improvements requested in May 1993 constituted a modest package, especially if "overall significant progress" had been assessed generously. The judgment in this case revolves around the question of whether the Chinese government might have agreed to a minimal package along these lines had the Clinton administration remained firmly united and the president publicly supportive of Secretary Christopher. No account of how the Chinese government decided to shift in early 1994 to a hard-line rejection of Christopher's demands is available. But even if, in the end, a minimally acceptable level of "significant progress" had been achieved, it would have been little more than token progress in order for President Clinton to have fulfilled his campaign pledge to link human rights and MFN renewal, with only marginal impact on the process of political change under way within China.

Targeted sanctions and national security interests.   Three principal issues in this category of unilateral sanctions are the nuclear sector sanctions linked to nuclear nonproliferation objectives, the on-again, off-again sanctions linked to Chinese exports of ballistic missile components and technology to third countries, and the wide range of dual-use export-licensing restrictions to inhibit Chinese military modernization. The nuclear sector sanctions on U.S. exports of light-water nuclear power equipment and technology are widely viewed as having had a significant positive effect in achieving U.S. objectives for Chinese commitments in the nuclear nonproliferation field. The export sanction was accomplished at considerable cost to U.S. commercial interests, however, possibly on the order of $10 billion or more, including initial exports and follow-on service and replacement parts. The strategy would have worked more effectively if U.S. allies had joined in linking commercial reactor sales to China to nonproliferation commitments, thus leaving China with Russian reactors as the only alternative. Presumably the allies were not prepared to do so, and therefore the United States made no serious attempt to develop a multilateral approach. In any event, this is a rare example of how a targeted unilateral export sanction probably helped achieve a U.S. foreign policy objective.

In contrast, the instances during the Bush and Clinton administrations when sanctions on U.S. exports of commercial satellites and other advanced technology products were imposed to pressure

China to join the MTCR and cease ballistic missile transfers to third countries did not achieve significant foreign policy results, as confirmed by the Rumsfeld Commission report. The Bush administration obtained a Chinese commitment to adopt MTCR guidelines, but without joining the MTCR, and subsequent Chinese ballistic missile shipments to third countries negated the credibility of that commitment. The Clinton administration reversed its early linkage of commercial satellite and other exports to MTCR membership as American firms faced losses to European competitors, dealing another blow to U.S. foreign policy credibility in the eyes of the Chinese leadership. Since 1994, the MTCR linkage has been abandoned.

The wide range of dual-use export-licensing restrictions related to Chinese military modernization has become less and less unilateral as the United States has liberalized export-licensing requirements for advanced-technology exports to China. Earlier unilateral restrictions—in that the United States imposed tighter standards than did its allies—may have had some restraining effect on Chinese military modernization, but in recent years, as the military modernization program gathers momentum, the unilateral dimension of U.S. sanctions has apparently become far less significant, although a detailed examination by sector is not available and would be very useful in confirming this judgment.

The most controversial sector in dual-use export restrictions is high-performance supercomputers. The United States has clearly been out front in liberalizing export restrictions as the demand for such computers grows rapidly throughout the Chinese economy in response to the information technology revolution and economic globalization, and American companies are the dominant suppliers. In this dynamic context, the definition of a high-performance computer is itself controversial. The performance level of a Cray supercomputer a decade ago can now be achieved by interconnected personal computers. The United States, as a consequence, took the initiative to increase the maximum performance level—from 195 MTOPS to 2,000 to 7,000—for computer exports to China that would not require highly conditioned export licenses. Subsequent U.S. computer sales provided substantial benefits to many Chinese industries and research institutions. In parallel,

Chinese military programs inevitably benefit, either directly through clandestine use of the computers, or indirectly through higher performance in the telecommunications, transportation, applied research, and other advanced technology sectors of the Chinese economy. Where to draw the line on performance levels of high-performance computers for export to China, related to the benefits such computers can provide to Chinese military modernization, is thus a highly technical and controversial question, and no attempt is made here to answer it.

4. Alternatives to Current Unilateral Sanctions Policy

Current U.S. policy toward China is based on "comprehensive engagement," particularly for economic relations, and a less clear "constructive, strategic partnership" with respect to U.S. national security interests. In this overall policy context, unilateral economic sanctions have been reduced to a relatively small role, although in the national security field multilateral sanctions—the ban on the export to China of armaments and certain dual-use civilian goods—are significant. Critics of this policy call for a more forceful approach to support democratization/human rights within China and to restrain weapons proliferation toward third countries and Chinese military modernization.

In terms of unilateral sanctions policy, there are two alternative courses to these ends. The first is to threaten or impose unilateral sanctions in a more substantial way, such as MFN withdrawal and more restrictive export restrictions on supercomputers and other advanced technology U.S. exports beyond those imposed by allies, with or without other basic changes in U.S. policy. The second alternative is to continue to minimize unilateral sanctions while adopting more proactive policies in other areas, principally diplomatic- and defense-related.[20] As done throughout this case study, a discussion of these alternative policy courses is presented first for human rights/democratization objectives and then for U.S. national security interests, with concluding comments on how the two are interrelated.

Human Rights/Democratization Objectives

Alternative 1: Increased use of unilateral sanctions. The principal issue remains MFN renewal, although less comprehensive, targeted sanctions also have considerable support within Congress and public interest, especially human rights and religious, groups. In view of the failed 1993–1994 MFN/human rights initiative by the Clinton administration, annual MFN renewal is now widely viewed as a virtual sure thing, but in 1998 166 members of the House still voted against unconditional renewal. Proposed legislation to restrict certain trade with China related to religious persecution had broad bipartisan support in Congress although the final version of the Freedom from Religious Persecution Act of 1998 eliminated or weakened the trade sanction provisions.

Supporters of an expanded unilateral sanctions approach, in view of recent experience, therefore need to demonstrate how such a course would in fact produce net benefits for U.S. foreign policy. During the spring of 1998, the two most frequent arguments for voting against unconditional MFN renewal were that it was a vote of no confidence in the Clinton administration's overall China policy and that MFN withdrawal would represent a statement of moral principle. But these arguments are difficult to sustain if actual implementation of the sanctions would have a net adverse impact on U.S. interests, including improved human rights in China. The moral principle argument is the familiar dilemma— "feeling good versus doing good"—encountered in the other case studies, and the consistent judgment offered here is that one cannot truly feel good by not doing good.

A central substantive argument that would have to be countered by prosanction advocates is that such sanctions provide only limited economic leverage against China, not enough to achieve the intended purposes, while in the process having particular adverse consequences. The examination of the experience during the early 1990s with the MFN/human rights linkage demonstrated how limited the economic leverage was in forcing political change on the Chinese government. In one respect, the Asian financial crisis since 1997 makes the Chinese economy more vulnerable to comprehensive sanctions on exports to the U.S. market, but the financial crisis also puts MFN withdrawal in fundamental conflict with other U.S. actions to prop up faltering Asian economies, wherein sustained economic growth in China is a linchpin to overall recovery of the regional economy. The assessment here is thus that conditional MFN for China as a credible U.S. foreign policy instrument is at a dead end. Other more targeted unilateral sanctions proposals need to be considered on their respective merits, but, in general, and including the 1998 legislation on religious persecution, the conclusion holds that the leverage is too inadequate to achieve significant positive results.

Another long-standing argument against unilateral sanctions, and especially comprehensive sanctions as would take place through MFN withdrawal, is that they would reduce U.S. private sector engagement in China as a force for positive change. This would be, in effect, one of the adverse consequences noted above and is also a recurring theme throughout the country case studies. Private sector engagement, particularly by American companies, in countries with authoritarian governments and largely state-controlled economies, such as China, can have wide-ranging positive impact for political as well as economic change.[21] Chinese working for American companies are generally treated with respect as individuals, with rewards based on merit. American companies have established voluntary profit-sharing plans with employees and employer home ownership programs. Compared with state enterprises, the far more productive modern private companies are clear models to all levels of Chinese society, including government officialdom.

American companies are also outstanding in providing training and support for community projects. U.S. law firms with offices in China play an active role in encouraging the rule of law, including training programs and visits by Chinese lawyers to the United States. AT&T donated $150,000 to train medical staff in a children's medical center, the Coca Cola Company has spent $1 million to build 50 primary schools and to provide books for 100 libraries in rural areas, and Motorola has sponsored 2,000 scholarships for Chinese students in technical schools. The fundamental values of American corporate culture are most effectively conveyed through the demonstration effect of daily contact with the Chinese people, and the message spreads. Finally, to a large extent, the media are the message, as U.S. and other telecommunications companies provide telephones, fax machines, satellite dish television, and now Internet connections to the Chinese people. Unilateral sanctions to curtail this private sector engagement, such as through withdrawal of MFN and inevitable Chinese retaliation, would greatly reduce these positive forces for political and economic change within China.

Alternative 2: Maintain MFN/open trade with more proactive support for human rights/democratization. This alternative would pursue comprehensive economic engagement in parallel with more proactive support, bilaterally and multilaterally, for democratic reforms and improved human rights conditions within China. Specific bilateral initiatives could include proposals developed by the House Policy Committee, also chaired by Congressman Cox, such as expanded Radio-Free Asia and Voice of America broadcasts in Mandarin and Cantonese and increased American Embassy staffing to monitor prison labor and other commitments by the Chinese government.[22] Multilaterally, stronger support would be given to UN and nongovernmental organizations engaged with China to promote a more open political system and greater respect for individual rights. A more proactive orientation of U.S. China policy does not mean confrontation with the Chinese government, but rather some distancing from it in ideological terms, or, to paraphrase the Clinton administration point of departure in 1993, a less coddling relationship with a still repressive communist government.

The rationale for this alternative is based on the judgment that a process of fundamental change is under way within China, in which democratic political reform and transition to a market-based economy are mutually reinforcing. The change is largely generational, with an increasingly educated and informed younger generation—including the 100,000 Chinese who have returned from university training in the United States—playing a major role, and the United States should thus reorient its China policy more heavily toward support of this younger component of the public and private sector power structure.

This alternative policy orientation is controversial. Those who see the U.S.-China relationship predominantly in geopolitical terms, in pursuit of mutual interests based on pragmatic negotiation and power relationships, would be opposed to a policy that stimulated a higher level of ideological friction. Some U.S. business interests, dependent on supportive actions by the Chinese government, could also be adversely affected. This approach would, however, appeal to those critics who believe that current U.S. policy is driven principally by commercial interests and at the expense of broader U.S. foreign policy objectives, and who espouse unilateral sanctions as a second-best solution while searching for a better alternative. For example, Gary Bauer, head of the Family Research Council, while sympathetic to unilateral sanctions, acknowledged U.S. private sector engagement as a force for positive change but wants something more:[23]

> Q [*Business Week* correspondent]: The administration's engagement policy with China is based on the premise that the magic of the marketplace will break down Marxist ideology. Do you dispute this?
>
> A [Bauer]: This clearly is not Mao's China. I'm sure part of the change has been due to interaction with the West. But I can make a more convincing case that trade with China is changing us rather than changing them. Suddenly, because of the fear of losing contracts, we begin to quiet our rhetoric on human rights.

The net assessment of this alternative to unilateral economic sanctions for supporting democratization and respect for human rights in China must, in the final analysis, be based on whether it will, in fact, produce net benefits for overall U.S. policy objectives, which include U.S. national security interests in the China relationship.

National Security Objectives

Alternative 1: Increased use of unilateral sanctions. This would involve tightening U.S. restrictions on dual-use exports substantially beyond those applied by friends and allies, through broader product coverage and/or increased end-use monitoring requirements. Sanctions could also be threatened more broadly on U.S. exports to or imports from China if China were not more forthcoming in curtailing exports to third countries related to the proliferation of weapons of mass destruction and ballistic missiles.

An assessment of such a unilateral approach is extremely difficult in view of the technical complexity and constantly evolving technologies of the goods and services involved. Enhanced restrictions on U.S. high-performance computer exports, in particular, would have to be assessed in relation to rapidly rising computer performance in general, the capability of non-American companies to develop reasonably comparable substitutes for U.S. exports, and the internal capability of China to upgrade computer production and performance. A renewed suspension of U.S. commercial satellite and related exports, either to pressure China finally to join the MTCR or to prevent the dual-use application of U.S. technology to the Chinese ballistic missile program, would entail considerable loss to U.S. industry through quick substitution by European and other satellite suppliers, while incurring relatively little economic cost to China.

The most likely prospect is for some tightening of end-use monitoring requirements, but from a practical point of view this would have to be limited to a relatively small range of products and would be at significant increased cost to U.S. suppliers vis-à-vis third-country competitors. The net impact of such a move to the pace of Chinese military modernization would probably be small, although hard analysis of this question apparently is not currently available even within the U.S. government.

Alternative 2: Strengthen multilateral sanctions and increased U.S. national defense capability. This alternative to unilateral sanctions has far-reaching implications for U.S. national security policy that are beyond the scope of this study. The discussion here is limited to defining the issues involved.

Two basic U.S. national security interests need to be addressed. The first concerns the relatively weak and ineffective multilateral framework currently in place to contain the proliferation of weapons of mass destruction and the ballistic missile capability to deliver them. China, along with Russia and North Korea, are the principal alleged suppliers of goods and services to third-country proliferators, while only partially committed to antiproliferation multilateral agreements that are themselves inadequate to the task. A substantial reordering of the international response to the rapidly growing threat to U.S. national security appears necessary, with a more credible threat of substantial multilateral sanctions against proliferators and others who assist them. For example, if allies had joined the United States in withholding exports of commercial satellites to China until China joined the MTCR, Chinese membership would more likely have occurred. The MTCR, in turn, could be strengthened, particularly with respect to implementation requirements. Finally, such threatened sanctions would be even more credible if targeted on Chinese (and Russian, et cetera) exports rather than imports. Multilateral targeted restrictions on Chinese exports to the North American, European, and Japanese markets would shift the threatened economic pain to Chinese rather than American and allied exporters, and could be justified in the World Trade Organization, even when China becomes a member, under the national security exclusion.

The second national security interest concerns the U.S. policy response to Chinese military modernization. Existing multilateral sanctions on exports of armaments and dual-use technology to China are having a modest inhibiting effect at best. China is engaged in a broadly based strategy of increased procurement, research and development, and overall modernization of its armed forces.[24] The United States, in parallel, is phasing down its force capability and procurement of new weapons systems in particular.[25] The U.S. foreign policy challenge noted earlier of maintaining a critical military superiority over Chinese capability in order to exercise effective American deterrence of the use of force by China requires, first, a clearer assessment of the convergence under way between increasing Chinese and decreasing U.S. weapons procurement and related military capability. Existing analysis, such as the reports cited in the chapter's endnotes 24 and 25, suggests the need for a substantial increase in U.S. defense procurement. This vital objective should not be obscured by debate over tighter unilateral sanctions that will have a marginal impact at best on the overall bilateral strategic relationship.

∿ ∿ ∿

The foregoing alternatives to the current policy of minimal unilateral sanctions against China can be considered in various combinations. The first alternatives—increased unilateral sanctions—can, of course, be pursued in conjunction with the second alternatives of strengthened prodemocracy and national security initiatives, but this would essentially be a variant of the first alternatives, which distinguish increased use of unilateral sanctions as against alternative policies. It is also possible to pursue greater use of unilateral sanctions for human rights/democratization while not increasing the unilateral dimension of targeted sanctions for national security objectives, and vice versa.

The most far-reaching alternative to current policy or enhanced unilateral sanctions would be the alternative 2 approaches for both human rights/democratization and national security objectives. In concept, they are mutually reinforcing, based on the assessment that a process of fundamental political and economic change is under way within China, but with conflicting implications for U.S. interests. The positive changes can be encouraged and accelerated through open trade and U.S. private sector engagement while the parallel upgrading of Chinese military capability needs to be contained as long as fundamental political and ideological differences persist. In bilateral terms, this central post–Cold War political/economic/security challenge is most stark and important for the China relationship, but it is, in broader terms, a global challenge. This challenge and the role of unilateral economic sanctions in responding to it are addressed in the final chapter of this study.

5. Conclusions and Recommendations

The principal conclusion related to the use of unilateral economic sanctions against China is that comprehensive sanctions—particularly MFN withdrawal—are no longer a feasible policy option if ever they were. Targeted unilateral sanctions need to be judged each on their respective merits, but their effectiveness is very limited, especially as third-country competitors become increasingly capable of substituting for U.S. exports and investment in advanced technology sectors. The withholding of U.S. commercial nuclear reactor goods and services linked to nonproliferation objectives was essentially an exception that proved the rule. Restrictions on the use of Chinese launch services for U.S.-built commercial satellites is self-defeating in terms of both U.S. foreign policy and commercial interests, although restrictions on U.S. company support services to Chinese authorities need to be strictly observed to avoid what appears to have been the problem in the Loral/missile launch failure incident. Where and how to draw the line on high-performance computer exports is highly complex and deserves serious review as undertaken by the Cox Committee.

Another basic conclusion, consistent with those in the other four case studies, is that U.S. private sector engagement in China is an important force for positive political as well as economic change toward a market-oriented democracy, which would form the basis for a more secure, cooperative bilateral relationship over the longer term. This foreign policy conclusion reinforces U.S. commercial interests for a continued U.S. policy of open trade and investment with China.

Conclusions with respect to U.S. national security interests, and in particular containment of exports to third countries related to weapons of mass destruction and Chinese military modernization, are less clear but of vital importance. The assessment here goes no further than to conclude that the role of unilateral economic sanctions, to the extent they are involved, is relatively minor and should not be overstated in formulating a policy response that must predominantly involve other areas of defense and national security policies.

The policy course recommended here is the alternative 2 approaches for both human rights/democratization and national security objectives, as explained in the final paragraph of the preceding section. This would reject unilateral economic sanctions, except in rare and narrowly targeted instances, as contrary to U.S. interests, while adopting strengthened and more forceful diplomatic and national defense strategies toward China.

Notes

1. This two-phase distinction is assessed in greater detail in Robert S. Roth, "China," in Richard N. Haass, ed., *Economic Sanctions and American Diplomacy* (New York: Council on Foreign Relations, 1998).

2. Former president Bush commented: "The Democratic leadership in the Senate fought me tooth and nail on MFN for China. Senator Mitchell and others saw my support for China as something that could be very damaging to me politically. On vote after vote they stood against what I felt was best." See George Bush and Brent Scowcroft, *A World Transformed* (New York: Alfred A. Knopf, 1998), 276.

3. This legislation would have ended MFN treatment for China and would thus have required a positive congressional vote to resume the annual renewal process—in other words, a more severe reversal than a simple one-year suspension through congressional override of a presidential decision.

4. See *New York Times*, September 29 and May 25, 1993.

5. The speech is quoted at length in the *Washington Post*, October 2, 1992.

6. *New York Times*, May 30, 1993.

7. Ibid., May 13, 1994.

8. Ibid., May 27, 1994.

9. Ibid., May 29, 1994.

10. The legislation, passed by the House in July 1989 and by the Senate in January 1990, also "urged" the president to continue postponing Exim Bank financing and called for a review of China's MFN status. But by the time the president signed the legislation, he had already approved selective Exim Bank financing despite the congressional urging.

11. A full presentation of this issue is contained in *U.S.-China Commercial Nuclear Commerce: Nonproliferation and Trade Issues* (Washington, D.C.: CSIS, September 1997), a report of a steering committee chaired by Brent Scowcroft.

12. "Executive Summary," *Report of the Commission to Assess the Ballistic Threat to the United States*, pursuant to Public Law 20, 104th Congress (July 15, 1998), 11.

13. See Iain K. McDaniels, "A Tangled Web," *Chinese Business Review* 25 (March/April 1998): 40. It is not clear, however, whether the levels of technology in the U.S. and Japanese products are comparable.

14. See Stephen D. Bryen, in a November 13, 1997, statement before the House National Security Committee. Forty-six U.S. supercomputer sales to China were disclosed by the Department of Commerce during the 18-month period through June 1997, after sanctions were relaxed. The higher figure estimated by Bryen is based on the following: not all companies had reported computer sales to the Department of Commerce, computers slightly under 2,000 MTOPS were not counted, and other computers may have been upgraded to supercomputer capability with relative ease.

15. Peter D. Rodman, *Between Friendship and Rivalry: China and America in the 21st Century* (Washington, D.C.: The Nixon Center, June 1998), 35.

16. See *Washington Post*, August 19, 1998. Implementation apparently began in late 1998.

17. *China: Foreign Trade Reform* (Washington, D.C.: The World Bank, February 1994).

18. Hugh M. Arce and Christopher T. Taylor, "The Effects of Changing U.S. MFN Status for China," *Weltwirtschaftliches Archiv* 133, no. 4 (1997): 737–753.

19. Still another measure of investment supplied by the Chinese government is for "investment commitments," but these figures obviously overstate actual investment because many commitments never materialize. In 1992, for example, the Chinese Ministry of Foreign Trade and Economic Cooperation reported $3.1 billion of U.S. investment commitments compared with only $0.9 billion of actual disbursements.

20. The trade policy dimension of the China relationship, as noted earlier, is treated as separate from this assessment of the use of economic sanctions for foreign policy objectives.

21. The specific examples cited in this paragraph are from "U.S. Corporate Practices in China: A Resource Guide," The U.S.-China Business Council, June 6, 1996. An elaboration of the general theme is presented by Michael Santoro, "Doing Good While Doing Well in China," *Wall Street Journal Europe*, June 12, 1998. Professor Santoro of Rutgers University is writing a book about multilateral corporations and human rights in China.

22. This comprehensive initiative, put forward on July 17, 1997, comprised 11 separate bills pertaining to human rights, free trade, and national security.

23. See *Business Week*, September 14, 1998, p. 160.

24. For example, the *Washington Times* (November 3, 1998) cites a Pentagon report that the Chinese army "is building lasers to destroy satellites and already has beam weapons capable of damaging sensors on space-based reconnaissance and intelligence systems. . . . The ability to damage or destroy satellites will provide China with a strategic weapon against the U.S. military, which relies heavily on the use of space-based equipment for communicating with forces and detecting foreign military activities, from troop movements to missile launches."

25. See Daniel Gouré and Jeffrey M. Ranney, *Averting the Defense Train Wreck in the New Millennium* (Washington, D.C.: CSIS, 1999).

7

General Conclusions and Policy Alternatives

T HE FOREGOING FIVE COUNTRY CASE STUDIES together constitute a disturbing and almost entirely unsuccessful experience
in U.S. foreign policy during the 1990s. This chapter summarizes
the experience in four parts. First, specific conclusions are drawn
from the economic analysis in the case studies, which provides
input to the following part, a concluding assessment of the effectiveness—or more precisely the general lack of effectiveness—of
unilateral sanctions in achieving their intended objectives. The
third part then examines weaknesses in the U.S. policy process as
observed in the case studies and related to the 1997–1998 legislative proposal, "The Sanctions Policy Reform Act," while the final
part addresses policy alternatives to the use of unilateral economic
sanctions.

1. Economic Impact

The most striking conclusion from the five case studies about
assessments of the economic impact of proposed unilateral sanctions is how little of it took place during U.S. government deliberations. There was no comprehensive assessment of the impact on the
target country economy in any of the five cases, and the assessment
of adverse impact on U.S. commercial interests was uneven, tend-
ing toward estimates of maximum possible impact—that is, the
entire U.S. export and investment position in a target country—
often presented by business groups who had an interest in high-
lighting the maximum possible negative effects. Although the
assessments of economic impact undertaken in the case studies are
admittedly limited by resources available and inherent analytic
problems, they were developed to provide an order of magnitude of

likely economic effects and significant qualitative characteristics of what has happened or would happen from the unilateral sanction in question. With these caveats, the following specific conclusions are drawn about the impact on the target country as well as on U.S. commercial interests and the systemic effects of U.S. private sector engagement in the target countries.

Impact on the Target Country Economy

The degree and nature of the "economic pain" inflicted on the target country is by far the most important economic assessment. It determines the leverage brought to bear on the target country government to change its behavior in accordance with the U.S. foreign policy objective involved. This fundamental point only highlights the extraordinary observation above that no attempt was ever made in any of the five country cases to make such a detailed assessment before the sanctions were threatened or imposed. Based on the analysis in the case studies, five specific conclusions from the economic impact on the target country economy are as follows:

1. The adverse impact from U.S. unilateral sanctions is relatively small. This finding should cause little surprise because all other nations continue normal commerce with the target country and are eager to have their companies substitute for U.S. exporters and investors. In terms of foreign exchange loss relative to total imports or GDP, Myanmar and Iran show the smallest adverse impact, Vietnam (still without MFN) and China (if MFN were withdrawn) somewhat more, and Cuba the greatest relative impact in view of its location at the center of the Caribbean Basin regional economy where the U.S. economic relationship is dominant and its absence therefore of greater relative impact.

2. The adverse impact is much greater for unilateral sanctions on U.S. imports than sanctions on exports to and investment in the target country. This conclusion also follows logically from the fact that whereas third-country companies can substitute for U.S. exporters and investors, a closing of the U.S. market to target country exports is often not replaceable elsewhere, especially for manufactured products, services, and nontraditional agricultural exports. In the case studies, Cuba is the outstanding example where the exclusion of American tourists (the preeminent Cuban export service industry) and exports to the United States of citrus fruit and labor-intensive manufactures deprive the Cuban economy of roughly $2 billion per year (or half the level of total existing exports), whereas the prohibition on U.S. exports to and investment in Cuba, as well as the extended sanctions to U.S. subsidiaries in the 1992 Cuba Democracy Act, are having relatively small to insignificant impact on the Cuban economy.

A related striking contrast is between Myanmar and Vietnam, where the Myanmar investment sanction has had no significant effect on the Myanmar economy, while the continuing withholding of MFN status for Vietnam (which effectively excludes Vietnamese manufactured exports to the U.S. market) has substantial adverse consequences for the Vietnamese economy. Likewise, the debate over MFN withdrawal from China was of relatively greater importance because the initial impact would be on the closing of the U.S. market and the potential loss of about half of Chinese exports to the United States. Even in the case of Iran, where the 1995 embargo on U.S. investment in and exports to the Iranian petroleum sector, in particular, had significant initial disruptive effects on the Iranian economy, now that Iran has made the transition to non-American suppliers the more important ongoing adverse impact on the Iranian economy from the U.S. embargo is on potential Iranian exports of carpets, pistachio nuts, and other nonpetroleum exports to the U.S. market.

3. The "economic pain" of sanctions falls more heavily on the people than on the target country government. This broadly recognized conclusion has much greater absolute significance for multilateral sanctions—as applied during the 1990s against Iraq and Haiti—where the sanctions indeed caused serious pain to the target country economy. In the case of unilateral sanctions, however, where the overall economic pain is much less, an authoritarian government can even more easily transfer to the people whatever economic pain is inflicted, through immediate reductions in the availability of consumer goods or postponement of infrastructure and social sector investment. In the case studies, the Vietnamese and Myanmar armies are by far the two largest among

ASEAN members, while the economic deprivation of the peoples, although caused far more by internal economic mismanagement and corruption than by U.S. sanctions, is clearly evident. A more mixed picture prevails in Iran, where earlier planned purchases of conventional weapons have been scaled back in parallel with economic hardship throughout the domestic economy, but again U.S. unilateral sanctions played only a small role in these developments. Finally, for Cuba, where the U.S. embargo is having the most substantial impact, the Castro government has reduced the size of its military, but domestically oriented police and other resources devoted to maintaining tight political control over the country take clear priority over the needs of the people.

4. The multilateral action of withholding economic aid, particularly through the multilateral development banks, can have a greater effect than U.S. unilateral sanctions. This has clearly been borne out in Iran, Myanmar, and Vietnam. For China, the withholding of aid would be of relatively less importance compared with the withholding of MFN status because the Chinese export sector is far more developed while economic aid is declining in relative importance. Cuba, again, is distinct because of its Caribbean Basin location. The withholding of economic aid has substantial adverse consequences for Cuba, but the U.S. embargo, especially on tourism, has at least comparable economic effects.

5. An unholy alliance can develop between the target country government and proponents of unilateral sanctions in the United States to greatly exaggerate the adverse economic impact on the target country. The target country government wants to blame the United States for its own economic problems while sanction proponents want to convince doubters that the sanction will, in fact, force change on the behavior of the target country government. This unholy alliance thrives when there is no available assessment of the relatively small economic impact of unilateral sanctions, as was the case in all five country studies. Cuba was by far the outstanding example of such an unholy alliance whereby Fidel Castro and the Cuban-American and other U.S. proponents of an ever-tighter embargo provided mutually supportive statements that exaggerated the actual or potential impact of the embargo. The China MFN debate elicited a similar mutual reinforcement, continuing on beyond the debate itself as in the more recent highly misleading Chinese claim, "American companies are fully capable of winning over a bigger slice of the emerging China market as long as the Clinton administration withdraws its meddling hand."[1] The Iranian government has also tended to blame the U.S. embargo for effects far in excess of the actual adverse impact. The Vietnamese government, in contrast, has been relatively quiescent about the very real negative effects from non-MFN access to the U.S. market, while the Myanmar generals have made the only basically correct assessment in stating that the U.S. unilateral investment sanction has had no significant effect on Myanmar because third-country investors quickly move in, as was the case of the Chinese investor in the Yangon port project and the UK company, Premier, that replaced Texaco.

Impact on U.S. Commercial Interests

The economic impact of unilateral sanctions on U.S. commercial interests is inherently negative for U.S. exports and investment because of the third-country substitution effect, which is clearly demonstrated throughout the five case studies. There is also some cost to American consumers through higher prices and reduced choice of imported products. But this effect has been very small because the substitution effect works in reverse for unilateral import restrictions, with third countries replacing target country exports, and the cost is spread widely among American consumers. Four specific conclusions about the more important adverse impact on U.S. exports and investment are as follows:

1. The adverse impact of sanctions on U.S. exports and investment is substantial, and larger than that on the target country economy. This logical implication from the nature of a unilateral sanction was the observed experience for Cuba, Iran, and Myanmar, where such sanctions were imposed during the 1990s. The absolute magnitude of the estimated losses of U.S. exports, moreover, was substantially higher than those contained in the widely cited global estimate of U.S. export loss from all sanctions of $15 billion to $25 billion per year, prepared by the Institute for

International Economics. One reason is that the institute limited its study to exports of merchandise, while U.S. service exports, including those for the petroleum sector in Iran, tourism in Cuba, and financial, telecommunications, transportation, and other services more broadly, account for more than a quarter of total U.S. exports.[2] The estimated losses to U.S. investment, of course, are additional to the loss in exports.

2. The adverse impact on U.S. exports is more lasting for capital and advanced technology goods and services than for agricultural commodities and consumer goods. Grains and other basic agricultural commodities, like petroleum and industrial raw materials, are sold on a global market, and unilateral sanctions against one country can lead, to a large extent, to offsetting changes in market shares elsewhere. This probably would have happened, for example, if MFN status had been withdrawn from China and China retaliated by cutting its grain imports from the United States. For U.S. consumer goods, trans-shipment through third countries to the sanctioned market takes place with relative ease although at a higher cost and without the benefit of sales promotion in the sanctioned market. Thus, for example, some U.S. consumer goods are available in Cuba and Iran. However, when the unilateral sanction leads to a substitution of Airbus for Boeing commercial aircraft, Komatsu for Caterpillar tractors, and to third-country sales of electric power generators, telecommunications switching gear, and petroleum drilling equipment, there is likely to be little or no offsetting market adjustment elsewhere short term. Even more threatening, the establishment of third-country technologies in target country markets can preclude future U.S. exports after the sanctions are lifted. Examples of this effect were commercial nuclear power reactors in China, telecommunications equipment in Vietnam, and, most important of all, the whole range of petroleum sector plant and equipment and their embedded technologies in Iran.

3. The adverse impact on U.S. investment is relatively more important than on exports. As noted in the previous paragraph, some U.S. exporters circumvent unilateral sanctions by shipping through third countries and, once sanctions are lifted, many can resume marketing relatively quickly. The situation for U.S.

investors is more constrained both during and after the sanctions. In Cuba, the European contract to rebuild the domestic telephone system could preclude U.S. telecommunications investors over a long term, as could Spanish, Mexican, and other non-U.S. hotel chains that have secured and built on prime Varadero Beach and central Havana properties. Again, the threat to U.S. investors in the Iranian petroleum sector is greatest of all if the Iranian government, as a practical as well as political matter, pursues the path of limiting the number of engaged major company investors to a relatively small number.

4. The indirect adverse impact in third-country markets, including questions about the reliability of American companies as suppliers, or joint-venture partners, cannot be measured, but it is real and almost certainly substantial.   The case of Caspian Sea oil development was examined in some detail in the Iran case study, and episodic accounts of other third-country impact are cited, such as the worldwide inability of American companies to compete for sole source airport services where they might have to service a Cuban aircraft. Other reports relate to American companies spreading their R&D, production, and supplier sources to European and other foreign locations so as to avoid actual or potential U.S. sanctions.

Systemic Effects of U.S. Private Sector Engagement

The issue of U.S. private sector engagement as a force for positive political as well as economic change was raised in each of the case studies and is a central question addressed in chapter 8. In terms of overall impact, such engagement, based on the case study observations, is assessed as playing, or potentially playing, an important positive role in support of the transition under way in each of the five countries from an authoritarian government with a state-dominated economy to a more productive, market-oriented economy based on the rule of law, respect for individual rights, and democratization. This does not mean that the engagement of American companies, or of all foreign private companies, will alone ensure such a transition, but rather that they constitute an important positive influence on the process and that, in their absence, which by

definition economic sanctions dictates, the transition will be greatly inhibited.

The five countries examined in this study all currently have
authoritarian or totalitarian governments—three communist, one
military, and one clerical—and dominant state influence and control over the economy. At the same time, however, each is moving
in the direction of a more open economy, with explicit priority on
attracting foreign direct investment as a means of modernizing the
economy based on market incentives. This economic change, in
turn, is moving forward in a mutually supportive way with political
change of a largely generational and educational character. Younger,
more educated men and women are calling for greater respect for
the rule of law, increased personal freedom, and a more democratic
process for selecting at least parts of the leadership structure. The
overall process is stimulated by what is referred to as an information age revolution in communications, ranging from books to
films to faxes to e-mail to especially potent foreign travel and education that, ironically, is often most accessible to the children of the
authoritarian elite.

The catalytic impact of foreign private sector engagement on
this process of political/economic change is observed in the case
studies to be substantial, and American companies are qualitatively
the most influential in communicating, through day-to-day
demonstration effect, how job creating, productive enterprise can
function, with emphasis on employee training and remuneration
based on merit, within an overall business relationship oriented
toward efficiency and the rule of law rather than political influence
and corruption. Such ongoing experience was recounted in some
detail in the two country cases where American companies are fully
engaged, Vietnam and China. The process of change in Cuba and
Iran is moving forward without the participation of American
companies, but the same demonstration effects are evident there as
well from non-American companies. Working for a foreign firm in
Cuba has clear advantages compared with work in a state enterprise
despite the Cuban government's 95 percent tax rate on wages
through exchange rate manipulation. Educated Iranians from all
levels of society who have observed the devastating mismanagement of state enterprises in recent years are mostly eager for more

efficient and rewarding international engagement. And Myanmar, the country most threatened by economic collapse and political violence, is also the least engaged with independent foreign private companies, owing to Western government political disengagement—and U.S. economic sanctions—as well as to the oppressive behavior of the military regime.

The vexing observation about current U.S. policy toward this important issue—and the associated use of comprehensive unilateral economic sanctions that precludes American private sector engagement—is that it is irredeemably inconsistent. The policy of "different strokes for different folks" is a statement of convenient opportunism driven largely by domestic politics. There is no rational explanation for the contradiction between highly praising U.S. private sector engagement in communist Vietnam and blindly condemning it in communist Cuba; saying yes for private sector engagement in China but no in Iran; and for Myanmar, pursuing an internally inconsistent if not incoherent strategy of a ban on new but not old U.S. investment and "a U.S. government policy of neither promoting nor prohibiting trade."

U.S. private sector engagement is, or should be, a force for positive political and economic change in all five countries. A U.S. policy of comprehensive economic sanctions thus has important negative consequences that need to be fully considered in judging the overall effectiveness of a unilateral sanctions policy.

2. Effectiveness of Unilateral Sanctions in Achieving Their Intended Foreign Policy Objectives

This is the central policy question addressed in this study, and the answer, derived from the five detailed case studies and other recent experience, is that during the 1990s unilateral economic sanctions, with rare exceptions, have failed to achieve their intended foreign policy objectives, while in the process causing substantial adverse effects on various other U.S. interests. Moreover, the rare exceptions occurred in such unique circumstances as only to prove the rule. The previous section that assessed the economic impact of the sanctions, especially on the target country, provided much of the analytic and empirical support for this conclusion. This section elaborates the assessment in broader foreign policy terms, with target country experience grouped on the basis of whether the foreign policy objectives were primarily related to human rights/democratization, national security, or "other."

Human Rights/Democratization Objectives

U.S. unilateral economic sanctions in the 1990s have shown a nearly total lack of success in achieving stated human rights and democratization objectives while consistently producing various adverse consequences. The people, for the most part, have suffered the economic pain caused by the sanctions, the positive influence of U.S. private sector engagement has been diminished or lost, and target country governments have made exaggerated claims, to good propaganda effect, that U.S. sanctions were the cause of what were really internal economic policy failures. This is also the policy area where the United States is almost entirely alone if not at odds with friends and allies—not to mention the Catholic Church—which further reduces the prospects for positive concrete achievement.

The basic reason why these unilateral economic sanctions are ineffective is that the foreign policy objective is to change the oppressive behavior of an authoritarian or totalitarian government, which constitutes a direct threat to its control if not survival. Such governments are consequently not prepared to make this kind of fundamental concession in response to the relatively small economic impact of unilateral economic sanctions. Even in the one case during the 1990s when far more devastating multilateral trade sanctions were applied in the cause of democratization—the three-year embargo against Haiti—the rag-tag Haitian military still held out, becoming more oppressive while the people suffered greatly and the economic infrastructure of the country was destroyed. In the end a U.S. military intervention was still needed to restore Jean Bertrand Aristide to the Presidential Palace.[3]

All of the case studies bear out this assessment. Even with the abrupt cutoff of Soviet aid in 1991, the Castro regime has maintained power, and almost all experts agree that Fidel Castro will retain control as long as he is physically able and willing to do so. In the process, he has adroitly used the U.S. embargo to split the

United States from its allies. The MFN/human rights linkage failed to achieve significant improvement in basic human rights in China during both the Bush and Clinton administrations, and President Clinton's decision to reverse course and jettison the linkage in May 1994 negatively affected broader U.S. credibility in dealing with the Chinese communist leadership. The unilateral sanction on new U.S. investment in Myanmar had no significant adverse effect on the Myanmar economy and has only tended to push the generals further into isolation from the rest of the world, except China, and into near total disengagement from the United States. A similar absence of any positive result is evident for the U.S. unilateral trade embargo against the Sudan in 1996. As for other embargo proposals linked to democratization/human rights objectives in recent years, those against Indonesia and Nigeria had the most important potential consequences, but in both cases they were not pursued for largely the same reasons observed in the case studies—limited economic impact if pursued unilaterally with little prospect of the authoritarian/military governments reacting in a significantly positive way.

Narrowly targeted economic sanctions, as distinct from the broadly based trade and investment sanctions addressed in the previous paragraph, must be examined on a case-by-case basis, but again there are no clear success stories during the 1990s. The problem here is that targeted sanctions are extremely difficult and complicated to administer, as, for example, would be a targeted sanction against Chinese companies owned by the military, while having very small to insignificant economic impact. Freezing overseas bank accounts of members of a communist politburo or a military command can be circumvented with relative ease in a world of instant electronic banking and numerous banking safe havens. The final version of the 1998 Religious Persecution Act remains to be tested, but it is doubtful that it, by itself, will result in much greater tolerance and less repression of religious beliefs in countries such as China, Iran, and Saudi Arabia.

A final relevant indicator of whether U.S. unilateral economic sanctions help or hinder the process of democratization and respect for basic human rights is the judgment of prodemocracy and human rights dissidents within the target countries, because they are in the front lines of the struggle, often at great personal risk. Attitudes are not monolithic, but the large majority of them are clearly on the side of U.S. private sector engagement rather than unilateral sanctions. The antiembargo statement of Elizardo Sanchez, quoted at length in the case study, represents the dominant dissident view within Cuba and should take precedence over anti-Castro Cuban-Americans living in Florida and New Jersey. The predominant view of prodemocracy activists in China, including Hong Kong, and Vietnam is also strongly supportive of U.S. private sector engagement.

Only in Myanmar is there a clear split among prodemocracy dissidents, including within the NLD, and the outspoken view of Aung San Suu Kyi against private sector engagement or even engagement by most humanitarian-oriented nongovernmental organizations and aid agencies has received broad international recognition and official support. Indeed, the actual imposition of the U.S. unilateral investment sanction in May 1997 by the second Clinton administration foreign policy team was triggered less by the "substantial increase in oppression" criterion contained in the Cohen/Feinstein legislation, than by Aung San Suu Kyi's call for the sanction shortly before. The judgment here, with all due respect for her courageous, democratic struggle, is that she is wrong in advocating foreign private sector and international agency disengagement from her country, with all the inherent short- and longer-term adverse impact this has on the people of Myanmar, as the means for changing the oppressive behavior of the military regime.

National Security Objectives

The unilateral sanctions experience related to national security objectives is more complicated than for human rights/democratization objectives, and, by definition, concerns issues more directly threatening to the United States. The national security issues involved—proliferation of weapons of mass destruction, the ballistic missile capability to deliver them, international terrorism, and modernization of the Chinese military—also include a more elaborate and evolving set of multilateral arrangements and policies that need to be related to economic sanctions policy. The unilateral sanctions policy assessment here is thus less conclusive than for human rights/democratization objectives, although it still points in the direction of relatively small positive results with significant downsides.

The Iranian case study was predominantly about U.S. national security interests as were parallel sanctions against Libya contained in the ILSA. Much of the China case study pertaining to targeted sanctions falls within the national security domain, and the 1998 sanctions against India and Pakistan in response to nuclear weapons tests, while not addressed as a full case study, are included in this summary assessment. Yet another national security threat with a sanctions dimension is North Korea, although in this case the "carrot" approach of economic aid to deter nuclear weapons development takes precedence over the largely meaningless trade sanctions, and this relationship is thus left for the later section on alternatives to sanctions.

With respect to Iran, the 1995 unilateral sanctions on U.S. investment and exports imposed by President Clinton through IEEPA and the 1996 secondary boycott against third-country investors in the Iranian petroleum sector contained in ILSA legislation have had relatively little lasting adverse impact on the Iranian economy, especially after the June 1998 South Pars waiver. The sanctions may have restrained Iranian purchases of conventional weapons to some extent, but even this restraint was driven principally by Iranian economic mismanagement and the drop in world oil prices. No discernible progress in other U.S. security interests in Iran can be attributed to the unilateral sanctions policy. The related experience with Libya has been devoid of significant results one way or the other because the ILSA technical provisions, primarily related to the Pan Am 107 shootdown, have not produced any significant sanction threats against third-country investors in Libya, while negotiations to extricate the alleged terrorists from Libya for trial in the Netherlands have taken place within a multilateral context linked to the multilateral sanction on commercial flights to and from Libya.

The Chinese case study shows mixed results from the targeted unilateral sanctions for U.S. national security interests. The sanction on U.S. exports to China related to commercial nuclear reactors as leverage to obtain stronger Chinese nuclear nonproliferation commitments is a rare example where a unilateral sanction appears to have had a positive effect, although in the unique circumstances of a timely Chinese interest in U.S. civilian nuclear technology. In contrast, the three instances of suspension of export licenses for commercial satellites and related equipment, twice by President Bush and once by President Clinton, to pressure China to cease exports of ballistic missile equipment and technology to third countries and to join the MTCR, achieved little if any positive result. Finally, restrictions on exports to China of armaments and dual-use goods and technology, intended to restrain Chinese military modernization, are generally imposed within multilateral arrangements, although with the conspicuous nonparticipation of Russia. The unilateral dimension, whereby U.S. restrictions are broader and more costly than those of others, was relatively small as of 1998, but this could change in the direction of tighter U.S. controls, with uncertain impact on Chinese military modernization.

The automatic imposition of unilateral U.S. sanctions against India and Pakistan in mid-1998, based on the 1995 Glenn amendment, was quickly protested by U.S. agricultural and industrial interests because third-country suppliers were ready and very willing to replace U.S. exporters. Legislation was promptly adopted to exclude U.S. agricultural exports from the sanctions, and further legislation gave the president flexibility to ease the remaining sanctions, such as a ban on Exim Bank credits, which President Clinton exercised to a large degree in November. Further sanctions in November 1998 against 205 Indian and 93 Pakistani entities, utilizing IEEPA, could become an administrative nightmare, while India has lodged a complaint in the WTO. As to any positive foreign policy impact from this brief experience with unilateral sanctions, the sanctions clearly did not deter the initial testing. India and Pakistan have long considered nuclear weapons development a vital national interest, and the limited impact of U.S. threatened unilateral economic sanctions was not a decisive deterrent.[4] As for ongoing multilateral and bilateral negotiations to obtain Indian and Pakistani adhesion to the nuclear test ban treaty and other commitments, which is linked to more important development assistance programs, it is extremely doubtful that the quick and somewhat confused imposition of U.S. unilateral trade sanctions and their equally hasty withdrawal under pressure from U.S. export interests had any significant positive impact.

The principal conclusion—and warning—in the national security area is that unilateral economic sanctions, however applied, can only play a small role in the overall strategy to confront what are clearly growing threats to U.S. national security in the specified areas addressed here. The far more important components of a successful strategy are enhanced multilateral arrangements, which could include more effective multilateral economic sanctions, and a fully responsive U.S. national defense capability.

Other Objectives

Almost all foreign policy–oriented unilateral sanctions have been directed toward human rights/democratization or national security objectives, but a few have addressed other issues. During the 1990s, three of these issues are noteworthy:

1. The MFN/MIA linkage with Vietnam.   This is the only instance of a broadly based unilateral sanction serving to advance a foreign policy objective—namely, Vietnamese government cooperation for MIA accounting and the related issue of emigration of Vietnamese detainees, both carryover issues from the Vietnam War. The unique circumstances of this linkage, however, were recounted in the case study, in particular the strong Vietnamese interest in normalization of relations with the United States and the fact that the U.S. objectives did not require any basic political or economic concessions on the part of the Vietnamese government.

2. Expropriation/third-country investment in Cuba.   The 1996 Libertad Act was primarily designed to pressure the Cuban government to democratize, but the specific sanction provisions dealt mainly with third-country investors in Cuba on properties expropriated without compensation from American companies and citizens, and the subsequent U.S.-EU negotiations on this issue led to an agreement that could greatly restrain such investments. In this limited context, the Libertad Act did help achieve a positive agreement in a new and untested area of expropriations policy. There are two qualifications, however, to this policy experience. First, it would have been preferable for the United States to have launched a strong, high-level initiative with trading partners in 1993, when Cuba began to solicit foreign investment, requesting negotiation of an agreement not to permit new investment on properties with outstanding expropriation claims, and with sanctions reserved as a threat if negotiations failed. And second, the Libertad Act has had little impact on foreign investment in any event—the hotels are not on expropriated properties, European telecommunications companies settled privately with IT&T, and Canadian mining and Israeli citrus investments have gone forward in spite of the act. The issue of the effectiveness of U.S. unilateral sanctions against Cuba as a means of fostering democracy involves predominantly the ban on U.S. trade, investment, and travel, and not the marginal effects of attempted third-country extensions contained in the Cuban Democracy and Libertad Acts.

3. *Swiss gold.* Threatened sanctions by New York City against Swiss commercial interests provided a strong incentive for Swiss authorities to arrange belated compensation to World War II Holocaust survivors and their heirs for gold taken from concentration camp victims and placed by Nazi Germany in Swiss banks. The circumstances again were highly unique, and a future initiative in this manner may be precluded by the November 1998 Massachusetts district court decision that a Massachusetts sanction against Myanmar related to foreign policy objectives is unconstitutional.

≈ ≈ ≈

In conclusion, the overall assessment is that unilateral economic sanctions during the 1990s, with a few exceptions, have been ineffective in achieving their foreign policy objectives while having various adverse effects on other U.S. interests. The record for sanctions directed at human rights/democratization objectives is especially bleak, while targeted sanctions for national security objectives, in one case at least, produced a positive result. The rare exceptions of positive results from unilateral sanctions, however, only tend to prove the rule in view of the unique circumstances involved in each such instance.

With this essentially negative overall assessment, the remainder of this chapter is devoted to steps that could be taken to improve the U.S. foreign policy process, and thus avoid counterproductive economic sanctions, and to the elusive subject of alternative policies to the use of unilateral sanctions.

3. The Policy Process

The case studies highlighted important problems of policy process, both for the imposition of unilateral sanctions and for lifting them. The imposition process is more complex technically while the decision process for lifting sanctions is primarily a matter of power sharing between the president and Congress. Each is considered in turn, first with respect to an assessment of recent experience drawn from the case studies and then in terms of proposed changes to improve the policy process, as contained in the 1997–1998 legislative proposal, "The Sanctions Policy Reform Act," sponsored by Senator Richard Lugar and Congressmen Lee Hamilton and Philip Crane.

The Process for Imposing Sanctions

The process of formulating and implementing unilateral sanctions, within the executive branch and Congress, is inherently skewed in favor of imposing the sanction, and often doing so quickly with little regard as to whether the sanction is likely to achieve its intended result. Sanction target governments operate against U.S. interests and values—developing weapons of mass destruction, harboring terrorists, suppressing religious and press freedom, and oppressing or killing their people. International diplomacy is slow-moving and only partially effective at best, which leads to public frustration to do something more forceful, but military intervention has little public support and other options can have large budgetary obligations. This leaves sanctions on trade and investment by American companies, and it is often politically unpopular for executive branch leaders and members of Congress to oppose sanctions on doing business as usual in countries with such oppressive or outlaw regimes. Moreover, these inherent pressures to support, or at least not to resist, sanctions increased during the 1990s when, in the absence of an overriding Soviet threat, the large majority of sanction target countries were no longer pawns on a global Cold War chessboard, nor were trade and effusive aid part of the strategy to keep "friends" from going over to the other side. Finally, the compelling pressure to impose a sanction is far greater for unilateral than for multilateral sanctions. The need to reach multilateral accord before imposing a multilateral sanction usually takes considerable time for detailed deliberations, thus reducing the likelihood of hasty, ill-considered actions.

These inherent weaknesses in the policy process for imposing unilateral sanctions were evident throughout the case studies. The lack of a clear definition of the intended objectives of a proposed sanction, of the likelihood of its being achieved, and of the impact on other U.S. interests, was the consistent pattern for congressional consideration of sanctions legislation and for presidential decisions. The legislative markup of the Libertad Act was done in haste after the shootdown in March 1996 while deliberations over ILSA stretched out over a year but mostly occurred behind closed doors with little systematic attempt to assess what would actually happen if the sanctions were imposed. The initial proposal by Senator McConnell for sanctions against Myanmar received a super-quick hearing in the wrong committee, with no testimony from the executive branch or the U.S. private sector, and the final compromise Cohen/Feinstein amendment was enacted in such haste that authority for the president to impose the sanction was omitted.

The executive branch record of the Clinton administration was at least as bad. Candidate Clinton committed himself to the MFN/human rights linkage for China before he had a foreign policy team to advise him. The March 1995 decision to ban U.S. investment in Iran was preempted by Secretary of State Christopher's press comment in Tel Aviv while cabinet discussion in Washington was divided over whether the sanction would have positive results. The ban on exports to Iran, announced in the president's April speech before the annual World Jewish Congress dinner, was based on secretive internal review that was as much about domestic politics as about the sanction's ability to achieve a particular foreign policy objective. The president's decision in April 1997 to impose the investment sanction on Myanmar was taken hastily by the new foreign policy team, with no formal review and little regard for the substantive criteria in the Cohen/Feinstein legislation. The principal executive branch villain of sanctions policy is the ultra-flexible IEEPA, used in both decisions for Iran, the Myanmar decision, the 1996 decision for sanctions against Sudan, and the November 1998 decisions for the "entities list" of sanctions against India and Pakistani firms. This authority has been abused out of all recognition, as when President Clinton was obliged to declare the internal political struggle in faraway Myanmar "an unusual and extraordinary threat to the national security of the United States."

The Sanctions Policy Reform Act, or SPRA, goes a long way in proposing necessary disciplines on both congressional and executive branch decisions to impose unilateral sanctions. Unilateral economic sanctions legislation would require the committee of primary jurisdiction to provide an opportunity for interested members of the public to submit comments on the proposed legislation prior to a committee vote. After the committee vote and before a floor vote, the president would be required to submit an assessment on various points, including whether the proposed sanction would achieve its stated objective, the impact on humanitarian conditions within the target country, and other affected national security and foreign policy interests. In addition, the secretary of agriculture would be required to assess the impact on U.S. agricultural exports. For executive branch actions, including those taken under IEEPA, the president would have to give 45 days notice of the intent to impose a sanction in order to permit public comments and to hold congressional consultations. The imposition of a sanction would also require a presidential assessment along the lines required for legislative proposals, including the finding by the secretary of agriculture. Finally, the U.S. International Trade Commission would be required to report on the impact of the sanction on the U.S. economy, including trade performance, employment, and the reputation of the United States as a reliable supplier. The president would have waiver authority to act faster, in the case of a real national emergency, but the various reports and assessments would then have to go forward promptly after the sanction is imposed.

All of these provisions are eminently sound and would have greatly improved the policy process in each of the five country cases examined here, while in none of the cases would the president have needed to utilize a national emergency waiver to speed up the process. There are additions, however, to the proposed legislation that should be considered, based on the country case experience:

1. Economic impact on the target country. This was the critical missing assessment in all five case studies, and such an assessment is not explicitly called for in the SPRA. A general statement by the president of likely effectiveness of a proposed sanction could well evade a hard economic assessment, and indeed it is not obvious where in the executive branch such an assessment could best be made. The State Department, as frequent sanctions advocate with limited economic analysis capability, would be suspect. The best procedure would probably be a CIA assessment, with a review panel of independent economists.

2. The secretary of commerce. Far more U.S. industrial exports and investment are at risk, qualitatively as well as quantitatively, than agricultural exports, as explained in the case studies, and thus a finding by the secretary of commerce for U.S. industrial interests, similar to that by the secretary of agriculture for agricultural interests, should be included.

3. U.S. trade representative. The Office of the U.S. Trade Representative never submitted a public statement of the impact of a proposed sanction, including the Libertad Act and ILSA, on U.S. trade policy commitments, including in the World Trade Organization. In fact, U.S. trade policy officials generally try to avoid making any statement even hinting that there could be problems, in the knowledge that they could later have to defend the sanctions in a WTO dispute panel. This was certainly the case for the Libertad Act. The U.S. trade representative should therefore be required to make a finding similar to those of other cabinet members about WTO and other U.S. trade policy commitments.

4. IEEPA. An independent review of recent experience with IEEPA is in order in light of the repeated abuse of its provisions for the quick imposition of unilateral sanctions. This section of the 1977 War and National Defense Act requires the president to declare a national emergency to deal with an unusual and extraordinary threat to the United States before exercising the sweeping authorities provided, which clearly was not warranted for invoking selective sanctions against Myanmar and the Sudan, or even Iran during the nonemergency circumstances of 1995 and India and Pakistan in 1998.

The Process for Lifting Sanctions

The issue here is whether the president should have complete flexibility in how and when to modify or lift the sanction, or whether Congress should impose limitations. When the president utilizes IEEPA, for example, he has total flexibility for terminating the sanction. At the other extreme, in the Libertad Act, the president's authority to lift the embargo against Cuba (Titles I and II) or permit travel to the United States for certain officials of foreign companies that invest in Cuba (Title IV) is zero. Other sanctions have waiver authority, such as ILSA and other parts of the Libertad Act, and then there is the annual review and possible voting process on MFN status for China and at some point for Vietnam. There is finally the question of whether sanction legislation continues indefinitely, as does the Libertad Act, or ends at a given date, such as ILSA with a five-year termination date in 2001.

The SPRA leans heavily in the direction of maximum flexibility for the president and automatic termination dates, or "sunset provisions." Unilateral economic sanction legislation should provide authority to waive the sanctions if the president determines it is in the national interest, and all legislation should have a two-year sunset provision. These provisions, however, are "guidelines" rather than "requirements." The executive branch, in contrast, is required to terminate a sanction after two years unless it is specifically extended with all the normal assessment provisions.

These proposals for flexible application and termination of sanctions are well justified based on the unilateral sanctions experience of the 1990s. One additional provision that should be considered would be to praise the success of the Jackson-Vanik amendment a quarter century ago for helping Jews emigrate freely from the Soviet Union and then to terminate this piece of obsolete legislation.[5] Such an action would not limit the ability to set tariffs at any level for China and Vietnam, but it would end the time-consuming and, if anything, counterproductive annual debates over a Jackson-Vanik waiver and MFN renewal.

Overall, the SPRA would therefore constitute a major improvement in how the U.S. government policy process deals with usually ill-advised unilateral sanction proposals. In 1998, the draft legislation had 39 Senate (25 Republican, 15 Democrat) and 92 House (53 Republican, 39 Democrat) cosponsors, and it was rejected in August by a close 52–47 vote in the Senate when proposed by Senator Lugar as an amendment to the agricultural appropriations bill. The Clinton administration remained conspicuously neutral, however, until near the end, and then, in a September 8 testimony by Under Secretary of State Stuart Eizenstat before the Bipartisan Task Force on Sanctions, it largely supported the proposed disciplines on Congress and opposed almost all disciplines on the executive branch. A reevaluation by the Clinton administration leading to strong support for disciplines on the executive branch as well as on Congress is thus clearly in order if the SPRA is to be adopted in 1999–2000.

4. Alternatives to Sanctions

If unilateral sanctions are usually ineffective, logic dictates a search for alternative policy approaches, but this is an elusive quest. By definition, alternative policies include all other foreign policy instruments, which, in turn, can be packaged in many ways on a country, regional, and global basis. Some basic policy alternatives were presented in each of the five case studies, and a particular alternative course was recommended, but extrapolating these recommendations on a broader geographic basis has limited practical relevance. The point of departure is that all sanction targets present difficult challenges for U.S. foreign policy, and there are no easy, cost-free solutions. The brief discussion here is consequently limited to comments on four foreign policy considerations that are often closely related to decisions on unilateral sanctions—the null hypothesis, multilateral versus unilateral sanctions, carrots versus sticks, and economic sanctions versus military intervention.[6] Chapter 8 follows with a broader statement about post–Cold War U.S. foreign policy strategy and objectives.

The Null Hypothesis

The simplest and most immediate alternative to a policy of unilateral sanctions against a given country is to maintain all other policies in existing form while lifting or not imposing the sanction. If this "null hypothesis" alternative produces a net improvement in terms of the pursuit of U.S. interests, even though it does not achieve the hoped for (but in any event not realized) objectives of the sanctions, it is still a preferable alternative and should logically be adopted. In operational terms, the unilateral sanction is lifted unilaterally or not imposed, and everything else remains the same.

This line of reasoning will not necessarily convince entrenched proponents of a particular sanction to change their position, but it is nevertheless the necessary first step in a systematic assessment of alternatives to a policy of unilateral sanctions. Moreover, if the null hypothesis assessment indicates a net improvement for the United States, the burden of proof for continuing or imposing the sanction shifts to sanctions proponents. In effect, the best defense becomes a good offense. In the case studies, the null hypothesis—that is, a unilateral lifting of current sanctions—was deemed to be preferable to continued unilateral sanctions for Cuba and Iran, and for Myanmar on a contingent basis. The Clinton administration and most members of Congress continue to support these sanctions, but they should at least be obliged to offer a counterassessment of how the continued unilateral sanctions are preferable to the null hypothesis, which through the end of 1998 they have not done. The recommendation for a bipartisan presidential commission to review Cuba policy would force such an appraisal for the Cuba embargo and thus serve a useful purpose. Indeed the commission mandate could be extended to include Iran and Myanmar as well.

Multilateral versus Unilateral Sanctions

The familiar statement that multilateral sanctions are preferable to unilateral sanctions is self-evident, but of limited content except where the United States is prepared to act forcefully with friends and allies. With respect to human rights/democratization objectives, the multilateral alternative is especially limited because almost all other countries favor "constructive engagement," including private sector engagement through trade and investment, to economic sanctions. Haiti was the exception during the 1990s,[7] but there do not appear to be any similar target countries ahead. In the national security field, broader opportunities exist, but they each entail difficult commitments, such as broadened dual-use export restraints or sanctions against Chinese and Russian companies involved in ballistic missile and other exports or technical support to third countries. The point is that the frequent recourse to unilateral sanctions has not been out of ignorance of multilateral alternatives, but out of the unwillingness to take on major initiatives of likely negative outcome.

A more limited though more pertinent issue of multilateral versus unilateral policies is whether the United States could achieve strengthened multilateral collaboration in diplomatic and other areas of policy in the absence of the unilateral economic sanctions. Cuba, Iran, and Myanmar are all good examples, as related in the case studies, and the issue can cut both ways. The Libertad Act unilateral sanctions did help achieve the U.S.-EU agreement on expropriated properties, but it has also isolated the United States in the United Nations, the Western Hemisphere, and elsewhere, from a concerted campaign to press democratic reforms directly on the Cuban government. Indeed the act has enabled Fidel Castro to wage a successful propaganda campaign against the U.S. embargo so as to divert attention from human rights abuses within Cuba.

For Iran, the 1995 ban on U.S. exports to and investment in Iran may have initially helped restrain other countries from providing official export credits to Iran, but subsequent entrenched differences between the United States and its allies over unilateral sanctions versus constructive engagement have precluded strong

U.S. leadership for concerted multilateral pressures on the Iranian leadership over international terrorism and other national security interests. For Myanmar, the relevant relationship is between the United States and ASEAN members, even more sharply divided over unilateral sanctions versus constructive engagement, including full Myanmar membership in ASEAN.

These multilateral versus unilateral questions need to be addressed carefully in each country situation. The conclusion from the Cuba, Iran, and Myanmar case studies is that significant opportunities for strengthened multilateral collaboration could be obtained by lifting the unilateral sanctions. Such collaboration would not likely achieve all of the objectives sought through the sanction policies, but neither have the sanctions.

Carrots versus Sticks

The dichotomy between positive incentives such as economic aid and economic pain through sanctions—carrots versus sticks—is not always a simple either-or choice, and the two categories of policy instruments are sometimes used in conjunction. In fact, there are often three distinct policy instruments in play: economic sanctions on commercial relations (as defined in this volume), the withholding of normal flows of economic assistance, both bilateral and multilateral, and the clearly positive incentive of additional economic assistance beyond what would normally be available to a target country.

The pattern in the five case studies and other recent sanctions experience is that the United States is usually alone or almost alone in going the trade/investment sanction route, while other aid-donor countries are more inclined to join the United States in holding back normal aid flows. This was the case in the post–Tiananmen Square China relationship and continues to be the relationship for Cuba, Iran, and Myanmar. It is relatively rare that both trade sanctions and additional aid incentives are used together, although this is current U.S. policy toward North Korea, as substantial financial support for petroleum imports is given as an incentive to curtail the North Korean nuclear weapons program while a unilateral economic embargo remains in place.

The preference for carrots over sticks or aid over trade sanctions follows naturally from a strategy of private sector engagement to support a process of market-oriented economic reforms and democratization. In such circumstances, however, the composition of aid programs becomes important. Initial economic assistance should be directed to nongovernmental organizations, private sector projects, social sector infrastructure such as schools and health facilities, and technical assistance directly related to economic and political reforms, with financial support to the central government and public sector projects coming later if at all.

The use of aid rather than sanctions in relation to national security objectives is far more complicated and can only be judged on a case-by-case basis. The North Korea aid program noted above is highly controversial, and aid projects in Russia to keep highly trained nuclear and other strategic weapons personnel gainfully employed in the civilian sector at home rather than in weapons development abroad is a partial solution to the problem at best.

In terms of alternatives to unilateral economic sanctions, the carrot of economic aid is thus always one policy instrument to consider, but there are many ways to offer economic assistance, which, if nothing else, makes this a more flexible and thus at times a more effective policy instrument than broadly based commercial sanctions.

Economic Sanctions versus Military Intervention

This is a complex but important question about alternative policies to economic sanctions. Economic sanctions and military intervention can be pursued jointly, in a mutually supportive way, as was done in Bosnia. There can also be a sequential relationship, attempting to achieve a given objective first through economic sanctions, and then, if the sanctions fail to achieve their objective, resorting to military intervention, as occurred in Iraq and Haiti.[8] The most troubling relationship is when economic sanctions are adopted as a convenient substitute for military intervention because the sanctions avoid putting American lives at risk and have no budget cost, while there is a felt political need to "do something." The potential problem in this case is that the sanctions can be oversold as a foreign policy instrument when in fact they are ineffective in achieving the intended objective while having adverse consequences for other U.S. interests.

These important relationships between economic sanctions and military intervention, however, are far more likely to arise in circumstances involving multilateral rather than unilateral sanctions. When the United States is alone and without support from friends and allies in the application of economic sanctions, it would certainly have to act alone militarily, probably in the face of condemnation from the UN and others. Such U.S. military actions, therefore, except for quick punitive strikes, as taken against Afghanistan and Sudan in August 1998, would rarely if ever be an attractive alternative to unilateral sanctions in the post–Cold War circumstances of the 1990s. The only instance of a tradeoff between tightened unilateral sanctions and a U.S. military intervention in the case studies was for Cuba, after the shootdown of the unarmed planes over international waters in February 1996, and even in this case the punitive military strike was rejected.

≈   ≈   ≈

These are some of the specific policy issues that almost always arise when assessing alternatives to unilateral economic sanctions. There remain, however, more fundamental questions about maintaining normal commercial—that is, sanctions-free—relations with oppressive and rogue regimes, which require more fundamental thinking about the appropriate answer.

Notes

1. The quote is from Zhou Shijian, a vice president of the China Chamber of Commerce, in the *China Daily Business Weekly*, August 2, 1998.

2. Gary Clyde Hufbauer et al., "U.S. Economic Sanctions: Their Impact on Trade, Jobs, and Wages," Working Paper (Washington, D.C. Institute for International Economics, June 1996). The estimated annual loss of U.S. exports by country cannot be compared precisely because of methodological differences, in addition to the exclusion of service exports in the IIE report, but the estimates produced for three case study countries that overlap the IIE listing are Cuba (IIE $1.1 billion; EHP $3.0 billion), Iran (IIE $0.8

billion–$2.5 billion; EHP $0.5 billion–$2.0 billion), and Vietnam (IIE $69 million; EHP $1.3 billion–$2.6 billion), with a cumulative total of IIE $2.0 billion–$3.7 billion and EHP $4.8 billion–$7.6 billion.

3. For a detailed, authoritative account of the tragic consequences of the embargo on the Haitian people, see Elizabeth D. Gibbons, *Sanctions in Haiti: Human Rights and Democracy under Assault* (Westport, Conn.: Praeger/CSIS, 1999). Her summary statement of the impact of the multilateral trade embargo is as follows: "Because the embargo could not differentiate between villains and victims and its effects reached far into the urban slums and rural hilltops, it proved to be the main cause of the sanctions' devastating impact on Haiti's people, triggering or accelerating a horrifying descent into absolute poverty for the vast majority of Haitians. Unemployment increased by half (from 50 percent in 1990 to 75 percent in 1994), agricultural output declined 20 percent, prices for basic foodstuffs increased more than 100 percent while annual per capita income declined 30 percent, bottoming out at $250. Child malnutrition doubled, and thousands of children perished in a measles epidemic; maternal mortality increased 29 percent; school enrollments dropped by a third; the number of street children doubled, and some 100,000 children were placed in domestic service to live as little more than slaves. Consistent humanitarian exemptions and a massive humanitarian relief program could not prevent Haiti's devastation and demonstrated their essential inadequacy in the face of economic and social collapse" (pp. 94–95). For a broader assessment of U.S. interests and the Haitian embargo, see Ernest H. Preeg, *The Haitian Dilemma: A Case Study in Demographics, Development, and U.S. Foreign Policy* (Washington, D.C.: CSIS, 1996).

4. For an account of how the development of a nuclear weapons capability has been an overriding national security objective for Pakistan, see Dennis Kux, "Pakistan," contained in Haass, ed., *Economic Sanctions and American Diplomacy*, 157–176.

5. A related measure that might also be considered by the congressional trade committees is to eliminate the column two Smoot-Hawley tariff rates from U.S. tariff schedules. No purpose is served by continuing to pay homage to these highest tariffs in U.S. history through their inclusion on thousands of lines of tariff headings. Such simplification of the U.S. tariff schedule does not preclude members of Congress from raising any or all tariffs as high as they wish, but there is nothing sacrosanct about this particular set of extremely high tariffs that contributed significantly to the Great Depression of the 1930s.

6. Another part of the CSIS unilateral economic sanctions project deals in far greater detail with the subject of alternative policies.

7. South Africa is often cited as a successful example of how multilateral sanctions achieved positive results for human rights and democratization by

ending apartheid. This was again a case of unique circumstances, however, including the critical fact that the South African government was democratically elected, however limited its participation, and operated under the rule of law. Circumstances are very different for the authoritarian governments targeted for unilateral sanctions during the 1990s.

8. The sequential relationship raises further questions beyond the scope of this study. For Iraq, the Bush administration began with economic sanctions knowing full well that they would not induce an Iraqi withdrawal from Kuwait, but they were considered necessary as a step to gain American public support for the later military intervention. In the case of Haiti, the Bush administration in 1991–1992 was adamantly opposed to a U.S. military intervention, as was President Clinton's first Haiti policy envoy, Lawrence Pezzullo, in 1993 and early 1994. Only when the killing and repression in Haiti greatly intensified during the final months of the embargo, in large part caused by the devastating economic impact of the prolonged sanctions on the isolated and threatened military regime, was a policy of U.S. military intervention adopted as the least bad alternative. In effect, the economic sanctions created the circumstances for an unintended military intervention.

8

Feeling Good *and* Doing Good[?]

THE TECHNICAL ASSESSMENTS AND ARGUMENTS made throughout this study demonstrate that unilateral sanctions do not achieve their intended objectives but do adversely affect other U.S. interests. Yet an overarching argument in favor of sanctions must be addressed before a conclusive judgment on sanctions policy can be made. It concerns basic American values and the perceived need for the United States to take tangible actions against the leaders of oppressive or rogue regimes as a statement of principle. Trade and investment may create jobs and help the people in target countries, but they also inevitably provide at least some financial benefits for regime leaders to use personally or to support activities that are the target of the sanction, and American companies should simply not be permitted to contribute to such illicit benefits. Moreover, the opening of trade and investment to currently embargoed regimes will be touted as a victory by them, a tacit recognition of their legitimacy, as was the case for the communist leadership in Vietnam in 1994 and as would be the case for Fidel Castro's communist government if the Cuba embargo were lifted while he continued in power. Americans should consequently feel good about taking a principled moral stand against such governments through the imposition of economic sanctions even though the actions involved have no immediate good effects.

The response to this line of reasoning needs to be based on critical observations about how international relationships are evolving in the changed, post–Cold War world of the 1990s. Specific actions by the United States, including the imposition or the lifting of economic sanctions, must be viewed in a broader conceptual framework of U.S. interests and foreign policy objectives.

The first critical observation is that the global economy is undergoing a rapid transformation, unprecedented in history, which is powerfully affecting all countries, politically as well as economically. The economic transformation derives from the application of wide-ranging new technologies on a global scale, driven by private sectors and, in particular, by multinational corporations. Since the mid-1980s, international trade and investment have been growing three to four times faster than global GDP—the economic globalization phenomenon—with a consequent result of much higher growth in per capita income, especially in "emerging market economies." The temporary economic setbacks of 1997–1998 reflect, primarily, the failure of governments to undertake financial and other reforms necessary to accommodate the forces of high growth-oriented globalization and not the end of the growth process. The deeply interrelated political transformation stems from inherent advances in education levels and the accumulation of knowledge through new telecommunications technologies, with the concurrent rapid growth of an educated, younger generation middle class pressing for greater individual freedom and more democratic government. The overall transformation can be characterized as movement toward a new information age of reason.[1]

Another critical observation is that the United States is at the center and the forefront of this historic process of change. New technology development up to this point has taken place predominantly within the United States and is transmitted internationally primarily by American companies. Economically, the leading-edge standards for applied new technology, management, employee training, and protection of the environment are set largely by these American companies. Politically, the U.S. corporate culture of respect for individual rights, compensation based on merit, and the rule of law provides a positive day-to-day model for public- and private-sector observers throughout the developing world, even in remaining communist states such as China and Vietnam.

Yet another and related critical observation is that private-sector leaders are generally out in front of government leaders in managing this global process of change. Government leaders in all countries, including the United States, are preoccupied with, and frequently overwhelmed by, difficult adjustments to the new globalization realities. Caught in a political crossfire between market-driven forces for change and resistance from traditional constituencies threatened by it, they tend toward indecision. By contrast, private sector leaders, in their quest to develop new productive—and profitable—enterprises within and across borders, have provided creative leadership for trade liberalization, deregulation, privatization, and financial reform at all levels of economic development, including the emerging market economies of Asia, Latin America, and Central Europe.[2]

These critical observations underpin the recurring assessment in this study that U.S. private sector engagement is an important positive force for political as well as economic change, even in the most recalcitrant states as encountered in the case studies. And from this broader conceptual context is drawn the policy conclusion that maximum U.S. private sector engagement can do substantial good by promoting democratization and improved respect for human rights, while at the same time it is something to feel good about. Such a conclusion applies to all five country case studies, with the ensuing policy recommendations for lifting existing unilateral sanctions against Cuba, Iran, and Myanmar. Fidel Castro can claim victory, but it will be a hollow one as the growing forces for private economic enterprise and democratization proceed to consign his centrally planned and politburo-controlled regime to the dustbin of history.

This unleashing of U.S. private sector engagement in countries with oppressive or rogue regimes should, however, be only one dimension of an overall strategy for promoting market-oriented democracies in such countries. Three other areas of policy, in particular, should be engaged in a mutually supportive way:

1. Diplomatic relations. The United States should have normal and in some cases reasonably good political relations with such regimes, in the practical pursuit of mutual interests, but underlying differences in values should not be obscured. Democratic governments based on the rule of reason and a cooperative, nonviolent political process are fundamentally different from those that maintain power through coercion and force, because these same principles at home, for each grouping, inevitably carry over to international relations as well. U.S. diplomatic exchanges with nondemocratic regimes, at all levels, should firmly articulate basic U.S. values, emphasizing outreach to the younger generation, prodemocracy constituencies that now exist in almost all such countries. The United States should strongly support international organizations and private groups that promote democratization and protection of basic human rights. Concerted diplomatic initiatives with other democratic nations should also be a priority, and such initiatives, in the absence of current U.S. unilateral sanctions, could be strengthened with ASEAN members toward Myanmar and with European and Western Hemisphere democracies toward Cuba.

2. Economic assistance. This "carrot" becomes relatively less important as private sector investment increasingly dominates overall development finance, but a substantial role still exists for official development assistance, especially in the poorest countries, which should include Cuba, Myanmar, and Vietnam. The qualitative choices in providing such assistance, however, are crucial. The priorities, especially for economic assistance to the authoritarian regime grouping addressed here, should be to support nongovernmental organizations assisting the poorest segments of the population, private sector-oriented projects, and technical assistance directly related to economic and political reforms. For the multilateral development banks, in particular, such support would require a substantial restructuring of programs away from the long-standing preponderant concentration on public sector project and budget support loans. In addition, both multilateral and bilateral aid programs should establish more explicit political reform conditions for lending programs. For example, the European Bank for Reconstruction and Development permits loans only to countries with democratically based governments, and the World Bank recently adopted project conditions to avoid official corruption, but these conditions should be extended and strengthened.[3]

3. The international economic system. Strengthening the international trading system, toward free trade and investment, and building a "new financial architecture" that will mitigate if not avoid the financial disruption encountered during 1997–1999, are essential to all of the foregoing points. And yet both face uncertain prospects and unfocused international leadership. Next steps in trade liberalization and deregulation have bogged down while the content of a new financial architecture has yet to be addressed adequately. A particular challenge for U.S. leadership that bridges the trade and financial arenas, and casts a threatening cloud over both, is the chronic and growing U.S. current account deficit.[4]

The line of reasoning and proposed policy framework up to this point provide the basis for both doing good and feeling good in support of democratization and respect for human rights, while avoiding resort to unilateral economic sanctions except in rare, narrowly targeted circumstances. There is, however, an inextricably linked darker dimension to this same technology-driven, economic globalization process—namely, the proliferation of national security threats from weapons of mass destruction, ballistic missiles for delivering them, and what is referred to as cyberwarfare. Ever simpler and more available technologies, at lower and lower costs, put these new weapons increasingly within reach of rogue states, terrorist groups, and organized international crime. Moreover, the political orientation of these new and growing national security threats is fundamentally different from the relatively contained U.S.-Soviet standoff during the Cold War and requires a corresponding new and redesigned policy response.

The interaction of private sector engagement as a force for positive change and the unavoidable contribution such engagement can make to the development of new technology-intensive security threats constitutes the central foreign policy challenge to the United States and the entire democratic grouping of nations for the decades ahead. The policy challenge can be formulated largely in terms of time sequence, of a race to bring the large majority of nations, population, and economic and military power up to the level of stable, cooperating democratic governments, capable of suppressing the new weapons threats, before rogue states and associated private groups are able to threaten or carry out wide-scale disruption and destruction. To win the race requires a reordering of foreign policy goals and instruments, keyed to the new national security realities.[5]

The integrated policy response offered here, in general terms, is to maintain the commitment to essentially unhindered private sector engagement while, at the same time, placing a higher priority, which almost surely involves a commitment of greater resources, on a strengthened and redirected national defense and international law enforcement capability. The specifics of such a strengthened and redirected capability are beyond the scope of this study, although as indicated in the case studies, there are very distinct challenges involved for dealing with the proliferation of weapons of mass destruction in unstable subregions such as the Middle East and South Asia, the overlapping yet broader threat of international terrorism, and the emerging geostrategic rivalry between the United States and China. Yet another important part of the new order of national security threats that did not surface in a prominent way in any of the five case studies is the rapid growth in technology-intensive international crime.

As for the role of unilateral economic sanctions in this overall scheme of things, it is in any event relatively very small, with potential net negative impact in most situations, and thus generally to be avoided through strengthened disciplines on their application and better awareness of their downsides by those in foreign policy leadership positions. Perhaps the most damaging use of unilateral sanctions, in this context, is to present them as a relatively cost free solution to growing threats in the national security field, and thereby to divert attention from the need to consider the hard choices for a genuinely effective response.

In conclusion, is it possible to remove the bracketed question mark in this chapter title? The answer is that it can only be removed contingent on a more effective response to growing national security threats, which are inextricably linked to the parallel pursuit of more productive and democratic societies throughout the world. In short, the United States should speak softly, but firmly, while carrying the big stick of a formidable national defense capability and an even bigger carrot of a fully engaged U.S. private sector.

Notes

1. The summary assessment of the globalization process in this paragraph, including the normative goal of a "new information age of reason," is elaborated in Ernest H. Preeg, *From Here to Free Trade: Essays in Post-Uruguay*

Round Trade Strategy (Chicago/Washington: University of Chicago Press/CSIS, 1998), especially the first essay, "Economic Globalization and the U.S. Interest: A Net Assessment."

2. The private sector leadership role within the new economic globalization process is explained and defined more fully in Ernest H. Preeg, *Traders in a Brave New World: The Uruguay Round and the Future of the International Trading System* (Chicago: University of Chicago Press, 1995), with a summing up on p. 236: "The utopian New Soviet Man never materialized, but the New High-tech Economic Person is already among us and exercising a growing influence. These new economic persons have a common educational grounding across national borders based on scientific inquiry and the rule of reason. They have an optimistic disposition, working within the enormous positive sum game environment of new technology development and application, and are negatively disposed to economic nationalism that holds back technological change. At the international level, they communicate freely with each other despite widely differing cultural backgrounds and provide the expertise and leadership for the economic globalization under way. They are engineers, scientists, economists, business-school graduates, and technicians nurtured on computers and jointly able to create amazing new technology-intensive enterprises oriented toward international trade and investment. They are the traders in a brave new economic world, and their eighteenth-century forefathers would be very proud of them."

3. A major shift of financing to private sector projects and the establishment of political reform conditions, as done by the European Bank, would require changes in the charters of other multilateral development banks, especially the World Bank. The United States should propose and pursue such changes, beginning with the Inter-American Development Bank, all of whose borrowers are democratically elected governments committed to free trade and investment in the hemisphere.

4. Key elements of the relationship between the existing financial architecture and the chronic U.S. trade deficit are presented in Ernest H. Preeg, "The U.S. Trillion Dollar Debt to Foreign Central Banks" (Washington, D.C.: Institute of International Finance, October 1998), available on www.iif.com (click to "essay competition").

5. A more detailed presentation of the interaction of the economic and national security dimensions of U.S. foreign policy, including the important factor of interrelated time tracks, is provided by Ernest H. Preeg, "The Economic-National Security Interface," in *Foreign Policy into the 21st Century: The U.S. Leadership Challenge*, Douglas Johnston, ed. (Washington, D.C.: CSIS, 1996), 140–142.

Appendix A

Unilateral Economic Sanctions and the U.S. Constitution

Denise Auclair

THE DEBATE ON UNILATERAL ECONOMIC SANCTIONS has focused primarily on the effectiveness of federal sanctions as a foreign policy instrument. Another important dimension to the sanctions debate, however, relates to the U.S. Constitution, in two respects. The first concerns sanctions adopted at the state and municipal levels that may conflict with the federal government's constitutional powers in the foreign policy field and thus be unconstitutional. In 1998 this issue came before the federal courts over a Massachusetts selective purchasing law against companies doing business in Myanmar (formerly Burma). The second respect involves the relationship between the president and Congress in the conduct of sanctions policy and is more a matter of the spirit than the letter of the Constitution. The most specific recent case in which Congress challenged the president's constitutional foreign policy leadership role is the 1996 Cuban Liberty and Democratic Solidarity Act, or Helms-Burton, which extends economic sanctions against Cuba while at the same time greatly limiting the president's freedom of action on Cuba policy.

State and Municipal Sanctions

The growing participation by states and municipalities in the global economy—through foreign trade missions and the opening of state offices abroad to promote trade and investment, for example—has magnified the potential impact of subfederal sanctions, increasing the economic leverage that can be applied to attempt to influence foreign behavior. Previous waves of sanctions have addressed Northern Ireland's Catholic-Protestant conflict and South Africa's apartheid regime in the 1980s, as well as the Arab boycott of Israel in the 1970s, while recent state and municipal sanctions have focused primarily on Myanmar's human rights violations. Besides questions of whether these sanctions are effective or how they affect U.S. relations with allies or the targeted country, the proliferation of these controversial sanctions in the past few years has also prompted the question of whether subfederal sanctions are constitutional.

The preferred form of subfederal sanctions has recently been "selective purchasing" legislation, which penalizes bids on government contracts by companies that do business in the targeted country. To date, one state and more than 20 municipalities have passed such legislation against Myanmar, Nigeria, Cuba, and Tibet. Potential sanctions under consideration have targeted these countries as well as Indonesia, Switzerland, and a range of countries in the category of human rights violators. Of the nearly 30 laws in place (some municipalities have enacted more than one such provision), 22 target Myanmar, which is the target of the only law enacted at the state level, in Massachusetts.

"Test Case": The Massachusetts Burma Law

On June 25, 1996, Massachusetts became the first, and thus far the only, state to pass a selective purchasing law against Myanmar.[1] Chapter 130 of the Massachusetts Act of 1996, entitled "An Act Regulating State Contracts with Companies Doing Business with or in Burma," commonly called the Massachusetts "Burma law," affects any U.S. or foreign company doing business in Myanmar that also wants to provide goods or services to the Massachusetts government. Any bid for a Massachusetts contract by such a company will have a 10 percent premium added to it, which puts it at a substantial competitive disadvantage. "Doing business" in Myanmar is defined to include a physical presence in the country, transactions with the government, or promotion of the country's exports, while "company" applies not only to the bidding entity, but also to its parent company if it is a wholly owned subsidiary. As a result, even a company that does not do business in Myanmar, but whose parent or affiliate does, cannot bid on Massachusetts contracts on a fully competitive basis.

The law requires the Massachusetts secretary of administration and finance to keep a "restricted purchase list" of those companies doing business in Myanmar. In September 1998 this list included 38 U.S. companies and 240 foreign companies, as well as numerous subsidiaries. The law stipulates that a company must be certified as having ceased operations in Myanmar in order to avoid the 10 percent pricing penalty. Companies on the list also may not purchase or lease state-owned property. Exceptions exist for bids that are the only offer or bids for which there is no comparable low bid; medical supplies for which there are no substitutes; and operations for the purpose of news reporting. The law in effect forces companies to choose between doing business with Massachusetts or doing business with Myanmar. Several companies have opted for the former by withdrawing from Myanmar, including Apple Computer, Hewlett-Packard, Eastman Kodak, Motorola, and Philips Electronics, all of which cited the law as a reason for withdrawal. Other companies on the list, such as Unocal (which is involved in a large offshore natural gas project), Caterpillar, and Procter & Gamble, have elected to stay despite the Massachusetts law.

Selective purchasing laws are not new to the Massachusetts political scene. The Burma legislation's sponsor, Representative Byron Rushing, also sponsored Massachusetts's 1988 selective purchasing law targeting South Africa, which was intended to help pressure South Africa to end apartheid. The Burma law similarly came about in reaction to human rights violations by the military junta that took power in 1988. The explicit intent of the law was to force companies to stop doing business in Myanmar, with the secondary intent, as publicly stated by Massachusetts officials, of eliminating this source of revenue as a means to pressure the Myanmar government to begin a transition toward a democratic system. Although Congress was simultaneously considering action on Myanmar in 1996, Massachusetts legislators were not content merely to try to affect the federal process by passing resolutions condemning the situation in Myanmar, the traditional and usually ineffective route. This time Massachusetts took a proactive stance, believing its action would set an example for a strong federal policy. In the words of Rushing, "That's why we're passing selective purchasing bills, because that gets [the State Department's] attention."[2]

As with the federal sanctions against Myanmar, human rights activists played a substantial role in initiating the legislation. The idea for the law developed from an encounter at a 1993 press conference to announce the termination of the state's South Africa sanctions. There Rushing met Massachusetts resident Simon Billenness, a Myanmar rights advocate and senior analyst at the self-described socially responsible investment firm, Franklin Research and Development. Rushing's enthusiasm for selective purchasing legislation, plus Billenness's belief that this method would be most effective in creating pressure on Myanmar, produced a bill similar to the 1988 South Africa law, for which Billenness simply crossed out "South Africa" and substituted "Burma." The Massachusetts Burma Roundtable, a loose group of organizations and individuals chaired by Billenness, was formed around the time the bill was introduced in the spring of 1994 and had as one of its major goals passage of the bill. The legislation did not gather momentum until it was reintroduced in 1995, and by the end of that year, the bill had passed the House without dissent and moved to the Senate, where it was approved in 1996 by a unanimous voice vote. Throughout the 1994–1996 period, questions were never raised about the measure's constitutionality by Massachusetts legislators, their staffs, private sector lobbyists, or the U.S. government. Although no expert on Burma, Rushing made a compelling case for the bill, while his "work on apartheid had established his credentials, and colleagues, who felt little pressure either way, were willing to go along."[3]

Domestic politics also played a role in the passage of the law. Massachusetts governor William Weld, who had previously opposed the linkage of sanctions to human rights concerns in the case of China, was engaged in a close U.S. Senate race with incumbent John Kerry. Weld "got religion"[4] and proclaimed his support for the Massachusetts Burma legislation, which set him apart from

Kerry and made Myanmar sanctions a campaign issue. Kerry, who had been slow to endorse federal sanctions on Myanmar, shifted after the Massachusetts law was signed in July 1996 with the backing of Weld and in August voted in favor of the Cohen-Feinstein "Policy toward Burma" amendment, which established the federal sanctions banning new U.S. investment in Myanmar.

As protests by frustrated U.S. corporations grew against the proliferation of sanctions at the federal, state, and municipal levels, one established business group decided to test the legality of subfederal sanctions by challenging the constitutionality of the Massachusetts law. At the request of several of its corporate members, the National Foreign Trade Council (NFTC) in the spring of 1997 formed an ad hoc coalition—USA*Engage—to fight unilateral sanctions, mostly at the federal level. The coalition included a committee on state and municipal sanctions, though it did not initially plan a suit against the Massachusetts Burma law. The idea soon arose for the suit, however, and it was eventually filed by the NFTC on April 30, 1998, before the U.S. District Court for the District of Massachusetts, located in Boston. NFTC officials called the suit a "test case" that could set a precedent for challenges of similar laws and pending legislation across the country. For some proponents of the suit, the concern was less about the direct fiscal effects of the Massachusetts law, or even the negative publicity it drew to the companies, and more about the recent wave of subfederal sanctions and the principle of states and municipalities limiting companies' ability to do business abroad. In response, Massachusetts legislators presented a united front against this attack on their procurement prerogative.

Both sides agreed that the issues at stake were so important that the case would likely go beyond the district level to an appeals court and finally to the Supreme Court. In the district court, oral arguments were held September 23, 1998, and the decision by Chief Judge Joseph Tauro was handed down on November 4, in favor of the NFTC. The judge then filed a formal judgment that the law was unconstitutional, halting implementation of the law. Massachusetts immediately announced its intent to appeal the ruling before the First Circuit Court in Boston and filed its appeal, accompanied by amicus curiae briefs from 11 states and 26 members of Congress, in February 1999. The NFTC submitted its response in March, backed by 10 members of Congress and the European Union, and observers predict an expedited ruling. In the meantime, supporters of the Burma law pressed for a new divestment law or consumer boycotts as alternative means to pressure companies to withdraw from Myanmar, while the city of Los Angeles, undeterred by the ruling, adopted its own provision similar to the Burma law. Although the district ruling was a victory for the NFTC, the final outcome of the suit has no high-level precedent, as neither the Supreme Court nor any federal court has ever ruled on the constitutionality of subfederal economic sanctions laws.

Principal Arguments of the NFTC Suit

The suit is based upon three arguments: (1) foreign policy is the exclusive domain of the federal government, (2) the Foreign Commerce Clause of the Constitution precludes state restrictions on international commerce, and (3) federal policy toward Myanmar preempts the Massachusetts legislation.[5] These arguments derive from the text of the Constitution and the interpretation of the courts over the years.

Exclusive foreign affairs doctrine.   The suit charges that the Massachusetts selective purchasing law constitutes the state's own foreign policy toward Myanmar, seeking as its final objective a change in the behavior of the Myanmar government, whereas the Constitution provides that foreign policy is the exclusive domain of the federal government. Article II, section 2 of the Constitution stipulates that "[the president] shall have power, by and with the advice and consent of the Senate, to make treaties . . . [and] appoint ambassadors." Article I, section 10 states: "No state shall enter into any treaty, . . . agreement or compact with another state," nor "lay any imposts or duties on imports or exports." An important legal precedent for the case is the 1968 Supreme Court case *Zschernig v. Miller*, in which the Court found unconstitutional an Oregon law that prohibited inheritance rights for nonresident aliens whose countries did not provide reciprocal rights for U.S.

citizens. This ruling came in spite of the fact that the federal government had submitted an amicus curiae brief registering no complaint with the law, and took into consideration such factors as effects on and protests by foreign nations, the number of similar laws across the country, and the scope or intent of the law related to foreign affairs—all relevant to the NFTC case.

Massachusetts responded that its law does not intrude upon the foreign policy powers of the federal government. It argued that the Burma law does not seek to "conduct" foreign affairs, but rather to "affect" them, and that the Constitution permits certain state actions that only indirectly affect foreign affairs.

The district judge's decision evaluated the NFTC argument and found that "the Massachusetts Burma law impermissibly infringes on the federal government's power to regulate foreign affairs." The ruling states that the Constitution "vests plenary power over foreign affairs in the federal government" and that the Supreme Court has consistently recognized this exclusive role. The judge's interpretation of an "impermissible burden" placed on foreign affairs relied principally upon *Zschernig v. Miller*, concluding that the Burma law has more than an "indirect or incidental effect in foreign countries." The ruling refers to the law's clear intent of changing Myanmar's domestic policy regarding human rights and to the amicus curiae brief submitted by the European Union as evidence of the Massachusetts law's "disruptive impact on foreign relations."

Commerce Clause and the market participant exception. Article I, section 8, clause 3 of the Constitution states that "[the Congress shall have power] to regulate commerce with foreign nations." The courts have ruled that the Commerce Clause forbids state laws that discriminate against or burden foreign commerce. The NFTC argues that the Massachusetts law significantly penalizes companies engaging in commerce with Myanmar, running counter to this clause. In the 1979 case *Japan Line, Ltd. v. County of Los Angeles*, the Supreme Court found unconstitutional a California law that levied an ad valorem property tax on Japanese cargo containers used solely for foreign commerce. The ruling includes the often-quoted phrase, "the Federal Government must speak with one voice when regulating commercial relations with foreign governments," and calls foreign commerce "a matter of national concern."[6]

However, the Supreme Court has also allowed for a "market participant exception" to the Commerce Clause, which says that a state may place restrictions upon those with whom it does business, as a sovereign participant in the market. Massachusetts officials and other supporters of the law have used this defense, stated as follows: "The citizens of Massachusetts, as well as every other state, have every right to decide criteria fitting with their principles on where and how they choose to spend their tax dollars,"[7] or more concisely, "No one can tell us how we can spend our money." The courts have in certain cases upheld the state's right to discriminate in interstate trade in favor of its own citizens. Advocates of the NFTC argue, however, that this is a narrow exception that does not apply in the case of the Burma legislation. They point out that Massachusetts does not merely seek to participate in a market, but to influence other markets in which it does not have a primary interest—namely, the business done between bidding companies and Myanmar. This could qualify Massachusetts as a market "regulator" rather than solely a "participant."

The district judge did not consider this argument, as the exclusive foreign affairs doctrine was sufficient for the ruling. He noted that although lower courts have extended the market participant exception to foreign commerce, the Supreme Court has never addressed a case involving international (rather than interstate) commerce.

Preemption. Preemption simply means that when state legislation and federal legislation on the same subject conflict, the federal policy preempts, or takes precedence over, state policy. The Supremacy Clause of Article VI of the Constitution states that the laws and treaties of the United States "shall be the supreme law of the land . . . anything in the Constitution or laws of any State to the contrary notwithstanding." Massachusetts contests preemption on the grounds that neither Congress nor the president has ever explicitly stated the intent to preempt state laws targeting

Myanmar. However, the Supreme Court has also defined two other means of federal preemption: actual conflict and implied preemption. The Massachusetts Burma law does not directly conflict with federal policy because it applies sanctions by means of a selective purchasing law, which affects trade rather than the new U.S. investment banned by the 1997 federal sanctions. The NFTC suit argues the latter type of preemption: because federal officials did not state an intent *not* to preempt, the federal decision not to limit trade with Myanmar as part of its sanctions should be understood as disapproval of such laws. However, the district judge dismissed this argument in the September 23 hearing and repeated in his ruling that the NFTC "failed to carry this burden [of proving implied preemption]."

U.S. Government Position

The Clinton administration has declined to take a position on the NFTC case, but is "following" the case closely. State Department officials have occasionally made statements relevant to the exclusive foreign affairs doctrine, asserting the federal government's control of foreign policy. Advised by its legal counsel not to directly confront the constitutionality issue, the administration has preferred to discuss the effects of state and municipal sanctions, particularly their detraction from a single, unified U.S. foreign policy. Under Secretary of State Stuart Eizenstat, the Clinton administration's point man on sanctions, testified before Congress in October 1997 that "it is the Executive Branch of the U.S. Government which is charged with conducting the nation's foreign policy, in consultation with the U.S. Congress, not states and municipalities. We should have only one foreign policy at a time."[8] Deputy Assistant Secretary of State David Marchick seconded this statement in a March 1998 testimony before the Maryland House of Delegates, stating that "we are concerned that state and local sanctions may impair the President's ability to send a clear and unified message to the rest of the world." However, Marchick did not address the constitutionality of state sanctions. State Department officials have preferred to handle the issue by publicly calling for states and municipalities to work with the federal government in the writing of sanctions legislation, rather than pressing for a halt to state and local sanctions.

Comments on the constitutionality of the law have often been confused by simultaneous comments on the extraterritorial implications of the Massachusetts Burma law. The European Union and Japan have protested that the law violates the 1994 General Procurement Agreement negotiated within the World Trade Organization, which prohibits consideration of political grounds in the awarding of official contracts. For example, State Department officials' descriptions of state and municipal sanctions as counterproductive have often been directed at how their extraterritorial reach has shifted U.S. focus during talks with its allies from a coordinated policy on Myanmar to a WTO dispute. The two issues have also been linked because an unconstitutionality ruling on the Massachusetts law would likely negate the WTO challenge. However, the law's possible conflict with U.S. international commitments is not directly related to the U.S. Constitution.

Some have suggested that the Clinton administration has been reluctant to publicly commit to a position against subfederal sanctions for domestic reasons, such as the risk of appearing not to support tough measures against governments that violate human rights. Although the Clinton administration has seriously considered filing an amicus curiae brief in support of the NFTC suit at the appeals level, it will likely withhold any position until forced to do so by court request, the odds of which increase as the case moves through the courts. The State Department is in any event hesitant to get involved in a dispute over the boundary between federal and state powers and points out that matters of constitutionality are the domain of the Justice Department. The Justice Department is responsible for filing an opinion on behalf of the United States, and the State Department role would likely be limited to advising Justice on the degree to which the Massachusetts law limits the executive branch's ability to conduct foreign policy. A precedent exists for the Justice Department's determination in its Office of Legal Counsel's 1986 opinion on South Africa divestment laws, in which the constitutionality of the laws was affirmed on the same three grounds present in the NFTC suit. This opinion would have to be distinguished before a filing by Justice in support of the NFTC suit. Although there may be institutional resistance to such an action, enough dissimilarities exist between the two situations to warrant a review of the opinion. In the absence of a formal U.S. position, the judge may take into consideration public statements by State officials such as those mentioned above.

Two Related Developments

The South Africa precedent. The Massachusetts Burma law evokes comparisons to the state's 1988 South Africa law and to the numerous divestment and selective purchasing laws that were in place against that country in the late 1980s. Indeed, supporters of the Burma law point to the South Africa legislation as its inspiration and as a model for bringing pressure on a foreign government to change. The characteristics of the situations may appear similar: for example, government human rights violations and internal opposition support of sanctions by the African National Congress in South Africa and Aung San Suu Kyi in Myanmar. Archbishop Desmond Tutu, a moral authority figure in the struggle against apartheid, has said, "I think the world needs to use pressure, the kind that was used against the South African regime: sanctions to isolate Burma."[9] However, there are several important differences. The majority of the South Africa laws were divestment laws, with differences in application that did not always require total divestment from companies doing business in South Africa. Moreover, the South Africa laws applied only to U.S. companies and their subsidiaries, rather than to U.S. and foreign companies alike, including their subsidiaries and parent companies. This characteristic of the Massachusetts legislation has provoked the ire of U.S. allies and lessened the support of the federal government for such measures.

The crucial difference is that the Massachusetts Burma law is not the welcome companion to federal efforts that subfederal measures were in the case of South Africa. In the late 1980s, not only was there a growing consensus in the United States about the utility of sanctions in putting an end to apartheid in South Africa—approximately 140 state and municipal sanctions were in effect

prior to the 1985 and 1986 federal sanctions—but the same mind-
set prevailed with U.S. allies, making the sanctions truly multilateral. Assistant Secretary of State Alan Larson addressed this issue in
his March 1998 testimony before the Maryland legislature, allowing that the South Africa measures may have strongly contributed
to the ending of apartheid, but that at that time states and municipalities "were swimming with the tide of public opinion, not cutting across trading rights or political rights of our major partners."
Although questions of constitutionality were present then as well—
in 1989 the Maryland State Court upheld the constitutionality of a
Baltimore divestment ordinance—U.S. companies were unwilling
to contest the more unified U.S. public opinion and wanted to
avoid appearing to support apartheid in South Africa. In the present situation, taking care to firmly state their opposition to
Myanmar's military junta, U.S. companies have taken advantage of
split views within government and the public on the utility of subfederal sanctions as a force for change and have vocally opposed the
recent wave of sanctions.

The Swiss bank settlement.   The threat of U.S. state and
municipal sanctions, especially by New York City, were an important impetus to the August 13, 1998, announcement that the two
largest private Swiss banks, Credit Suisse and Union Bank of
Switzerland AG, had agreed to settle claims by Jewish victims of
the Holocaust and their heirs for $1.25 billion. New York City offi-
cials led a group of state and local representatives that had threatened to phase in sanctions on Swiss banks beginning September 1
of the same year if a settlement was not reached.

The federal government, which had been claiming that it could
not prevent states or cities from imposing such sanctions, reversed
its position in July after State Department legal counsel advised
that such a claim could negatively affect the U.S. position in the
Massachusetts case, in which U.S. precedence over state sanctions
was at issue. Although Under Secretary of State Eizenstat, who was
principally engaged in both the sanctions debate and the "Nazi
gold" case, made several statements against state and municipal
sanctions, the government's influence in negotiations with the
Swiss banks probably benefited from the pressure created by the

specter of subfederal sanctions. This may have contributed to the reluctance of the Clinton administration to take a position on the Massachusetts case. In any case, although the threat of state and municipal sanctions seemingly helped the federal government informally pressure the Swiss, the Switzerland analogy does not answer the question of whether enacted subfederal sanctions are constitutional.

Conclusions

The Massachusetts Burma law is only one of nearly 30 similar subfederal economic sanctions. The final decision in the NFTC suit will have a strong impact on the future of such laws and on the balance between the federal government's foreign policy powers and state and municipal governments' procurement powers. Precisely because past cases have not resolved this issue, a Supreme Court decision would be tremendously helpful in decisively answering the constitutional questions raised by the case.

With such matters at stake, the U.S. government cannot afford to sit on the sidelines of this case without voicing its own opinion. The Clinton administration has raised practical concerns about state and municipal sanctions, such as their effect on the executive branch's flexibility in formulating foreign policy. However, this is not enough: the State Department should ask the Justice Department to thoroughly review the NFTC challenge of the Massachusetts law, while taking a clear position as to how these sanctions intrude upon the foreign policy powers delegated to the federal government by the Constitution.

Executive versus Legislative Control of Sanctions Policy

The use of sanctions as a foreign policy instrument also raises constitutional questions within the federal government, although they are more likely to be related to the spirit, not the letter, of the Constitution. The increasing number of sanctions laws initiated and passed by Congress in the 1990s has prompted the question: who controls this area of foreign policy?

The most important case in which this question arises is the Cuban Liberty and Democratic Solidarity (LIBERTAD) Act of 1996, commonly called Helms-Burton after its cosponsors. From 1960 to 1996, Congress granted the president broad discretionary power for the implementation of the embargo against Cuba, a central instrument of U.S. Cuba policy. The Cuban Democracy Act of 1992, while tightening the embargo in some respects, also encouraged the president to "be prepared to reduce the sanctions in carefully calibrated ways" in response to positive steps by the Cuban government. When Republicans gained control of Congress in 1994, Helms-Burton developed in part out of a concern that President Clinton might actually take advantage of that clause and move toward an easing of the embargo.

Titles I and II of Helms-Burton, although less publicized, substantially limit the president's flexibility in Cuba policy. Title II mandates that suspension of the embargo be preceded by presidential certification of several conditions, including a Cuban transition government in power that has released all political prisoners, has planned to hold democratic elections within 18 months, and has taken appropriate steps to settle claims on expropriated property. Should he wish to modify the embargo in any respect, the president is bound by the codification of the embargo in Title I, which states that all elements of the embargo are to remain in effect, subject to Title II's requirements for determining a transition government. Title IV of Helms-Burton, which denies visas to "traffickers" in expropriated U.S. property and their dependents, breaks controversial new ground in the area of expropriation policy and is therefore particularly noteworthy in that the president lacks any discretion—waiver authority—in its implementation.

Drafters of the Helms-Burton legislation believed that they were well within their constitutional bounds on Title II. In their view, the title merely made explicit a role for Congress in U.S. Cuba policy that Congress has always had—that is, the authority to pass a joint resolution disapproving the president's decision to suspend the embargo. The real change, then, was in the requirements delineated by Congress for the president to make his determination to lift part, or all, of the embargo. This does "tie the president's hands" in the sense that Congress has set strict conditions that may not all be present when the president wants to respond to change in Cuba. The administration viewed Helms-Burton in this light, and during hearings on the legislation, Under Secretary of State Peter Tarnoff went as far as to warn that the legislation could infringe upon the president's constitutional authority to conduct foreign policy.[10] However, most administration complaints took the form of protests against the practical limitations on the executive branch's flexibility to respond to positive events in Cuba and negotiate during an imperfect transition. Secretary of State Warren Christopher threatened a presidential veto if changes were not forthcoming, such as addressing the lack of presidential discretion in Titles II and IV. Although Congress made some changes in the bill to deflect criticism, the administration abandoned its negotiating position after the Cuban shootdown of two unarmed aircraft over international waters in February 1996. The incident created great pressures to adopt the entire bill, including the codification of the embargo written in just after the shootdown, and the president signed the law on March 12.

Article II, section 2 of the Constitution states: "[The president] shall have power . . . to make treaties . . . [and] appoint ambassadors," albeit with the advice and consent of Congress. Interpretation of this passage has generally assigned primary responsibility for foreign policy to the executive branch. In practice, the balance between executive and legislative control of foreign policy has seesawed over the years. The legislative branch dominated foreign policy for much of this country's history, with the executive branch's prominence in the latter half of this century related to the phenomenon of the Cold War, during which the United States needed a strong, unified foreign policy. Thus complaints against congressional sanctions laws have tended to be related more to their practical effects on policymaking than to the Constitution, and the problem is often rephrased in terms of Congress's "micromanaging" foreign policy.

Sanctions policy also concerns foreign commerce, however, for which Congress is responsible under Article I, section 8, clause 3 of the Constitution. Although this fact could conceivably have been used to defend against charges of Congress's overstepping its constitutional bounds in Helms-Burton, members of Congress responded to European threats to challenge Helms-Burton in the WTO by claiming that the issue was a matter of foreign policy, not trade policy, and thus outside the WTO's mandate. In fact, sanctions policy is both trade policy and foreign policy, or trade policy for foreign policy objectives.[11]

Not only is the Constitution vague on the intersection of foreign and trade policies, but court cases on this subject have not resulted in any definitive delineation of powers, and no case has challenged a law similar to Helms-Burton. An important case, often quoted by State Department lawyers in matters of presidential powers in foreign affairs, is the 1936 Supreme Court case *United States v. Curtiss-Wright Export Corp.* The case concerned a situation opposite to that of Helms-Burton, in which Congress granted broad discretion to the president, authorizing the president to halt weapons sales to Bolivia and Paraguay. The Court refuted the plaintiff's charge that the resolution was overstepping congressional power. The opinion stated, "We are here dealing not alone with an authority vested in the President by an exertion of legislative power, but with such authority plus the very delicate, plenary and exclusive power of the President as the sole organ of the federal government in the field of international relations—a power which does not require as a basis for its exercise an act of Congress."[12] However, in 1952 the Court rejected broad presidential powers in a national security situation in *Youngstown Sheet & Tube Co. v. Sawyer,* which nullified President Harry Truman's seizure of steel mills to prevent work stoppage during a national emergency declared after the 1950 North Korean invasion of South Korea. The ruling set up a continuum in which the president's powers increased in tandem with the level of congruence between his actions and congressional authorization. This framework led to the determination that the president was on weakest ground constitutionally when acting in opposition to the stated intentions of Congress. This set a precedent for a lead role for Congress when a national security situation involved commerce in any way, clearly relevant to Cuba.

Concerns about executive versus legislative prerogative at this intersection have become more urgent in the context of the recent surge in the use of unilateral sanctions as a foreign policy instrument. Two important issues are who decides to pursue these sanctions—based on what kind of assessment—and how much flexibility is granted to the president. Congress has taken frequent initiative on sanctions in the 1990s, although 1998 sanctions reform legislation sponsored by Senator Richard Lugar and Representatives Lee Hamilton and Philip Crane argues that improvements are needed in the process, such as a prior economic assessment of the sanctions' impact on U.S. commercial interests. As sanctions can be a politically sensitive policy instrument that may be most effective when applied or modified quickly, the executive branch, with its comprehensive direction of foreign affairs, is better suited for policy implementation. This need for flexibility has made waiver authority a prominent issue in congressional sanctions laws. Both extremes are present in current sanctions laws, from the lack of discretion in Titles II and IV of Helms-Burton to the broad authority granted in the Iran-Libya Sanctions Act. In these two cases, as with federal Myanmar sanctions, the initial legislative proposals contained far more limitations on presidential flexibility than did the final version of the laws.

Despite working to preserve executive waiver authority in each of these laws, the Clinton administration poorly managed congressional initiatives on sanctions policy in 1996. Those working with the administration at the time believe that it did not fully understand the impact that the sanctions legislation would have on the executive branch's foreign policy authority. In 1997 and 1998, however, the Clinton administration made a concerted effort to obtain greater flexibility in sanctions laws. This was especially apparent in the administration's strong opposition to early versions of the 1998 Freedom from Religious Persecution Act, which required the president to impose sanctions under broad circumstances and allowed only limited waiver authority. During the recent, ongoing debate on sanctions, administration officials have even broached the idea of permanent presidential waiver authority. Meanwhile, President Clinton signaled his desire to regain some

control of U.S. Cuba policy by his May 1998 decision to increase
the permitted level of remittances to Cuba and to lift the ban on
direct flights to Cuba and by his January 1999 authorization of
similar small measures. These actions were taken despite Helms-
Burton recommendations (though not binding) that he not do so
unless the Cuban government permitted "unfettered operation of
small businesses" and "abrogation of the sanction for departure
from Cuba by refugees, release of political prisoners, recognition of
the right of association, and other fundamental freedoms."[13]

Conclusions

A court case challenging the constitutionality of congressional
sanctions laws is unlikely. Congress has historically played a role in
foreign policy and has a firm constitutional basis for its prerogative
in trade policy. Rather than protesting the interference of Congress
in sanctions policy on constitutional grounds, then, the executive
branch needs to firmly protect its own foreign policy authority
when necessary. At the very least, a middle way between the
extremes of no waiver authority and unlimited waiver authority is
necessary to satisfy both branches. The executive branch must take
seriously the policy objectives driving congressional sanctions legislation and work to negotiate the best compromise that addresses
both the concerns of Congress and the need for presidential flexibility for successful foreign policy.

∾   ∾   ∾

Although the foregoing constitutional issues at the state and
municipal level are quite different from those within the federal
branch, the two levels share one important characteristic: both
derive from recent unilateral economic sanctions. In the post–Cold
War period, the principal justification for a single U.S. foreign policy has disappeared, leaving in its wake multiple policies advocated
by various actors in the political system. Yet in the context of globalization and a constantly evolving world, the success of sanctions
as a policy instrument is dependent upon the clarity of the policy
and its responsiveness to change. The president and secretary of
state must be able to implement a clear and coherent foreign policy.

Both subfederal and congressionally mandated sanctions may be detrimental to executive foreign policy flexibility, but this is not inherent. The best scenario is for all branches and levels of government to work together toward a consensus-driven U.S. sanctions policy, allowing maximum flexibility and prerogative for the executive branch in the use of unilateral sanctions. Given the present lack of a clear overall foreign policy vision articulated by the executive branch, however, it is more likely that for the foreseeable future, states, municipalities, Congress, and the president will continue to struggle over the application of unilateral sanctions, lessening their efficacy as a foreign policy instrument.

Notes

1. The government of Burma changed the name of the country to Myanmar in 1989. However, the United States follows the highly unusual procedure of officially calling the country Burma. Standard international procedure is to accept the legitimacy of a government, and its name for the country, if it effectively controls the national territory. In this context, the country is referred to here as Myanmar, which implies no value judgment.

2. "50 Different Departments of State," *The Export Practitioner*, July 1997.

3. "State and Local Sanctions Trouble U.S. Trade Partners," *Wall Street Journal*, April 1, 1998.

4. "A State's Foreign Policy: The Mass That Roared," *The Economist*, February 8, 1997.

5. The description of the legal basis for the NFTC suit and relevant court precedents draws heavily upon Daniel M. Price and John P. Hannah's article, "The Constitutionality of United States State and Local Sanctions," *Harvard International Law Journal* (Spring 1998). This article is based upon an outline of the possible suit by Powell, Goldstein, Frazer, & Murphy LLP.

6. 441 U.S. 434 (1979), as quoted in Price and Hannah, "The Constitutionality of United States State and Local Sanctions."

7. Letter from 10 labor union presidents to U.S. Trade Representative Charlene Barshefsky, August 7, 1997, reprinted in the August 15, 1997, issue of *Inside U.S. Trade*.

8. Testimony of Under Secretary of State Stuart Eizenstat, *Hearing on Use and Effect of Unilateral Trade Sanctions before the House Ways and Means Trade Subcommittee*, October 23, 1997.

9. "Pressuring Burma," *Boston Globe*, May 13, 1996.

10. Testimony of Under Secretary of State Peter Tarnoff, *Hearing on the Cuban Liberty and Democratic Solidarity Act before the Senate Foreign Relations Western Hemisphere Subcommittee*, May 22 and June 14, 1995.

11. Congress's role in sanctions policy is further complicated by the fact that bills concerning export barriers come under the jurisdiction of the foreign affairs committees, while those concerning import limitations fall under the trade committees' jurisdiction.

12. 299 U.S. 319–320 (1936), as quoted in Harold Hongju Koh and John Choon Yoo's "Dollar Diplomacy/Dollar Defense: The Fabric of Economics and National Security Law," *International Lawyer* (Fall 1992).

13. Cuban Liberty and Democratic Solidarity Act of 1996, section 112.

Appendix B

Steering Committee and Experts Group Membership

1. Steering Committee Membership

Cochairs

Frank Murkowski
U.S. Senate

James Kolbe
U.S. House of Representatives

Dianne Feinstein
U.S. Senate

Robert Matsui
U.S. House of Representatives

Lee Hamilton
Former member
U.S. House of Representatives

Jon Christensen
Former member
U.S. House of Representatives

Members

Morton Bahr
President
Communications Workers of America

Archie W. Dunham
President & Chief Executive Officer
Conoco

William Brock
Counselor, CSIS
Former U.S. Senator, Secretary of Labor,
U.S. Trade Representative

Lawrence S. Eagleburger
Baker, Donelson, Bearman & Caldwell
Former Secretary of State

Harold Brown
Counselor, CSIS
Former Secretary of Defense

R. Michael Gadbaw
Vice President & Senior Counsel
General Electric Company

Zbigniew Brzezinski
Counselor, CSIS
Former National Security Adviser

Carla Hills
Chairman, Hills & Company
Former Secretary of Housing and Urban
Development and
U.S. Trade Representative

Thomas Buergenthal
Professor of Law, George Washington
 University
Member, United Nations Human
 Rights Committee

Whitney MacMillan
Chairman Emeritus
Cargill, Incorporated

Ray Marshall
University of Texas at Austin
Former Secretary of Labor

Theodore E. McCarrick
Archbishop of Newark

Sam Nunn
Chairman, Board of Trustees, CSIS
Former U.S. Senator

Stephen W. Percy
Chairman and Chief Executive Officer
BP America

James R. Schlesinger
Counselor, CSIS
Former Secretary of Defense, Director of
Central Intelligence, Secretary of Energy

William Schreyer
Chairman, CSIS Executive Committee
Chairman Emeritus, Merrill Lynch

Leighton Smith
Admiral, USN, ret.
Former Commander, Allied
Forces Southern Europe

2. Experts Group Membership

Elliott Abrams
Ethics and Public Policy Center

Anthony Albrecht
U.S.-ASEAN Business Council, Inc.

Jahangir Amuzegar
Former Finance Minister of Iran

Hugh Arce
U.S. International Trade
Commission

Bradley Babson
The World Bank

Teo Babun
Teo Babun Group, Incorporated

Claude Barfield
American Enterprise Institute

Dan Bob
Office of Senator William V. Roth Jr.

Benjamin Bonk
National Intelligence Council

John Brandon
The Asia Foundation

Ian Brzezinski
Office of Senator William V. Roth Jr.

Frank Calzon
Center for a Free Cuba

Michael Canes
American Petroleum Institute

Barry Carter
Georgetown University Law Center

Andrew Claster
U.S. Government

Patrick Clawson
Washington Institute for
Near East Policy

William Clements
General Electric Company

Gillian Gunn Clissold
Georgetown University

Isaac Cohen
UN ECLAC

Joseph Collins
Center for Strategic &
International Studies

Kenneth Crosby
Merrill Lynch & Co., Inc.

Timothy Deal
U.S. Council for International Business

Don Deline
Halliburton/Brown & Root

Arthur Downey
Baker-Hughes Inc.

Thomas Duesterberg
Hudson Institute

Robert Ebel
Center for Strategic &
International Studies

Everett Eissenstat
Office of Representative James Kolbe

Joseph Eldridge
American University

Kimberly Elliott
Institute for International Economics

Mark Falcoff
American Enterprise Institute

Georges Fauriol
Center for Strategic &
International Studies

Dan Fisk
Former Senate Foreign Relations
Committee

Virginia Foote
U.S. Vietnam Trade Council

Henrietta Holsman Fore
Holsman International

Mark Frazier
National Bureau of Asia Research

Paula Freer
Marathon Oil Company

Howard Frey
American International Group, Inc.

Antonio Gayoso
World Council of Credit Unions, Inc.

Larry Goldstein
Petroleum Industry Research
Foundation

Gerrit Gong
Center for Strategic &
International Studies

Leon Hadar
CATO Institute

Marie Huhtala
Department of State

Shireen Hunter
Center for Strategic &
International Studies

Charlyn Iovino
Mobil Oil Corporation

Mike Jendrzejczyk
Human Rights Watch

Robbin Johnson
Cargill, Incorporated

Douglas Johnston
Center for Strategic &
International Studies

Robert Kapp
U.S.-China Business Council

Julius Katz
Hills & Company

Geoffrey Kemp
The Nixon Center

Richard Kessler
Senate Foreign Relations
Committee

Christopher Krafft
Department of State

Mark Lagon
Project for the New American Century

Deborah Lamb
Senate Finance Committee

David Lampton
Paul Nitze School of Advanced
International Studies

William Lane
Caterpillar Inc.

Mia Lee
Consultant

James Lilley
American Enterprise Institute

Brink Lindsey
CATO Institute

Carl Lohmann
Department of the Treasury

Winston Lord
Former American Ambassador to China

Rodney MacAlister
Conoco

Todd Malan
Organization for International
Investment

Marino Marcich
National Association of Manufacturers

Greg Mastel
Economic Strategy Institute

Iain McDaniels
U.S.-China Business Council

Eric Melby
Forum for International Policy

David Moran
Department of State

Elaine Morton
Consultant

Julia Nanay
The Petroleum Finance Company, Ltd.

Richard Nuccio
Harvard University

Daniel O'Flaherty
National Foreign Trade Council, Inc.

Deanna Okun
Department of State

Peter Orr
Consultant

Sandra Oudkirk
Department of State

Douglas Paal
Asia Pacific Policy Center

Robert Pelletreau
Afridi & Angell

Hong-Phong Pho
Department of Commerce

Matthew Porterfield
Georgetown University Law Center

Daniel Price
Powell, Goldstein, Frazer & Murphy

Stephen Rademaker
House International Relations
Committee

John Rafuse
Unocal Corporation

Michael Ranneberger
Department of State

Frank Record
House International Relations
Committee

Otto Reich
RMA International, Inc.

Dianne Rennack
Congressional Research Service/Foreign

Peter Rodman
The Nixon Center

William Rogers
Arnold & Porter

Mark Roth
Department of Energy

Richard Sawaya
ARCO

Stephen Schlaikjer
Office of Senator Frank Murkowski

David Schmahmann
Nutter, McClellen, & Fish LLP

Jeffrey Schott
Institute for International Economics

Leslie Scott
Consultant

Andrew Semmel
Office of Senator Richard Lugar

Daniel Shapiro
Office of Senator Dianne Feinstein

Richard Smith
Consultant

Linda Specht
Department of State

David Steinberg
Georgetown University

Bruce Stokes
Council on Foreign Relations

Roscoe Suddarth
Middle East Institute

Karen Swazey
Department of Commerce

Mark Taylor
Department of State

Michael Townshend
BP America Inc.

Michael Van Dusen
House International Relations
Committee

Sidney Weintraub
Center for Strategic &
International Studies

Keith Weissman
American Israel Public Affairs
Committee

Howard Wiarda
Center for Strategic &
International Studies

Guenther Wilhelm
Exxon Corporation

Willard Workman
U.S. Chamber of Commerce

Frances Zwenig
U.S.-ASEAN Business Council, Inc.

Index

About the Authors

ERNEST H. PREEG is a senior fellow at the Hudson Institute in Washington, D.C. He undertook this study while holding the William M. Scholl Chair in International Business at CSIS. He holds a Ph.D. in economics from the New School for Social Research and was U.S. ambassador to Haiti, 1981–1983, well before the devastating economic sanctions against that country in 1991–1994, which caused enormous suffering to the Haitian people and destruction of the nation's economic infrastructure. Ambassador Preeg's earlier country case study work includes *The Evolution of a Revolution: Peru and Its Relations with the United States, 1968–1980* (1981), *Haiti and the CBI: A Time of Change and Opportunity* (1985), *Neither Fish nor Fowl: U.S. Economic Aid to the Philippines for Noneconomic Objectives* (1991), *Cuba and the New Caribbean Economic Order* (1993), and *The Haitian Dilemma: A Case Study in Demographics, Development, and U.S. Foreign Policy* (1996). His earlier work in the trade policy field includes *Traders and Diplomats: A History and Analysis of the Kennedy Round of Negotiations under the GATT* (1970), *Economic Blocs and U.S. Foreign Policy* (1974), *The American Challenge in World Trade: U.S. Interests in the GATT Multilateral Trading System* (1989), *Trade Policy Ahead: Three Tracks and One Question* (1995), *Traders in a Brave New World: The Uruguay Round and the Future of the International Trading System* (1995), and *From Here to Free Trade: Essays in Post-Uruguay Round Trade Strategy* (1998).

Denise Auclair is an analyst at Mercer Management Consulting. A graduate of the Georgetown University School of Foreign Service, she served as CSIS research assistant for this unilateral economic sanctions project.